AMERICA, I LOVE YOU

AMERICA, I LOVE YOU

by Ralph de Toledano

With annotations by Karl Hess

THE NATIONAL PRESS INC.
128 C STREET, N.E.
WASHINGTON, D.C. 20002

Library of Congress Catalog Card No. 68-17209

Printed in the United States of America

Contents

Introduction

This, I propose, will be the ultimate solution of the Toledano problem.

First, to establish that it *is* a problem:

Whereas, on the American left, it seems possible precisely to discriminate between the positions held by, say Sidney Hook (social democrat, libertarian tendencies) and Arthur Schlesinger, Jr. (social democrat, authoritarian tendencies) it is either difficult or considered insignificant to discriminate between positions on the right.

Thus, the right-watchers speak in lumps. This "lumpenrecht" contains in a glob everyone from Robert Welch to the undoubtedly most effective critic of the American left, Mr. Allen Drury, author of *Advise and Consent*, etc. etc. and, hopefully, etc.

Along the way we come to the Toledano problem. No one, it seems, wants to claim him although some have embraced him. He has remained, at a time when, left and right, the institutionalization of authors has been the practice, his own odd man out. Out, that is, of the institutionalized slot.

To understand that a Toledano is not only possible but inevitable on what often is called the right, is to take an important step toward a discriminating view of the politico-philosophical landscape.

Here is the way that landscape appears to me. It is not the pleasantly leafy scene that some political Georgia O'Keefes have painted. It is, instead, a series of crags, outcroppings, and tors.

The perspectives of the landscape are several. There is the economic, the political, and the philosophical. The differences between left and right cannot, usually, be made apparent across these perspectives but only through comparisons of one or two at a time.

Take the economic. To say that you can distinguish between left and right purely on an economic basis is to court disaster. At a meeting of Iron Curtain and Western economists in 1967 it was apparent to those observing that many of the Western economists where there to explore and enthuse over highly blueprinted or planned economies, mixed economies at the very least, while many of the gentlemen from behind the Iron Curtain were there to explore and enthuse over the possibilities of a more open, or market centered economy.

It cannot safely be said at all that it is economic differences which divide what we know as the left and right these days.

Highly bureaucratized industries, for example, tend to look upon their role as a "partnership" with government. They could scarcely be said to be advocates of capitalism. They are advocates of "getting along" with government and getting what they can from it. They are, to be sure, profit centered, but not necessarily profit-productivity centered. It would be more accurate to say they are profit-privilege-plan centered; expecting a decent profit, but anticipating that the way to get it is through the inherent privileges that large companies have with large governments. (The zeal of some industries in seeking government protection, either through franchises, special tax rates, tariffs, or insurance sums up the attitude.)

If, then, we are to find a left and right perspective, economically, we must look well beyond the shape of things as they are in industry and business generally in the United States. We must look, in practical terms, to the tough, usually small entrepreneurs, often technically oriented, who wish that the government would get the hell out of the way and let people compete (no matter how fiercely) strictly on the basis of their own energy, creativity, and productivity. Philosophically, we have to look to the few constant philosophers of capitalism such as Ayn Rand, Henry Hazlitt and, when he is not being "pragmatic" by suggesting such things as a negative income tax, the most economically learned of them all, Milton Friedman.

In between you find various establishmentarians. The labor unions comprise such a bloc, with the notable exception of the fledging and fine Association of Skilled Trades. Members of the Chamber of Commerce and the N.A.M. generally comprise such a bloc. They are seeking economic order or advantage and are quite willing to let government regulate here and there, or everywhere, to achieve it. They are not notably hot for what they feel is "cut throat" competition.

The differences between these blocs is probably negligible in the long run, adding up only to who is on top of whom rather than *how* we are to do business—by grand plan or great competition.

Toledano, economically, is a sort of establishmentarian. He has taken his side, generally, with the business-industry establishment.

Thus, when it comes to that side of things he is a good reporter with a good and obvious bias. But it is not as a writer of economics that his true significance arises.

How about politics?

If there is an easy way precisely to differentiate between the political left and right, I have yet to learn it. Frankly, I think that the terms are meaningless.

About the best that we can come up with are leanings, not directions. Toledano is a case in point. He is said, by those who call themselves leftists and rightists, to represent the most responsible of conservative political positions. That, in turn, is supposed to mean that his position is somewhat right of center. But what that, in turn, means is rather like interpreting the Bible. It depends on your particular bag.

Toledano is plain unshirted hell on any form of tyranny. He has fought the Fascists and the Communists. He has bent as many lances against as many impregnable statist windmills as any man I know.

Yet, he shares with the left a deep-down dependence on state power to accomplish certain important things. He opposes, but accepts, enforced military service. Leftists approve of enforced service to the state also, and for roughly the same reasons (you owe it to the rest of the folks, etc.). Leftists may love forced service while conservatives may only accept it reluctantly, but accept it both do.

Of course, on the right and certainly on Toledano's part of it, the willingness to accept any form of coercion by the state recedes rather rapidly and the enthusiasm for even those enforcements thought necessary diminishes apace far beyond anything that a leftist would feel.

Yet, we are still involved with tendencies, not flatfooted positions. Right and left believe in the sacrifice of a good many freedoms in order to achieve order and stability for the state. The big difference today seems to be in just how far you go. There seems to be no limit at the extremes of either side.

The lady elected head of the lady Republicans in 1967 made, as her first major proposal, the suggestion that all youngsters be drafted for national service when in their teens. This struck her as being fair. It would, of course, have struck Adolph Hitler as wonderfully fair also. Surely it would have raised no eyebrows in the Soviet Union, or even in Red China. Yet this conservative lady undoubtedly could go to bed thinking that, by golly, since we all do owe the nation (she would say republic) a debt for all the goodies of freedom, we should be willing to spend a little time in service to it.

Toledano, of course, would never go that far. I am sure he was as shocked as I at the horror of what this gracious lady so graciously had proposed.

But . . . but . . . but I can clearly recall that, perhaps in pique, but still revealingly, Toledano has said that one way to straighten up young people might be to draft them for a healthy turn in the armed forces. And General Hershey, that bastion of the draft and hero of many a conservative, has said that he wouldn't even want his grandchildren defended by volunteers. He actually reveres forced servitude.

The point is that politically there are leanings to left and right but few straight lines. Again, the straight lines would be drawn by such philosophers as Ayn Rand (for the regnant individual to whom the state is just an administrative convenience to enforce contracts, pay the cops, keep the medium of exchange straight, and maintain courts for adjudication of meaningful disputes) or Pope John (for the absolute subjugation of the individual to the "community").

Thus, although in the logistics of politics there is no keener observer than Toledano, it is not in politics that his most meaningful writing is to be found. There, as with economics, he is mainly a reporter, although a reporter of extraordinary perception and accuracy.

All right now, where is and what is the real Toledano problem? The real problem, dear reader, is that Ralph de Toledano is most significant for the most basic reason of all but for the very one which many, many of us prefer to ignore—perhaps in hope that if we do it long enough, it will all go away.

Toledano is a significant writer because he has consistently and clearly spoken for God—beyond politics, beyond economics, beyond everything else. Even before Whittaker Chambers made his points for religious mysticism more tellingly than had anyone since St. Augustine, Ralph de Toledano was writing the same things, even if between the lines.

He may dislike my putting him ahead of Chambers even more than what I will say subsequently, because he has so long and so deeply loved Whit Chambers and everything that he wrote in his agonized conversion from the mysticism of Communism to the mysticism of Christianity.

Nevertheless, I think it is true and I think that this book strongly will support the point; the point that Ralph de Toledano has importantly and persistently spoken for one side of the argument which is the basic one in our time and all time. It is not an argument of economy, although such an economy as that of capitalism depends absolutely on one side of the argument (and a side which might surprise even many who feel they are capitalists). It is not an argument of politics although political organization of people also depends sooner or later on which side of the argument you take (with the sides, as I see them, being a good deal different from the view of those who say, for instance, that you cannot be an anti-Communist unless you also are a deist).

Now we are at the crux of our time and the crux of Toledano. He is one of my oldest friends. He and I will die as friends, I hope. Yet he stands on one side of this argument and I on the other. He is a mystic in the Christian tradition. I am an atheist. He holds that the relationship of man to God is the prime issue of our and all time. I agree, to the extent that I feel that so long as man is devoted to any, repeat, any supernatural concepts that he cannot fully know himself or be himself as natural man.

We coexist, Ralph and I, because we do not want to destroy one another. We do not even want to destroy one another's ideas, although we both would sleep more easily if the root ideas of the other would vanish from the earth.

The way in which we can coexist is to live in a time and in a place where neither has the power to apply violent power to the ideas of the other. It is as simple as that, and the fact that neither of us believe in violence except in self-defense.

The reason that, for instance, Communism, with its (in Miss Rand's memorable phrase) "mysticism of muscle" cannot coexist with Christianity's "mysticism of mind" is not that, for instance, Popes and commissars always disagree, because they don't, but that mystics of muscle even by definition believe in physically suppressing those who resist not its ideas but, simply, its power.

Toledano fights for freedom, or more precisely, in the direction of freedom, the direction of orderly freedom and away from the direction of orderly totalitarianism. We fight together there. But I do not revere community order as he does. I revere the mind of man and the independence of men from the oppression of other men beyond any portion of the community, any function of the community, any privilege or plan of the community. Ralph de Toledano is too good, and sincere, a patriot to go that far. The flag, the "country," the traditions, all mean more to him.

But they mean things to him honestly and wonderfully and never viciously, as with those who feel the urge toward the tar bucket whenever anyone objects to, say, interminable oaths to a state which, ordinarily, free men should be bucking, not bowing down to.

There is no question that Ralph is in love with all the feelings, the mystical meanings of America. I happen to share most of them also because it was America that set the mind of man fully free to seek whatever heights it could. It was America that sloughed off birth and privilege and put all its chips on talent and energy. But there was nothing mystic in it and the things I feel about it are not as viscerally emotional as obviously are the feelings, so often poetically so, of Ralph de Toledano.

I turn on when I see a good lathe operator whizzing away at his work or, even better, when I hear somebody describing a new invention that will turn the world on its ear and to hell with stable markets. Ralph turns on, practically, when you even say America. And I must say it is an emotion which, in him, I always have found attractive.

But back to the point, *the* point. Toledano is more than a reporter, more than a polemicist. He is the best that the side of religious mysticism has to offer and he has been that for decades. He is no spiritual Johnny-Come-Lately. He has always been on God's side. Way, way down where the heart of the matter is, Ralph's writing always shows where the soul of the matter is.

This is what is important. This is what provides the ultimate solution to the Toledano problem. He is not a conservative. He is not a political polemicist. He is not left and he is not right. He is, if you are looking for significance, a Christian scribe. There are few preachers these days who, in relation to Ralph de Toledano, are worthy to do whatever it is that the Bible says you aren't worthy to do when you aren't worthy, etc.

Toledano takes this business seriously. Surely Bishop Pike, to name just one Christian disaster, does not.

Toledano is what you need to know about if you want to understand properly and profoundly the mysticism of the mind with which the mysticism of muscle is at war these days—and the mysticism with which these believers in Man Alone, such as I am, coexist even if uneasily as we all search our minds for, let's face it, the meaning of our minds.

Toledano takes a flatfooted position when it comes to that. So do I. The world, dear reader, may well turn upon whether you do.

So. Here, speaking for one side, is one of the very best men that that side can produce, Ralph de Toledano.

(s) Karl Hess

America, I Love You

The considerable significance of this essay lies in its deeply religious conclusion—making powerfully the point made in the introduction to this volume. It can be observed also that the poetic reflections on the nation state are just that, poetic rather than rational. But it should also be observed that this was poetry written at a time when in no major journal of opinion, or even of popular circulation, was there any house room at all for even the simplest appreciation of this marvelous land, and its marvelous people. Instead, it was written at a time of the highest skepticism and the harshest criticism of the land and the people. It was written when it was absolutely cornball to love your country and absolutely chic to refer to any such thing as loutish flag-waving. Even for those of us who have absolutely no reverence for the nation state beyond our respect for the way that its citizens make it operate at any given time, I must say that Toledano's optimistic, uplifting lilting waving of the flag is light-years preferable to the sour, dour grumping of the "sophisticates."

From the deck of the Army transport, we watched the low flat shore of Louisiana sinking into the Gulf. We stood as millions of other American soldiers had stood at landfall, feeling homesick and forlorn. And suddenly, in that small moment of farewell, we knew that we loved America very dearly—for reasons great or trivial, for the hallowed faith of this republic, for that small spot of landscape which had nourished the roots.

1

No one said it, no one could say it, but America-I-love-you was on every face. The simple love of one's home soil, of the contour of the land or the houses of the cities, of the hard or tender speech which gave voice to our traditions—these were not things to be discussed. "Patriotism" belonged to those who had given us the send-off at the staging area, to the tub thumpers and the orators. There were rumors of Nazi submarines, and we could be studiously matter-of-fact about them.

It was a moment of great clarity—a moment in which the sudden despairs and infinite longings of our brief tenure took on meaning. It shared, but transcended, the quality of those other moments when we stood rigid at Present Arms, touched by the sunset light, as the bugle parsed the brief music of Retreat and the flag slowly descended in the Army's most moving ritual.

But it was more than a moment of emotion which had broken through unabashed. The years of absence from our household gods were not so sterile as we had supposed. In the great surge of war, we had learned much about America—and even more about ourselves. In time, combat troops and the rear echelon boys came back hugging their secret—and in time they packed it away in moth balls, along with their old uniforms.

We came back to find the old.attitudes and the old ways lying in ambush for us. After a small struggle, many of us succumbed. I am not speaking from the vantage point of hindsight. In a note-book, I recently came across words written in those early post-war years: "The tragic fact, the shocking and ironic fact, is that there are no Americans left. Or, to be quite fair about it, only a small number, holding out against odds—the Vanishing Americans of this epoch. The rest are trampling out a vintage of hate or crankiness."

These were bitter words for 1946. The dismal day when a Presidential candidate could approvingly quote Dr. Johnson's sour epigram about patriotism and scoundrels had not yet come upon us. Nor had we reached that terrifying era in which former First Ladies and Supreme Court justices could trumpet to Europe that fear and fascism were astride this nation. Our leaders still had the decency to keep their dishonor a privy matter, nor did they play for laughs among Europe's intellectuals by taking prat-falls for television commentators!

Nevertheless, those words were not the bilious plaint of a veteran elbowing his way into the posture of commerce. The shock was very real. I felt then, as I do now, that being an American is a state of faith and a state of mind; that many of our people are less American than the refugee boy I knew whose accent was the butt of the barracks; that the Iowa farm boy who taught me how to roll a pack had more of an inner sense of his function in the American scheme than half a dozen J. Robert Oppenheimers; that to betray, in no matter what form, the soil and the tradition which it is man's nature to honor is an obscenity.

Looking back, it is easy to see that we were confronted by a nation which had accepted the heritage of the twenties and the thirties. The optimistic materialism of Boom and the pessimistic materialism of Bust had created a new state of mind and given a new coloration to the state of thought in this country. The writers of the post-World War I "disillusion" had said, "Throw away the old, let's not be hypocrites."

They did not understand that hypocrisy is in itself the tribute of the insincere to the sincere, that it is a wry-mouthed affirmation of traditional values, and that it therefore serves a social good. They only understood that all noble sentiment was foolish, that the Constitution was a declaration of selfish interest, and that economic "law" had supplanted the First Commandment. In this atmosphere, the medicine men had sapped the moral fiber of America with a brew of sneers at such old-fashioned nonsense as "My country, right or wrong"—and eventually tongue-twisted it into a belief that my country was always wrong.

On the one hand, this had produced a whole jabberwock of alien ideologies and movements—the Bund, the Christian Front, the Communist Party, and their splinter groups of reaction and revolution. On the other, it had created a limbo of distrust which alienated the Vanished Americans from all things truly and traditionally American. No longer did the lilacs in the dooryard bloom, and the hills of home were more suspect than Mother Machree.

Even during the war, the alienated intellectuals could not pray for an American triumph. Their hopes were for a United Nations victory, a semantic difference which found its expression at Yalta when Franklin Delano Roosevelt—taking time out from toasts to the murder of 50,000 German officers—sacrificed his country's interests on the altar of Big Three "unity."

And in the postwar years? The poor, benighted soldiers returned to find that the great moment had been tossed into a folder marked, "Defile and Forget." At every hand, there were former Americans ready to believe the worst of their country, to swallow, without straining, the most fantastic libels, to accept the fantastic explanations and vituperations of the anti-American coalition forming across the seas. And the concomitant rejection of those few allies remaining to us, in favor of our enemies and false friends, seemed—and was—a symptom of the illness which ran epidemic in our streets. Both here and abroad, men were vilified as reactionaries, or worse, who realized that the last, best hope of earth was the projection of the American mystique.

And what has happened to the echo of the sunset gun? In the years since the war, I have crossed and recrossed the American continent, moved always by its magnitude and magnificence. I have seen the great plains and the pushing cities, the energy and purpose and goodness, the great wealth which is accepted but never truly worshipped.

It is all there for Americans to see—but most of the Americans have vanished. Their heirs and assigns tell us that it is all foul or tarnished or unreal. The look of wonder which says America-I-love-you is even more unfashionable today than it was those years ago. The nation's honor is a commodity of politics, not an article of faith. Treason is a commonplace—the unheroic treason of termites—and apathy is its handmaiden. No one asks for proof in the night that the flag is still there.

No one, perhaps, but the Vanishing Americans, the last patriots. They are the men who believe that America's freedom is invested in the whole Constitution, not merely the Fifth Amendment. They draw their philosophy from Burke, not Locke. They stake their lives on the hope of Heaven, not the security of Marx.

They find the beauty of America in a vision of its determination, not in the squalor of its compromises. They are not afraid of America's power, though they live among cowering men.

They are vanishing, but not vanquished. They remember that on a bitter day, one American knelt in the snow and, out of the strength of his faith, asked God for guidance. And they know, out of the strength of their own faith, that if one American remains, the hand of God can yet descend to stay the course of history.

This We Face

There was a time when, because he had the time to devote to it, Ralph de Toledano was far and away the most perceptive and accurate reporter on the affairs of the Communist Party, U.S.A. He has broadened his field of fire considerably since then and the high specialty of CPUSA watching has passed to other eyes. Yet, the same curious fact remains. Here, in an area in which so many people feel that ideology is the be-all and end-all we also find the least of ideology and the most of pure and simple mechanical, if you will, old-fashioned plotting, subverting, and conniving. Despite the deep lines of ideology that guide it, the deepest fact of Communist subversion is that it is subversion, organized and actual. It is not a theoretical assault upon the republic. If the assault often is waged with idea, rather than guns, it is simply because the time of the guns is not appropriate—it is not because guns are banned from the fight. Toledano's great contribution in covering such matters is that he has never lost sight of all of those facets of Communist subversion and always has seen them, properly, in perspective.

With missile rockets hurtling through space at the speed of seven miles a second, the problem of Communist subversion seems old-fashioned almost to the point of quaintness. Yet all the revolutionary technology of the nuclear age has not made obsolescent what may appear like the horse-and-buggy concepts of civil war and civil disturbance. The Communists, with their plans for the internal assault on this nation, are still very much with us.

7

The great mushroom which bloomed over Hiroshima added but one new factor to the strategy and tactics of Communist subversion. Whereas in the past subversive conspiracy was but one arrow in the sling of revolutionary states, it has become the main weapon in the Soviet arsenal. It may manifest itself in many forms, but the categorical destructiveness of nuclear weapons has neutralized them. Our armies and navies, our air forces—these are vitally necessary in the elaborate process of stalemate which has become the function of Western and Soviet armed might. This process must continue. We are lost if the West—particularly this nation—does not understand, assimilate, and employ the methodology of applied subversion.

Americans do not understand this methodology—in fact, they think there is something a little overripe about those who devote their attention to the problem. When Whittaker Chambers remarked some years ago that "there are spies and traitors all about us," those who mold our minds were either outraged or convulsed. The fact he was stating, however, should have been apparent to anyone whose reading of history extends beyond elementary school texts.

Since the overthrow of King Charles I, civil war and subversion have been endemic to the Western world. Communist revolutionists did not invent the techniques so successful today. Lenin's seizure of the Constituent Assembly and Cromwell's overthrow of the British monarchy, by their controlled interaction of troops and mobs, were brothers under the slogans. The eighteenth and nineteenth centuries were a series of internal upheavals linked by an international *Weltanschäung* which in 1919 concretized itself in the Comintern. Today; civil war is all about us in a thousand manifestations of subversion and conspiracy, of stupid acquiescence and cynical resignation. It is the toy of millionaires and the self-abuse of intellectuals.

The A-bomb, the H-bomb, the ICBM are, in the active sense, significant and commanding only insofar as they are not used. The arsenal of nuclear weapons serves a psychological rather than a military function. For the Soviets, it is designed to destroy the will to resist in the free world, to make Goliath stretch out before David and ask for the stroke of the sword.

Nuclear weapons serve to stir the Gargantuan mind and pica-yune understanding of Bertrand Russell, who urges us to disarm unilaterally and to accept Communist domination rather than what he chose to call "the end of the human race." They encour-age the outbursts of a Cyrus Eaton who rattles his dollars and seeks to discredit the guardians of our internal security. A justice of our Supreme Court writes the introduction to a book by a notorious fellow traveler—a book which belabors the United States for its defense of the Korean Republic and equates us with the Communists.

Communist strategists know what we do not: that the secret weapon of any state when confronted by internal subversion and disturbance is the will to resist.

It is a prime axiom that no revolution in modern history has succeeded without a concomitant destruction of the will to re-sist in legitimate governments.   There is much talk of belly-communism, talk which thrives on a complete falsification of history. The French Revolution is always the example given.

Generations of school children, since the days of William Wordsworth, hold the passionate belief that hunger and oppres-sion led the Jacobin mobs which guillotined Louis XVI and Marie Antoinette. The meticulous and inspired reporting of Alexis de Tocqueville, ignored by the popularizers, proves conclusively that France was going through the greatest prosperity in several decades when sans-culottism swept in and that the Bastille—presumably crowded with political prisoners—was literally empty and had been for a long time—when the mobs of Paris stormed its ancient walls.

We forget that Lenin himself described the Kerensky regime which preceded his as the freest government in the world—whereas desperate heroism, hunger, ideological fervor, and the desire for freedom could not prevail in Hungary. The successful revolutionary assault, therefore, is not on the government but on the national will.

The immediate function of any Communist Party, therefore, is not the violent overthrow of the government—in the limited legal sense demanded by our contemporary courts—but in the sapping of allegiances, the dissemination of confusion, the instillment of fear, and the poisoning of faith in our institutions, in ourselves, in our God. Its aim is to halt the civil peristalsis. The Communist Party is a paramilitary force, true—but its ammunition is far subtler than bullets and hand grenades.

With this in mind, it becomes important to consider first the nature of the Communist who makes up this paramilitary force. For the sake of precision, let me refer to him as the Bolshevik. The Bolshevik is not a "liberal in a hurry." He is a Marxist only to this extent—that he accepts a general theory of the organization of the state. "Scientific socialism," the totality of a regimented world structure, certain outward patterns and certain semantic stridencies—all these he has incorporated into his thinking.

But the ancestors of Bolshevism are not Karl Marx and Friedrich Engels. They are two men, one hardly known to the West, Bakunin and Nechaev—two faces merged into the Janus-like configuration of Leninism and Stalinism. There is no facet of the Communist world revolution which does not reflect the baleful light of these two Messianic Russians—one self-deluded, the other so obsessively evil that he served as a model for Dostoevski's *The Possessed.* The Bolshevik practitioners, piling faggots on the world's trouble spots, may think that they were suckled on the Communist Manifesto, but they drew their milk from a forgotten little pamphlet, twenty-five hundred words in all. It is called *Catechism of a Revolutionist*; it was written by Bakunin and Nechaev; this is how it begins:

> The revolutionist is a doomed man. He has no personal interests, no affairs, sentiments, attachments, property, not even a name of his own. Everything in him is absorbed by one exclusive interest, one thought, one passion, the revolution.

The Byronic concept of the revolutionist—or its more intellectualized counterpart in a man like André Malraux—is cast aside. So too is the doctrinaire conformity demanded of the orthodox

Marxist. Morals, the accoutrements of culture, the softening decencies of everyday associations—these no longer exist. The revolutionist of the Bakunin-Nechaev school—and hence, the Leninist
school—makes a pact with the revolution which prepares him for
torture or death. His enemy is established society, a society he
categorizes neatly. Some members of society are to be con-
demned to death and ruthlessly liquidated. Those of the ruling
class who contribute to the revolutionary spirit by their acts of
brutality against people are to be encouraged and preserved. They
will goad the inert mass into unreasoning violence. And, the
Catechism adds:

> One may conspire (with the liberals) in accordance with their pro-
> grams, making believe that one follows them blindly, and at the same
> time one should take hold of them, get possession of all their secrets,
> compromise them to the utmost . . . use them as instruments for stir-
> ring up disturbances in the State.

The Bakuninist-Nechaevist has a basic contempt for the "doc-
trinaires" who spend their time "talking idly in groups and on
paper." This contempt we have seen in the utterances of Joseph
Stalin, and in his disregard of the Marxist dialectic. *Catechism of
the Revolutionist* argues that these "Talmudic" debaters of revolution are to be tugged into the arena of force and violence which
will destroy most of them but serve as "real revolutionary training" for a hard core which will break loose and join the true faith.
Agents in what Harold Laski called the "organization of catastrophe," and makers of despair, these revolutionists are urged to
seek out the "bold world of bandits" and to combine with it.
Have we forgotten that Stalin robbed banks?

Here then is the iron law which binds the Bolshevik, reiterated
many decades later by J. Peters in his *Manual of Organization*, a
Communist *vade mecum*, summed up poetically by Bertoldt
Brecht in that chillingly luminous line, "Sink into the mud, em-
brace the butcher, but change the world," and chanted in tender
ditty by the German Communists as the Weimar Republic sank
into its own morasses: "Grease the guillotine with the fat of the
tyrants/Blood, blood, blood must flow."

If we are to understand what faces the free world, we must
first come to grips with the Leninist concept of the revolutionary.
Not every conspirator or subversive is cut from the same heroic
pattern or shares the same determination. There are timeservers
and bureaucrats in plenty, all helping to make up the corpus of
international Communism. There are weak men and scoundrels
and men of soul who defect to freedom. But the weak and
the dishonest do not command the paramilitary forces of
Communism—they are merely a part of them. If military victory
were a simple function of unanimous courage, what wars would
be won?

We once thought of the Communist as an unkempt type fu-
tilely debating in a Union Square cafeteria. It would be an equally
serious mistake to accept the stereotype of the steely eye and the
commissar manner. Alger Hiss was, and is, one of the prototypes
of the Bolshevik. Yet on the surface and in ordinary discourse, he
was a man of somewhat mincing step and manner and, behind the
charm, a crashing bore. Richard Sorge, perhaps the most effective
espionage agent turned out by the Red Army's Fourth Bureau,
was hard-drinking and hard-lusting, yet he plundered the secrets
of the very Nazis and Japanese whose whiskey he drank and
whose wives he seduced. The leaders of the American Communist
Party seem flabby, even a little fey—yet the incidence of combat
decorations among them is startlingly high.

It is from this diversity that Communism fills its table of organization. Each comrade has his rank and his assigned role. Each
comrade delivers himself to a military discipline. Thousands of
intellectuals, to the lecture platform born, in 1948 accepted party
orders to join the campaign of "industrial concentration," a process of colonization and infiltration of the nation's key plants and
factories.

"Plant you now, dig you later," the Communist Party said.
One man held in reserve until the calibrated moment can do more
damage than a dozen rioting mobs, just as a single sniper can
immobilize a company of troops.

A strategic minority can achieve much with little—on somewhat the same principle. Neither theory is original with the Communists, nor is it exclusively theirs. Walter Reuther, with less than

a hundred men, employed the theory of the strategic minority in the 1930's. With this fulcrum he broke management resistance to the UAW and launched a powerful mass union.

Size, therefore, is secondary in Communist organization. When the "revolutionary situation" comes about, sergeants become colonels as new recruits are trained by the Bolshevik cadres. For those who find the size of today's Communist Party a cause for encouragement, let it be recalled that Lenin disapproved of mass membership in the precombat stages, and that he developed the technique of the continuing purge to keep the party vigorous. Organization must fit the situation, and in the CPUSA that organization is triangular.

There are, then, three Communist Parties in this country, directed by parallel chains of command from Moscow, the Soviet Embassy, and a highly mobile "field headquarters." These three parties are: The so-called Open Party, the underground party, and the reserve or sleeper apparatus. (I have not listed any of the dozen apparatuses, working in tandem, which carry out the Soviet Union's espionage missions. These fall into the category of military intelligence and are directed by the Red Army, the secret police, the Comintern, or the torture brigades known as Smersh.)

Of these three parties, the "open party" is the least important. It is made up of the expendables, the old hacks, the swing men of the front groups, the shouters and debaters. It has a double mission: to draw fire and to bring in the recruits.

The underground party is organized on Bakuninist lines, concretized by one B. Vassiliev in 1931, under the title: *Organizational Problems in Underground Revolutionary Work.* This Communist outline runs to five pages. It merits serious study. Vassiliev directed:

> In proportion as the legal apparatus of the party is liquidated, the directing functions will inevitably require a regrouping of party forces and the reorganization of the party apparatus. This reconstruction of the work will pass more and more to the illegal apparatus.

This has been going on, carefully and methodically, since the inception of the cold war. The underground party has been split up into several thousand fragments, the base being a cell of no more than ten, but usually five, members. Maximum security is maintained in liaison between cell, section, district, and national leaders. There is frequent use of couriers—telephones are banned—with the time-honored use of "cut-outs" to evade discovery. The party's financial structure has been overhauled to make the millions of dollars previously invested in legitimate enterprises more easily available. Caches of money—one of about half-a-million dollars—are kept.

Each member of the underground party operates like a soldier behind enemy lines. The more important comrades are provided with a false identity, false Social Security cards, and a false driver's license. For the top echelons, party doctors are available to change the color of hair, shape of eyebrows, size of nose. In Vassiliev's detailed instructions, it was mandatory

> (a) to find a building for storing Party archives; (b) to organize an illegal printing plant in which it would be possible to print the Party organ in case of suppression and closing of the legal Party papers and journals; (c) to form an apparatus for distributing illegal party literature; (d) to prepare a definite group of leading Party activists to pass into illegality; (e) to prepare addresses and houses for illegal correspondence, for secret sessions of the leading Party organs and also for housing the illegal Party activists and for conferences between them and the workers who continue to be on a legal footing; (f) to prepare a minimum number of workers who understand the elementary rules of the technique of underground work . . .

Every one of these organizational plans is now operational. Combat veterans in the party have been organized into hard-hitting flying squads for use in riot work. Beyond this, the Communists have set up a Red equivalent of the underground railroads which existed prior to the War Between the States. The policy of "industrial concentration" has put more than 75 percent of the underground party's mobile effectives into plants and factories where they can mold trade union policy now and sabotage by slowdowns and flash strikes in times of international crisis. Today, they have successfully infiltrated the largest local in the United Auto Workers union, and have begun the slow recapture of other unions. Less muscular troops have been carefully planted in everything from Parent-Teacher organizations to the grass roots echelons of legitimate political parties—and this includes the Republican Party. For the first time in a decade, spheres of influence have been reestablished in the Congress of the United States.

The third grouping of Communists is the most dangerous and the most potent. I refer to the "reserve" or "sleeper" apparatus. It is made up of people who have never joined a Communist front or identified themselves with a secret party cell. Record of the membership is kept in Moscow, and an approach to one of them may not be made for months or years. The member of the reserve remains on tap for one great assignment which exposes him, or for the small, subtle undermining of the will to resist of the nation.

There is another function of the sleeper apparatus, effective but beyond the reach of counter-intelligence. It operated silently during the Hiss case when—from the bars of Wall Street clubs to the comfortable reaches of Park Avenue—its poison dripped down every day and in every way, never defending treason but always besmirching those who exposed it. Editors and editorial writers on great newspapers, commentators, artists and entertainers— those responsible for the propaganda fallout which deforms the minds and thoughts of people in these terrible times—are included in the sleeper—part of the three-way drive to destroy America.

This is the paramilitary organism which threatens us. Seizure of power is its ultimate goal, but not by any frontal attack. The civil war to which it is directed has been going on for years; and, despite our smug complacencies, its victories have been considerable and steady. Let me enumerate:

1. In the past decade anti-Communists in this country have been systematically discredited and destroyed. With wise looks and smart sayings, those with specialized knowledge have been driven out of the market place of ideas. By innuendo, they find themselves deprived of standing in the intellectual community. They are accused of being "hysterical," of "seeing Communists under beds," of having lost a sense of proportion. And in time, they are elbowed out of the scholarly projects, the entertainment

field, the bookstores. Foundations, which control so much of the nation's intellectual life, shun them.

This is not accident. It is all planned—the work of the sleeper, but never sleeping, apparatus—and in most cases those who carry out the plan do not know that they are being manipulated.

2. Communists and pro-Communists who were painstakingly forced out of positions of influence in the mass media and the field of communications are returning. They are back on the networks, in Hollywood, in the publishing houses. They are strong enough to keep the paperbook field relatively clean of anti-Communist material. They are back in the teaching profession. Even convicted traitors—like Alger Hiss—are now being renovated by press, TV, and the academicians.

3. At every point of vulnerability, campaigns are being mounted and are meeting with increasing success: Stop nuclear testing, with or without adequate safeguards; recognize Red China, however it may open the way for Communist domination of the critically important overseas Chinese. Lower barriers on trade with Iron Curtain countries, even if it means strengthening their war potential. Curb the FBI, whatever the cost to internal security. Abolish Congressional investigation of subversion. Rip away all forms of government secrecy, legitimate or not, in the name of press freedom. And most of all, let's not be beastly to the Russians; turn the other cheek.

4. Coincident with these campaigns, voices urge the superiority of the Soviet system—its science, its education, its armaments, even its creaking productive capacity. At every hand so-called experts loudly deplore presumed American inadequacies—till the average citizen believes that this nation is hopelessly weak and unable to withstand the Communist onslaught. In this contest, Bertrand Russell's plea that we surrender begins to make sense.

This is not to imply that every man who raises his voice in behalf of these causes is broadcasting on a Moscow wave length. No one asks for a nation of tub-thumpers. But it is a fact that the intellectual atmosphere which agitates decent people over these issues—and the direction that agitation takes—is a function of the civil war now being waged in this country.

When a union newspaper attempts to terrorize its readers into a belief that their milk is poisoned by strontium 90, this is as much a manifestation of the civil war as the drilling squads of underground party activists. Those squads exist, trained in the use of baseball bats, picket sticks, hat pins, and the rest of the close-order drill of riot duty. But they are used almost never—when the order comes to put them into the field, the battle will be over. It will be over because the will to resist will be dead. The activists will storm an empty Bastille.

Not too many years ago the Office of Naval Intelligence was ordered by President Roosevelt to disband its Red Desk and destroy its files. Those files were never destroyed. They were carried out, as an admiral later admitted, on the backs of high-ranking officers who would not let politics triumph over patriotism. Would the Navy do as much today? Or has the will to resist begun to crumble?

Civil war and the violent seizure of power are easy to understand. The will to resist is intangible; once destroyed it may never be recreated. Not all the nuclear weapons of an atomic age, not all the brilliant strategic plans devised, not all the genius of production and logistics can prevail, once that will is gone.

This is what the Communists understand.

That is what they mean by civil war, by internal subversion.

Karl Marx once wrote: "Neither a nation nor a woman can be forgiven for the unguarded hour in which a chance comer has seized the opportunity for an act of rape." Can there be less forgiveness for those who today watch the rapist at work?

The American Mercury
April 1959

Notes on a Journey
to Russia

*If ever Toledano had to tilt against a windmill it was in
trying to shatter the whirling arms of that dervish conviction, bred of so much socialist hero worship, that
the Soviet Union somehow had moved mountains and
made miracles in its revolutionary industrialization.
When Toledano wrote these deflationary notes he was
bucking that mythology head-on. It is only now that
the tide has begun to turn, proving the prophetic accuracy of his plain, solid reporting. The latest data from
the worker's paradise, as most now know, tell us with
unblushing clarity that the "miraculous" industrialization of the U.S.S.R. is a pure and simple fraud. As
Warren Nutter, perhaps the foremost American
authority on the Soviet economy has put it–the truth
is that the industrialization of the U.S.S.R. under the
Communists has proceeded at no greater or effective a
pace than under the czars. So much for the miracle and
so much for one reporter who spotted the fraud early
on.*

This is an account of one reporter's observations of two weeks
in the Soviet Union and Poland. It pretends to be no more than a
series of notes, compromised perhaps by the fact that I have
limited myself to what I saw rather than to what I might have
seen had I the omniscience of some commentators who never left
American soil.

Moscow is a drab, ugly city—the only city I have ever seen which builds its slums new.

Moscow's handful of skyscrapers—the product of Stalin's vainglory and his love of wedding-cake, neo-Roxy architecture—had, like Stalin's face, the pockmarks of time. It was also a city of surprises.

The airport, which by rights should have had at least some of the superficial virtues of a Potemkin village, was a series of runways, one administration building, a single hangar able to service perhaps three planes, and an apron on which sat a long line of TU-104s (the Soviet two-engine jet) and some conventional aircraft. We were to see those TU-104s everywhere in the Soviet Union—for they have been produced at a rate which outstrips their use and so must sit through Russian winter and summer till they rust or turn into the medium-range bombers they were designed to be.

There are no superhighways in the Soviet Union—or at least we saw none. With passenger car production at 100,000 units a year and trucks at 400,000, there is no economic need for anything beyond the three and four lane roads which were the best we saw. Not far from the airport, the Intourist guide pointed out a collective farm—an abandoned movie set, it might have been—of empty fields, a cluster of old and primitive-looking shacks, and some farm buildings, but no people. In the middle of a field, we spotted a tractor, deserted by its driver. (When we passed that way days later it was still there, and the fields were still empty.)

On the outskirts of the city, we entered a tremendously broad avenue—Lenin Prospect—flanked by rows of apartment houses in various states of completion but all built to the same plan. The guide proudly announced that when it was completed, the development would house 300,000 people. Asked when work had been begun on this project, the guide was vague. Asked when it would be completed, he was vaguer still.

Since Catherine's day, Russians have built in the Italian style—stucco over brick. These houses were, even when occupied, still bare of their stucco—and we were shocked by the bad quality of the brick, the amateurish way it was laid, the slovenliness of the prefabricated concrete slabs used in construction. We noticed, too, that a wing or several floors of an unfinished house would be occupied. Many were so weathered that plainly they had been left to the elements in mid-completion long ago—a fact we later verified. It is difficult to say what depressed me most—the sameness, the disregard of what man's labor had wrought or the shoddiness of construction.

I have said that Moscow is a slum. This is true of the physical plant. Except for the old buildings of the Kremlin, the foreign embassies, and such show-spots as the MVD headquarters which houses the Lubianka, it is hard to find any structure in Moscow which does not need plaster, paint, or renovation—which has not been raddled by the grey termite of regimented poverty and heedlessness. The shops, flyblown and pathetic, will display a single sleazy jacket or a dusty pyramid of tinned food. There is, of course, GUM, the city's one big department store, whose glass-roofed arcades add a festive spirit, and its goods are plentiful. The click of the abacus, which tots up all money transactions in Russia, is loudest in the food departments.

The terrible drabness of Moscow is in its people. Stroll through the streets in the evening for a view of the working future. No children play on the sidewalks, and there is no sound of laughter. People move rapidly about their business, the figures of women dumpy, lost in shapeless clothes. The best-dressed girls were the Intourist guides, but they would have looked in envy at the wardrobe of a $50-a-week American typist.

This is the overlay. Beneath it there is the greater reality of the secret police. At the Ukraina Hotel, a 30-story Stalin-built "show-place," that reality is built in. As the lights flash on the elevator's panel board, the floors are ticked off—"10, 11, 13, 14" and "19, 20, 22, 23"—with "12" and "21" missing. On these two floors, the MVD has its equipment for tuning in on every room to record conversations or telephone calls. Here also is storage space for the photo equipment which the men in blue smocks carry about in small kits to photograph the papers in your bag. Outside the hotel, an MVD car sits day and night. At the Ukraina, my locked bag was searched twice, the steel frame of the two-suiter being bent in the process. The papers on my desk were scanned. This sounds comic now. But late at night, as the chemical smell of the Moscow River rose in the breeze and the bedbugs sought nourishment of me, it was not a comforting thought that terror lurked two floors below.

Those first days in Moscow were not all grim. If the other food was bad, it was possible to make a meal of the best grey caviar, bread and butter, and vodka—for less than 30 rubles. After the first shock of coping with an army of some seventy American reporters, Muscovites relaxed and showed signs of friendliness. That friendliness increased with every hostile mention of Vice President Nixon in *Pravda* or *Izvestia.* The U.S. Exhibit, tremendously popular, brought hundreds of people from as far away as the Crimea. They lacked the Moscow gloominess and sought us out, if only to shake hands. In time we realized that Communist propaganda, however warped an idea of the world it may have given the average Russian, had not been able to corrode his feeling toward Americans. We also realized that the occasional flash of hostility we encountered was usually motivated by a Russian's sense of the meagerness of his own existence, his knowledge that we lived better and dressed better than he, that we moved on a freer and fuller plane. It was not precisely envy but the need to sustain national pride. If we gave a child a small American coin, he always insisted that we accept something in exchange—and the same applied to adults.

It is this national touchiness, this subconscious rebellion against inferiority, that makes the average Russian respond to Nikita Khrushchev. I watched him for several hours during that unprecedented encounter with Vice President Nixon, noting the way he played up to the crowd in his gutter Russian, a *moujik* come to power, a natural politician skillfully manipulating emotions. At the first surge of people he had waved away his hard-faced security guards, hugged old women, nudged workmen, and put on a great show. But what had delighted the Russians who jostled about him was the obvious tactic of boasts and hyperbole with which he upheld the superiority of the Soviet way of life.

Surrounded by the fairyland of the Exhibit, and its manifestations of capitalist excellence, he could make statements palpably
contradicted by his surroundings and the Russians loved it. They
were not convinced; convincement was not the point at all. He
was on the attack against a world which represented all their
desires, and by a paradox in the human psyche he was satisfying
and justifying their need for it.

The next stop was Leningrad to which we flew in a TU-104B.
The Russians were very proud of this plane, so we praised it
politely. For them it is a luxury craft, but its appointments are
far below the level of the crudest American non-sked. Its jet
engines are set close to the fuselage which increases their thrust
but decreases stability and tends to induce a roll. Unlike American and other Western passenger jets, it lacked reverse thrust to
slow down the landing—relying on parachutes shot out from the
tail to cut down speed. We flew in the same plane throughout our
Soviet travels—not a happy experience after I had noticed that
the join of metal plates on the wing near the right engine had not
been riveted properly and gaped. At high altitudes, moreover,
screwheads inside the cabin iced up.

The terrible oppressiveness of Moscow began lifting in Leningrad. For one thing, we had weathered several crises in our relations with Soviet bureaucracy. For another, we were somewhat
more reconciled to Intourist and its shady business practices.

Before we left for Moscow, we had been assured by the Soviet
Embassy in Washington that there would be no censorship for us
and that we would be allowed to move freely. We had also been
assured that we would accompany the Vice President into Siberia.
Once in Moscow, the press office of the Foreign Ministry attempted to impose restrictions on the flow of copy. Herbert
Klein, Vice President Nixon's press secretary, stormed into the
Ministry and threatened that unless these restrictions were
removed, he would take the matter to Mr. Nixon who would
carry the fight to Premier Khrushchev. The Foreign Ministry
capitulated, then said the press would not be allowed to go to
Siberia "because hotel accommodations are insufficient." The

Vice President moved in on this one. "If the press doesn't go, neither will I," he told the Soviets—and the problem of accommodation suddenly melted away. But if the Russians could not censor our copy, they could slow it down, and Klein repeatedly had to "pop off to Popov"—Popov being the official in the ministry encharged with our destinies.

Intourist's financial shenanigans began when we were forced as a condition to receiving our visas to pay $30 a day in advance for thirteen days, though we were scheduled to remain only eleven days. This charge included $6.50 a day for meals, plus room and the services of an Intourist guide and car at all times. As it worked out, only eight to ten guides were ever available, cars often not, and when we most desperately needed one or both they were nowhere to be found. Before we left Moscow for Siberia, moreover, Intourist picked up our meal tickets for twelve meals and four teas—2,600 rubles or $260 at exchange—for which we were actually served eight meals, with the government pocketing the difference. By tactics such as these, the Soviet Union made a few extra thousands of dollars out of our trip—and lost millions in the good will of the more naive members of the press party.

In Leningrad, as I have noted, we felt a different atmosphere. The hotels, relics of the Tsarist past, put us up three, four, and five to the room. But the signs of a former graciousness had not been eradicated completely. And in the streets, there were voices and life well into the night. At the opera house, we sat through four acts of Khatchaturian's ballet *Spartak*—beautifully staged and costumed, and nostalgic for us since the composer had bodily lifted "Night and Day," "Over There," "Lover" and pages of Verdi in a kind of hit-parade potpourri. The TU-104B cannot fly non-stop from Leningrad to Novosibirsk. With a refueling stop, we made the trip in about five and one-half hours. There was excitement on the plane as we put down, for here, we had been told, was the new Russia of vast industrial development. Novosibirsk had once been under MVD government, but now it had reverted to civil administration. It was also billed, in Russian hyperbole, as the "Chicago of Siberia." Perhaps someday it will

be, when the grandchildren of those who welcomed us are growing into manhood.

Novosibirsk is strategically placed where the Trans-Siberian
railroad crosses the great Ob River. It is linked by air to European
Russia and the Far East. When the Russians get around to building a paved highway between this growing city and Moscow—right
now large stretches of road are rivers of mud except during the
summer dry season—Novosibirsk will also become a trucking center. Today, it is a long city paralleling Krasnyy Prospect, most of
whose side streets are still unpaved, with clusters of new apartment houses whose "modern" kitchens are equipped with wood-
and-coal burning stoves. Driving down the main street, we had a
view between the apartment houses of potato fields—thousands
of acres of potato fields—and a few small stands of corn. The city
is primitive, raw, frontier.

What interested us most in Siberia was the promise of seeing
the great model plants which turn out machine tools and heavy
machinery. But our visit to the Efremov industrial complex was a
real eye-opener. This, the Soviets told us, was their very best—but
that best turned out to be several decades behind our average.
Production lines were badly organized. Overhead cranes could
deliver only down the center of the plant. Automation was nonexistent. In time we realized that for the Soviet mentality, it is
enough to say—whether true or not—that a factory or plant is the
biggest in Russia or in the world. That its technology is outdated
and its production slow does not matter. ("Do you have plants
like this in the United States?" a Soviet official asked proudly.)

In Novosibirsk and Sverdlovsk, we wondered where the skill
and industrial power to build sputniks had come from. Every
plant we were shown was proof positive that we had been sold a
bill of goods by Soviet propagandists. Certainly by a great focus-
ing of effort, by the massing of labor, and by the use of limited
numbers of specialists, the Soviet Union could build rockets and
missiles and mass produce a jet. But taking Soviet industry, and
the economy as a whole, we were still dealing with a backward
country whose main incentive was to work as little as the state

power would tolerate. If the coffee break was an American invention, the Soviet Union had anticipated it by the all-day goof.

Going through the plants near Sverdlovsk–Uralmash where the Russians once made their heavy tanks, the copper mines, the rolling mills—we saw bigness, but nowhere the ability to produce both well and in great numbers. Said one correspondent who specializes in industrial reporting: "Maybe the Russians will catch up to us, but it won't be under this seven-year-plan or the next."

It was in Sverdlovsk, the sleepy city where the Czar was murdered and the Revolution born, that it finally penetrated through our sputnik-bedazzled minds that the Soviet Union had neither the transport, the industrial capacity, nor the trained work force to fight a long war. And it occurred to some of us that there was both method and chagrin in Nikita Khrushchev's missile-rattling whenever he was backed into a corner by Vice President Nixon. There had also been plain, stubborn ignorance in his remarks about the United States. Reporters who had firmly argued against his visit to America, then in a rumor stage, began to change their minds. "Let him see what the U.S. is like," they said. "Not only the big factories but the cities and roads and streets, the traffic jams. The worst we've got is better than this."

We returned to Moscow. We took one look at the wax figures in the mausoleum on Red Square—the Lenin which Russians believe is an embalmed human body and the Stalin which may be. We bought our souvenirs at GUM. And we took off for Poland.

It was with a sense of joy and relief that we boarded an American jet, that we slumped into seats made for our creature comfort and received the treatment from stewards and hostesses which we had almost forgotten existed. We put down in Warsaw never expecting the welcome of 250,000 shouting, cheering, and weeping Poles. "Long live Nixon!" they shouted. "We love America. We love Poland." The devastation of war still remained standing, mountains of rubble, shell and rifle-fire scars. But what was rebuilt was solid. The return of Gomulka had brought limited free enterprise, and the private shops were well stocked. The women in the streets had attractive figures—the first we had seen in close to two weeks. Men wore neckties. There was the breath of humanity in the air. People argued on street corners.

We discovered that there is a considerable amount of free speech in Poland—that criticism of the government and of the Soviet Union can be heard in loud and emphatic tones. We discovered that Russia and all things Russian were passionately hated by the Poles. It was a little puzzling to find expressed everything from mild concern to real support for the newest development in American-Soviet relations. Boiled down, this was to an announcement that President Eisenhower had invited Nikita Khrushchev to Washington:

"Yes, it may be that this will be another Hitler-Stalin Pact in which we will be caught in the middle. On the other hand, no matter what beasts the Russians are, America will not betray us. You sent your Vice President to be here when the announcement was made. His visit to Warsaw was a sign. And while the United States and the Soviet Union are busy discussing peace, perhaps Khrushchev will leave us alone." On the grounds of the University of Warsaw, a woman handed me a bouquet of flowers and said something I could not understand. The people in the crowd smiled and applauded. A young man in the crowd said in English:

"This is a great day for Poland." "You mean Mr. Nixon's visit or the announcement?" I asked. "Both," he said. "Long live America."

National Review
August 1959

Columns Right

REPORT FROM RHODESIA

*It can only be hoped that Toledano's reporting, as em-
bodied in this report from Rhodesia, will turn out to
be as vindicated as his reporting from Russia. Indeed,
one of the most cruel spectacles of the Twentieth Century has been the way in which American intellectuals
who dare call themselves liberals have stood by silently
while tribal despots wage genocidal war against whole
peoples in Africa while reserving their full and only
anger for such regimes as that of Rhodesia, whose great
crime has been to base its voting eligibility upon property requirements, precisely as some of our Founding
Fathers so earnestly and honestly wanted to do. It is
also worth noting, lest anyone get the truly foolish
notion that Toledano is some sort of racist that it has
been Toledano, and not any supposedly liberal journalists whom I can recall, who has persistently fought
racial segregation in that most steadfastly segregated of
all institutions, the American labor unions. It all adds
up, I think, to making Toledano's reporting on Rhodesia a good deal more worth listening to than the
'liberal' reporting either on Rhodesia–or America!*

American policy on Rhodesia represents the triumph of ideology over actuality. To excuse American intervention in what
should be the purely private conflict between the British Government and Rhodesia, it is argued that the chain of circumstances

leading to Rhodesian independence was improperly motivated—the result of a racist philosophy and a uniquely selfish economic interest. This position is based on a profound ignorance of the forces at work in Rhodesia—as well as in the rest of Africa.

The aim of both Britain and the United States is to bring down the constitutionally-elected government of Prime Minister Ian Smith and replace it by a puppet regime, to be followed by a "one man, one vote" formula—thus applying, in an undeveloped continent, a highly sophisticated Western political system divorced from the realities of the present situation in Rhodesia. Since that country has been significantly in the news for many months, it might have been expected that the American press would have sent numerous able reporters to Salisbury, the capital city, to report developments there at first hand. Instead, news reaching the United States has come almost exclusively from British circles taking their lead from Labour Party publicists. Dubious sources at the United Nations have added their mite to the muddle of misinformation.

Certainly, it is no secret that Assistant Secretary of State for African Affairs G. Mennen Williams has used what influence remains at his disposal in Washington to discourage on-site inspection by responsible legislators and newspaper correspondents who believe that United States foreign policy should lead from the strength of knowledge rather than the fanaticism of *a priori* judgment. Important publications have been told that the Rhodesian government is not admitting accredited journalists—a totally false charge. In actual fact, the Rhodesian government is not only willing but anxious to open its doors to those able to report what their eyes and ears register. "We have nothing to hide," Prime Minister Smith told me when asked if he would receive a Congressional delegation.

Planned myopia seems to be the technique of American policy makers—the same planned myopia which led millions of Americans to accept with no attempt at verification the myth that the Chinese Communists were "agrarian reformers" and Mao Tse-tung the George Washington of the Far East. A new myth now prevents a careful reading of the Rhodesian situation and halts debate by describing that country as a crumbling bastion of white supremacy which must "inevitably" fall before the progressive onslaught of African nationalism. To the propagators of this myth the "petrol bomb" used by Rhodesian nationalists to intimidate their fellow Africans has seemingly become just an instrument of democratic persuasion, acceptable despite the terror it engenders.

The steps being taken in Rhodesia to maintain and extend a high level of living for all, to preserve public tranquility, and to lift the economic, social, and political level of the African population may or may not be morally or pragmatically justifiable. But before any approbation or opprobrium is meted out, there surely must first be an accurate estimate of the situation. And this estimate cannot be valid unless it answers the following questions, which have been largely ignored by policy makers, the mass media, and those who derive their positions from both.

Is the Rhodesian government of Prime Minister Smith stable?

What degree of active or passive support does it have from the Rhodesian people—white and black?

Is the Rhodesian economy sound, and how is it threatened by the sanctions which Britain has imposed and America accepts?

If these sanctions succeed, who would suffer most?

Can the country survive a political and economic collapse, yet still continue as a respectable member of the family of nations?

Is the philosophy of the present Rhodesian government racist?

What, in fact, is its philosophy, and where does it lead?

What are Rhodesia's strengths and weaknesses as a nation?

What is the nature of the African population?

Most important of all, would the enshrining of the "one man, one vote" principle in Rhodesia be possible today without subjecting the country to the chaos, despotism and barbarism which have all to often taken over in the so-called "developing" nations of Africa?

Americans, in contemplating the Rhodesian situation, are either unaware or refuse to take cognizance of its complete uniqueness among all the other colonies, possessions, or participants in the systems set up by the European powers in Africa.

For example, few know that Rhodesia moved directly from its status as a chartered region to self-government. Until 1887—or two years before the Crown granted a charter to the British South Africa Company—the area now called Rhodesia was the battle-ground for bloody tribal wars between the militarized Matabele tribes and the relatively peaceful Mashonas. An ancient and end-less conflict had kept the Mashonas in a constant state of physical terror and economic uncertainty. These wars, and the incursions of disease and early mortality, had held down the African popula-tion to about 300,000. It has now risen to some four million—and it is estimated that barring starvation, cataclysm, or the kind of "freedom" which Britain wishes to impose, it will double in the next twenty years.

The white settlers who emigrated from Britain or South Africa were not looking for fast profits in gold and emeralds. They came to live as farmers, homesteaders, and businessmen. Rhodesia for them was not a way station on the road of Imperial convenience, but a way of life. Under the governance of the British South Africa Company, they built cities, established trade, opened up the land, set up a school system, and organized the country with the same goals of permanence that European settlers carried with them to America. They did this with a minimum of damage to the tribal system and its customs, and they did not act with the rapacity which led settlers on the American continent to wipe out entire indigenous populations or to take over the entire area in their civilizing course.

By free choice, after a referendum, the Rhodesians voted in 1923 for responsible self-government as a member of the British Commonwealth, rather than for joining the Union of South Africa as a fifth province. The status was replaced by an assertion of full sovereignty by a legitimate and legally elected government in 1965, at a time when the British government—with the blessing of the United States—was systematically granting independence to all sorts of former possessions with little or no training or tradition in self-government. The outcry at No. 10 Downing Street over Rhodesia's unilateral act of disassociation may be understood in terms of Commonwealth interest and the general inclinations of Prime Minister Harold Wilson. But to argue "constitutionality" under the circumstances, or to insist on the right of the British government to determine the internal organization of the withdrawing state, should have sounded strange to Americans who seized their own independence by force of arms and set up their own government without the permission of George III or his ministers.

The test of legal validity will not be found in the animadversions of Britain's Labour government. Despite the reservations of Prime Minister Wilson, it remains a fact that the Rhodesian government of Mr. Ian Smith was elected by an overwhelming vote of those who held the franchise. It remains a fact that the fourteen African members of the Rhodesian parliament, elected in the same election—there are 65 M.P.s in all—do *not* favor the surrender of the country to the African nationalists. And it remains a fact that the present Constitution differs only in nonessentials from the 1961 Constitution which Mr. Wilson holds so dear. For Britain to attempt to inject itself into the internal affairs of Rhodesia, and especially its political life, when it has signally refrained from doing so in many former British possessions that are now frankly African police states, is hardly consistent, let alone fair.

The structure of the Rhodesian state and its qualifications for granting the franchise will be discussed later in this report. That it meets the requirements of the Rhodesian situation is an observable fact. Salisbury, the other cities of Rhodesia, and the agricultural countryside are tranquil to a degree unknown in many sections of the civilized world. The streets are policed by African officers far more relaxed than their law-enforcement counterparts in New York, Los Angeles or Washington. Crimes of violence, an index to social *malaise* and instability, are relatively few. Political crime—consisting mostly of incinerating people in their beds by tossing "petrol bombs" onto thatched roofs—ceased almost entirely when the perpetrators were arrested, much to the relief of the African population. The tell-tale signs of racial tension are nowhere to be seen. Neither is that atmosphere of repression so visible in states where power is held against the will of the governed. Sanctions have, in fact, consolidated the hold of the Smith government by winning over to its side such scattered opposition as existed before their advent. For many of the Africans, the fear is not of more white government but of a return to that brief period when nationalist terrorists, financed by Peking, Cairo et al., were allowed to employ the "persuasion" of bomb and knife.

Rhodesian Minister of Law Desmond William Lardner-Burke stated to me in this regard what others later confirmed. "We don't stop people from speaking," he stated. "The only time we get cross is when there is a bit of subversion." There was a heightening of that subversion when the African nationalists themselves split into two factions, each vying for the financial support of the Committee of Nine (the OAU "Liberation Committee") in Tanzania. During that period, with a cash subsidy of $30,000 set aside by the Committee, African fought African with gasoline bombs and hand grenades. Much of the violence was directed against children, and the schools were virtually closed as a result of nationalist threats. When witchcraft was invoked to silence witnesses against the terror, the Rhodesian government had no option but to disregard the finer points of law. This was admitted by Mr. Lardner-Burke when he said, "You cannot allow complete chaos because of due process." In the United States, this would be heresy. For the population of Rhodesia, black and white, it was a stark necessity.

If there is any noticeable apprehension on the part of the white or African population, it does not derive from the steps taken by the Smith government to put an end to violence and subversion. The fear is that Rhodesia's course towards a viable and responsible multi-racial state will be interrupted by some overt military move against the country from either the British or a neighboring African country—with or without the support of the United Nations. These military adventures might take the form of outright invasion—which Britain's allies in Africa have already threatened, should economic sanctions fail to topple the present government. Neutral observers in Salisbury, London, and Paris discount the possibility of British military intervention, however. Such a maneuver would profit Britain little and cost her much. A former American official noted that if the British were to send in anything less than two divisions, they would be wiped out. An overwhelming force, moreover, would find a devastated country, put to the torch in "scorched earth" fashion. At least half the white population, with Africans at their side, are ready to fall, "rifle in hand"—a phrase heard with startling regularity in Rhodesia. The balance of the white population would probably leave the country permanently, emigrating to South Africa or to other countries which could absorb them and make use of their pioneering skills.

The African country most vocal in its incitements to violence is Zambia, which shares a border along the world's greatest man-made lake and also the hydroelectric installation at Kariba. But the Zambian economy has been sadly sapped by the sanctions which were to destroy Rhodesia in "a matter of months," and its government has so far survived only because of substantial aid from Britain, Canada, the United States, South Africa, and to some extent Rhodesia. Though demagogic passion often burns with a hard, senseless flame, it seems unlikely that the Zambian government will risk its own downfall by launching an attack across the Kariba Dam against the well-trained and determined Rhodesian army and air force. So far, there have been no overt acts to disturb the calm along the Zambia-Rhodesia border. On the Zambia side, there are no border guards, and the curious can cross over from Rhodesian territory without being challenged or molested. In the Rhodesian interior, Zambian workers continue to hold their jobs. They have made it plain that they do not want to return to the relative poverty of their Zambian homes.

There is, however, some concern that the more hot-headed African nations may mount a massive infiltration of saboteurs and activists whose aim will be to cause the kind of economic disruption which can be publicized abroad as "proof" of political unrest and a reaction to Rhodesian "tyranny." But here again, the government is prepared. An increase in unemployment, already making itself felt as a result of economic sanctions, can create the kind of unrest which feeds subversion. But with little official prompting, Rhodesian farmers and industrialists are spreading the work so as to lay off the fewest number of people. And unemployment will cease to be a problem if the Smith government is given time to rearrange the economy sufficiently to take up the slack. This rearrangement is already taking place as Rhodesia moves to manufacture at home many products once imported from Britain and the rest of the world.

Here again, the loser will be Great Britain. Though Rhodesian trade is not a major factor in the British economy, its loss is of sufficient importance to increase a balance-of-payments unfavorable to England and to force further retrenchment in an already distressing situation. Rhodesia, on the other hand, once she has survived this transition period, will find herself economically stronger and less dependent on the vagaries of Commonwealth politics. Even in the matter of oil, often called the lifeblood of a modern state, Rhodesia is not as pinched as Prime Minister Wilson or the American State Department had hoped. What stocks of oil existed at the time sanctions were imposed is a state secret. So, too, is the amount of oil coming in from Portuguese Mozambique and independent South Africa. There are still cars on the streets, however, and South African "neutrality" has not prevented a small but steady stream of oil from pouring across the border. At the same time, the Rhodesians are preparing to convert their transport, if necessary to the use of industrial alcohol for fuel— and since there is an abundance of sugar, this may be the ultimate solution.

The present danger to the Rhodesian economy is to be found elsewhere. Sixty percent of the country's export trade was in tobacco. It is its major cash crop, and Britain was Rhodesian tobacco's major customer. To soften the blow, the Rhodesian government has set up a corporation to buy at a fair price the entire tobacco crop—but this will put a considerable strain on the budget. Unless a substitute market is found, this will be a source of trouble for Prime Minister Smith. There are signs, however, that Rhodesia may have found an ally in Britain's tobacco industry. The *Times* of London has already reported considerable perturbation over the ban on Rhodesian tobacco. Grade for grade, it is considerably cheaper than American tobacco. If the ban is maintained, the profit margin will either be wiped out for British cigarette manufacturers—or they will have to raise prices, which they feel will bring serious complaints from smokers who have already sustained a long series of increases.

In other areas, British sanctions have failed to cause any real pinch. Stores in Salisbury are well stocked with luxuries and necessities—and goods on order prior to the imposition of the ban on trade are still coming in. There is no inflation so far, though Rhodesian businessmen bemoan the fact that the greatest boom in their history was cut short by Britain's action. Food is no problem; Rhodesia raises its own. The country has been ridden by drought, but Rhodesians find a silver lining in this. Food was an export, but with home-grown supplies down there will be no surplus to rot in warehouses. To date, there has been no hoarding of food or of other consumer items—a tribute to the self-confidence and self-discipline of the Rhodesians.*

When Britain's Prime Minister Wilson declared economic war on Rhodesia, there were expectations that this would (1) drive a wedge between the Smith government and the people, (2) cause widespread defections in the civil service and the military establishment, and (3) encourage the Africans to rise up. It has already been noted here that points (1) and (2) were dismal miscalculations. The effect of sanctions was simply to bring the people together—and if there have been any important defections from the government's civilian or military service, no one in Rhodesia knows about them. Point (3), however, continues to intrigue those who seek the overthrow of Prime Minister Smith and the ouster of his Rhodesian Front party. Yet here again, their hopes are based on false premises and a profound ignorance of the attitudes and desires of the Africans in Rhodesia. In conversations with African members of the opposition in Parliament—and with

---

*Fears of the boycott proved groundless. As time passed, the British resumed their trade with Rhodesia through intermediaries. The U.S., desperately in need of Rhodesian chrome, purchased it from the Soviets at a mark-up over the price the Kremlin paid to Rhodesia.

the one white oppositionist M.P.—it became abundantly clear to
us that no one in Rhodesia wants to see the kind of upheaval
which the African nationalists and their foreign supporters seek.

Among those Africans who have risen to public prominence,
there are of course some who demand instant applications of the
"one man, one vote" formula. But for the most part, the desire to
rule is tempered by the knowledge that at this point in Rhodesia's
development, the precipitate introduction of Western political
ideas would benefit no one. P. H. Mkudu, chief whip of the
opposition, has freely conceded that his people need much training before they can take over the reins of government. He puts
the time period required at "not less than five years" and calls for
increased educational opportunities and an end to social discrimination. And he has small patience with his colleague in the
Parliament, I. H. Samuriwo, who insists that the Africans should
be given the opportunity to rule—and *then* trained to administer
the government and the economy of the country. The African
opposition as a whole calls for a five-point program:

1. Change the franchise.
2. Institute a crash program in education.
3. Institute a crash program of agricultural development.
4. Change ownership rights and property rights.
5. End social discrimination.

What these points mean and how rapidly they are to be im-
plemented are another matter. Specific proposals are shunned.
Nor are the five points advanced as a panacea for Rhodesia's
problems. The most articulate spokesmen contend that the acceptance of the five points will insure tranquility and prosperity
for Rhodesia. The strongest argument offered in their favor is
simple: Without the "change" that is demanded, the country
faces bloodshed and turmoil. With it, there is "a possibility" that
these eventualities can be avoided. But the demands for a "crash
program" in this field or that fail to take into account the
cultural context of the country. The changes that Rhodesia requires to make it a truly multi-racial nation cannot come into

being overnight. In a society as technologically sophisticated as Rhodesia, integration must take place gradually, on an individual basis, and the gauge must be merit rather than color of skin. Merit, moreover, must be measured by objective standards.

The philosophy of the Rhodesian government—and it is shared almost universally by the white population—is derived from these beliefs and from the practices that have evolved from them. But beyond this, there is a concept of the role of the races in Africa which commands respect. It is, as the Prime Minister has insisted, completely divorced from any trace of Herrenvolkism, as well as from the *apartheid* policy of South Africa. Rhodesians see the "one man, one vote" principle as a form of reverse racism, for in practice it would destroy the white community completely and deprive the country of all the techniques of a modern society.

In broad strokes, this has been painted by P. K. Van der Byl, the young Minister of Information. "In Rhodesia," he points out, "there are two distinct societies. One is Western, parliamentary, and democratic. The second is an African tribal society. This tribal society is authoritarian and hierarchical. In between, there is a no-man's land—an intermediary African group—for whom the tribal system has lost much of its meaning. This group belongs to neither the tribal nor the Western system. They are the problem in Africa today."

Like most other Rhodesians, Mr. Van der Byl believes that the whites have no right to tamper with the tribal society "except by example and persuasion." To take this view, however, does not mean that the Rhodesian government will sit idly by and see its institutions destroyed, nor that it can condone violence and disregard of the law. "We must put a damper on such things as the killing of one of twins. But the Africans must be the arbiters of their own destiny. It would be morally and pragmatically wrong for Western society to impose its own *mores*. On the other hand, we will put no obstacle in the way of those who wish to leave the tribal society and join the Western system. There is no inhibition on an African getting the vote. But it is our belief that the franchise should call for a high degree of education or other qualifications."

The experience of the other "new" African nations would seem to confirm Mr. Van der Byl's contention that if those qualifications are forgotten or mechanically lowered to produce an overwhelmingly large percentage of enfranchised citizens, "it debases the entire system." It therefore boils down to two questions: (1) Is the electoral system theoretically impartial, and (2) is it also impartial in practice? There is no doubt that the Rhodesian whites have worked very hard at setting up an electoral machinery which will apply to all three categories of its population. There are two voting rolls—the A roll, which is dominant and which elects 50 members to the Parliament; and the B roll for those in the transitional stage, which elects fifteen members. The qualifications for the A roll are higher than those for the B roll. But there are Africans in the A category and white men in the B category. Within the Parliament, members elected on either roll have the same rights and privileges.

To ascertain the practical impartiality of the Rhodesian system, factors other than the strict application of the electoral code must be considered. First, there is the attitude of those Africans still living within their tribal organizations. Among them, there is scant interest in the exercise of the suffrage. They are, therefore, pretty much represented by their chiefs, who have official status. Eventually, the Rhodesian government hopes to institutionalize the role of the chiefs by setting up a second legislative chamber somewhat analogous to the American Senate or the British House of Lords—replacing the present Council of Chiefs. Such an innovation will enhance the status of the Africans and give them a greater voice in government affairs without debasing the franchise.

But this is secondary to a matter of far greater significance in assessing the Rhodesian system. Are the whites sincerely dedicated to raising the educational and economic levels of the African population? Or are the inhibitions on the suffrage merely a polite way of preventing qualified Africans from using their numerical preponderance to take control of the country? On this point, the opposition is most vocal. It claims that the government of Ian Smith—or any other white government—will simply create new impediments to granting the franchise as the level of the African population rises to meet the present inhibitions. But this charge goes to the matter of motive and psychological imponderables. As such, it is almost impossible to weigh objectively. All the evidence at hand, certainly, points to an opposite conclusion.

Has the Rhodesian government, for one thing, really *tried* to bring education to the African? The answer lies in economic statistics and an analysis of the school population. At present Rhodesia's ratio of children in school to total population is comparable to Britain's—even though there is a wide disparity (in favor of Britain) in the national incomes of the two countries. The following table of ratios tells a story which goes far to contradict those who reject the sincerity of the Rhodesian whites:

Great Britain . . . . 1 in 5

Rhodesia . . . . 1 in 6

Malagasy . . . . 1 in 11

Tanzania . . . . 1 in 18

Dahomey . . . . 1 in 20

Mali . . . . 1 in 43

Ethiopia . . . . 1 in 80

African education is the single target expenditure of the Rhodesian government, and it has trebled in the last seven years. It is significant in this context that 98 percent of all direct taxation is paid by whites. Despite this financial inequity, the Rhodesian government has been able to meet the demands of an African school population of some 2 million children under 17 for a primary education. As this demand is met, the government has moved ahead to provide secondary school education for those who desire it. But here the government has run into several problems. First, the 10 percent of the primary school population which is female has been kept out of the secondary schools by parents who take their daughters out of school when they become nubile and "sell" them into marriage. Secondly, the demand for the admittedly few but steadily increasing places in secondary schools has yet to equal the supply.

As a matter of educational philosophy, moveover, the Rhodesian government has subscribed to the Western idea of providing as much education as possible for all, rather than to the practice prevalent in former French and British colonies of training a small elite group and ignoring the rest of the African population. The Rhodesian school system, moreover, is relatively young. (After all, the country has been under settlement for less than 75 years). Rhodesians note that in Britain, with its ancient traditions, only 34 percent continue to go to school after age 15—and in the United States, which boasts of its public education, there are today some 23 million adults who never went beyond elementary school.

The opposition has criticized the government for not providing more vocational schools. But the Rhodesian experience has been one of apathy among Africans toward this kind of training; and what demand there was has tended to fall off in the past year. The government nevertheless has pressed for longer periods of education, particularly in the secondary schools. It has organized correspondence courses and night schools. There are, again, no discriminatory practices against Africans, and all African students at the University are eligible for government support. At the present time, those African students at the University of Rhodesia receiving scholarships, grants, and loans would not have qualified had purely academic standards been imposed. Instead, the school authorities have "discriminated" in their favor—hardly a sign that there is official reluctance to raise educational opportunities for Africans. Nor is it a sign of foot-dragging that the amount spent for African education doubled between 1963 and 1965—with the figure still rising—and that African pupil enrollment has tripled in the past ten years, with approximately 700,000 students now attending school.

Simultaneously, a strong effort—some of it governmental and some private—is being made to raise the economic level of the African population by introducing better methods of working the land and by opening up new land for African use. Since 1920, farm and grazing land assigned for African occupation rose from 21.6 million acres to 44.3 million acres, whereas white acreage has been reduced by 12 million. There are 5.9 million acres open for sale to either whites or Africans—but African lands (for which no rent or purchase price is paid in the tribal areas) are protected from encroachment by the more prosperous white farmers. The opening up of increased acreage for African use has been a continuing process, to meet demands by the Africans themselves.

What is done with that land is another matter. The charge has been made that the farm land occupied by whites is much better than African land holdings. This, however, is not sustained by the facts. For example, a tract of "worked out" land was taken over by an agricultural school. On this presumably worthless "sandveld" proper farming methods have produced a high yield of corn—yet African farms in the same area have remained on a subsistence farming level. Soils in the African area roughly match the fertility of those in areas being farmed by whites. Studies have further shown that 37 percent of Rhodesia has a rainfall in excess of 28 inches—and half the African areas are within the preferred zone. The government recognizes that it requires more than good soil and adequate rainfall to produce cash crops. Capital is necessary, and this is provided to African farmers in loans and grants.

At the same time, white farmers have banded together to help the African farmer increase his yield. They have provided seed, tractors, and instruction in agricultural know-how to those willing to join the program for a minimum period of three years. But they have run into what sociologists call a "high leisure preference" among Africans—as well as a tendency to retire from the economic contention once they have put aside enough money to provide subsistence for the immediate future. To counter these tendencies, the government and white businessman have attempted to increase the level of consumer demand by stocking the shops with the kind of items which will be attractive to the wives of African farmers and to the farmers themselves—washing machines, radios, bicycles, etc. Whether this modified form of the Madison Avenue technique will provide the drive that Europenas and Americans take for granted is not yet susceptible of proof. But the fact remains that more and more African farmers are able to buy new farms in the unreserved areas, to pay substantial sums in cash for homes and farm equipment, and to derive incomes equal to or better than those of the white settlers.

It should be noted here that this previously steady development ran into trouble when the African nationalists began their campaign. An Englishman who has lived for some years in Rhodesia reported that "Agricultural agents would go to African farms to show how to improve the yield. Then the nationalists would follow and say, 'If you do that, we'll burn your house down.'" Since there were 35 "petrol bomb" raids a month before the Rhodesian government clamped down, the effect on African farmers was considerable. The terror was not only physical, for many of the Africans still under tribal sway have not relinquished their belief in witchcraft and in the "power of the spirit." The nationalists invoked these beliefs and powers and would still be using them if the government had not proved that it was impervious to nationalist magic.

That, in brief, is the Rhodesian picture. A stable government, geared to the needs of a country in south-central Africa, commands the virtually unanimous support of the white population and the respect of a preponderance of the Africans. A sound and growing economy faces the threat of strangulation, but is moving energetically to adjust itself to new conditions. Should it fail, all of Africa will suffer. For the black people of Rhodesia, it would mean a return to the tribal wars which ended less than 70 years ago. It would mean the collapse of the economy as thousands of white farmers, businessmen, and technicians either died in the convulsions of a forcible takeover or migrated to South Africa. Under those circumstances, the burnt-out case of Rhodesia would become another and more terrible Congo. Chaos would innundate order, and Africa would not fail to read the message that Western civilization had abdicated. The joint achievement of white and African in Rhodesia would go up in acrid smoke.

It would be comforting to assume that sanity will prevail, that the ideologized fury of Britain's Prime Minister Wilson would be recognized for what it is and not for the principled assault on racism that it claims to be. It would be pleasant to believe that, in

American policy toward Rhodesia, facts will triumph over ideological commitments, leading to the withdrawal of this country from participation in the sanctions Britain has imposed; that knowledge will vanquish ignorance. It would be only human to hope that fanaticism over "majority rule" will bow to the realization that Rhodesia's 4 million Africans and 220,000 whites are not living in Chicago or Birmingham but are slowly evolving a sound and democratic compromise which will give the white minority a realistic chance of survival and the black majority an opportunity, almost unique in Africa, of achieving political and economic equality.

But these are not the reasons which lead to our conclusion, which is: that Rhodesia as now constituted will *not* be crushed by Mr. Wilson and the Labour government of England. On the beautiful streets of Salisbury, there is a firm determination to stand up to whatever the British, the neighboring African states, and the United States can throw at them. There is a conviction that Rhodesia is pointing the way to the kind of Africa which can develop its tremendous resources for the good of all; that it can sustain a deepening democracy against the totalitarian forces which one by one have taken over the less fortunate nations of the continent. Firepower wins wars, but guns are sometimes loaded with more than bullets. The Rhodesians will feed themselves and find new markets for their goods, whatever the effort may temporarily do to the way of life they have created on the African veld. They are pledged to this without drama, without vainglory, without hatred. Unless the world goes mad, this spirit of resolution is better than firepower and, stronger than economic sanctions. It alone can build the Rhodesia that is desired, and deserved, by all her peoples.

February 1966

DEATH, THE AEC, AND
ATOMIC RAT-HOLES

*The useful point of this series on the Atomic Energy
Commission is in its discussion of inept bureaucracy.
The not so useful point is its somewhat alarmist view
of nuclear energy as a source of power. As such, the
power of the atom has advanced far more rapidly and
effectively than most of its detractors possibly could
have imagined. It is true, however, that the advances
have been made, it would certainly seem, wherever and
to whatever extent the bureaucracy has got out of the
way and permitted the engineers and the businessmen
to get on with the job. As a great fan of the atom, I can
only regret that Toledano, in this instance, finds it unfriendly. But, as a great foe of any and all bureacracies,
public, private, or holy, I must say that any attack on a
bureaucrat is better than no attack at all.*

At every level of government, but particularly in the cloak-
rooms of House and Senate, there is talk of economy. With
billions of dollars melting away in the Vietnamese conflagration,
and with billions more being sought to make America's cities safe
from extremists, there are just not enough tax dollars to keep the
Great Society in blue chips.

Yet in all the debate over ways and means to trim the Federal
budget and to reduce the expected $29 billion deficit, not one
word is said about the Atomic Energy Commission's $2.5 billion
budget request or its fantastically costly drive to "nuclearize" the
United States. Nor is any thought given to the consequences to
the health and safety of the American people from the AEC's
program to replace adequate power facilities with nuclear reactors.

If the Congress and the White House really wish to cure the
Federal budget of its chronic elephantiasis, the place to begin
might be with the AEC. But this will never be done until the

American people are made aware of the atomic rat-hole down which the taxpayer's millions are being poured and of the hazards that the AEC's reactor program are creating. The facts, however, as this series of columns will demonstrate, remain incontrovertible.

It can be demonstrated that—

1. Millions, if not billions, are being wasted in the construction of nuclear power facilities which do not work simply because the engineers have not yet solved the problems that derive from the use of atomic fuels.

2. Lives are being lost and other lives are being jeopardized by the faulty or careless production and deployment of radioactive materials.

3. The AEC and the utilities involved in uses of nuclear energy have not found a safe answer to the problem of disposing of the radioactive waste which is the lethal bi-product of such uses.

In a recent column, I wrote of the tragic death of Robert Peabody as a result of an accident at an atomic energy laboratory, and of the secrecy which the AEC, in violation of Executive orders, clamped down on the case. The AEC, perhaps unaware that I had read its regulations, denied that secrecy existed and argued that, in sealing its files on such accidents, it was merely protecting those involved.

This is simply not so. The attorney for Mr. Peabody's widow was forced to get a Federal court order to allow him to examine AEC's records on the accident—and he is still being balked. This secrecy makes it difficult, but not impossible, to get a clear picture of AEC's operations, errors, and failures. But there is enough on the record to tell the tale.

The AEC's passion for secrecy—and the highly expert propaganda which accompanies it—have obscured the fact that industrial atomic power is an infant science, still unreliable and technologically deficient. At the six "working" atomic plants, as of December 1966, there were repeated interruptions of service. Some of them went out of power production for as long as six months—hardly an encouraging record for those who want to keep America's lights (and freezers and air-conditioners) going.

But these so-called "working" atomic plants are only a small part of the story. After an investment of $111 million, the Enrico Fermi plant near Detroit was taken out of service and replaced by an oil-burning facility. At Oak Ridge, Tennessee, another nuclear power plant was closed down, with $57 million going down the atomic rat-hole. A Hallam, Nebraska, plant, built at a cost of $54.7 million in January 1963 was shut down in August 1965— and the AEC has announced that it will be torn down because of "technical difficulties"—namely that the reactor was too "hot" for safety.

The cause of these multi-million dollar misunderstandings—and I have cited but a few examples—can be summed up simply: Neither the scientists nor the engineers have as yet the full know-how to build nuclear power plants. They are experimenting with the taxpayer's money. But these experiments should be confined to the laboratory, not to populated areas where mistakes can blow your city or mine to Kingdom Come.

The Atomic Energy Commission, in its great zeal to "nuclear-ize" America's electric power facilities, has stated flatly that "in the more than 20-year history of the nation's nuclear program, there have been only seven radiation-associated deaths." In the same "report," the AEC also claims that there have been only "some two-dozen accidents."

In any assessment of the AEC and its practices, these statements command the question: Are they true? They fall by the AEC's own testimony. In a 1965 AEC publication, the figure for atomic accidents was set at 33. This kind of backward arithmetic seems to be par for the course at AEC. The commission's real attitude on such accidents, moreover, may well have been summed up before the Joint House-Senate Atomic Energy Committee on May 4, 1967, when its representatives took the position that "progress" in the nuclear field was far more important than any death-dealing activities.

This view was underscored by Representative Chet Holifield (D.-Calif.), vice chairman on the joint committee and the AEC's champion on Capitol Hill, when he callously dismissed a union official's testimony on the deaths by radioactivity of uranium miners. "Maudlin sentimentality," Mr. Holifield said.

Have there been only "seven radiation-associated deaths" in the potentially lethal atomic power field? The Washington Post reported recently that an estimated 115 uranium miners had died of radioactivity. And United Mine Workers President W. A. Boyle, in a hard-hitting and eloquent Labor Day speech, charged that "the government in Washington has permitted this outrage to go on for more than twenty years . . . It's too late for an estimated 6,000 men—who will die miserable deaths in the next few years."

As to the "two-dozen accidents"—or is it 33?—there is the rebuttal of Leo Goodman, the AFL-CIO's expert on atomic energy problems. "I have tabulated 1,400 accidents," he has said—and all of them involved radiation hazards. That the facts have been kept from the American people by what the United Mine Workers president calls "a conspiracy of silence" by the AEC and its "stooges on Capitol Hill" is a demonstrable fact. At every turn, the AEC cries out, "Classified!" and quotes its release No. K-158, a document which violates anti-secrecy laws passed by the Congress.

From behind a bastion of self-ordained censorship, the AEC claims that "there have been no civilian reactor accidents which have caused loss of life or endangered public health and safety." Does this statement bear scrutiny? Forgetting its assertions of purity, the AEC in another document admits to "adverse effects" on health and safety as a result of accidents and negligence at a New York nuclear power plant.

Last fall, according to the AEC itself, that New York plant dumped five million gallons of radioactive waste into surrounding waters. Radioactive contamination spread into presumably "clean" areas of the plant. And radioactive gases from the plant's stack were not monitored. The Scientists' Institute for Public Information further contradicts the AEC, noting in a May 1967 report that "there have been 10 serious reactor accidents since 1949, and four reactors have been discontinued as a result." Among those accidents: A "core explosion" at a reactor in Idaho which "resulted in the death of three men and a significant release of radioactivity to the environment."

So far, the United States has not had an accident such as the one at Windscale, in England, which resulted in the release of 20,000 curies of radioactive iodine to the atmosphere. Since the lethal dose of radioactivity is measured in *micro*curies, the meaning of that accident is appalling.

Americans can take less comfort from the conclusions of the Scientists' Institute that "an explosion, meltdown, or other accident resulting in a major release of radioactivity is always possible." The scientists add that any degree of radioactivity is dangerous—so that quibbling about "low level" radioactivity, as opposed to "high level" radioactivity begs the deadly question. It is as tasteless as the old joke about the girl who was just a little pregnant.

The advocates of nuclearized electric power contend that they will eliminate the pollution caused by coal-burning steam generators. But all they propose to do is to substitute one kind of controllable pollution for another, and uncontrollable, pollution. In the debate, the AEC is of no help. It has a vested interest in the proliferation of nuclear power, and it will fight to the last press release to have its way.

Eleven foreign experts on nuclear power are in the United States to learn from the Atomic Energy Commission how the United States disposes of radioactive waste. What they discover will depend on their capacity to penetrate the curtain of AEC's joyous propaganda. The commission's chairman, Dr. Glenn T. Seaborg, has asked Congress to give him $17.9 million—an increase of $1 million over last year—for a delicately stated drive to "increase the number of trained people in the nuclear field and to disseminate information related to nuclear science and technology."

How much of that money goes to "public relations" is anybody's guess, and hardly to be forked out of the highly censored AEC testimony before the House Appropriations Sub-committee.

The fact is that the AEC is still "looking for a permanent method of disposal" for the high-level radioactive waste that is a by-product of its vast power-reactor program. (The quoted words are those of George M. Kavanaugh, the assistant manager for reactors of the AEC.)

Let me quote what the Scientists' Institute for Public Information and the Committee for Environmental Information jointly say about this radioactive waste:

"Activity levels in the liquid may be as great as several *thousand* curies per gallon . . . Since typical exposure limits for human whole body doses are of the order of microcuries—millionths of a curie—a *single gallon* of the waste would be sufficient to threaten the health of several million people. One ton of processed fuel will produce from 40 to several hundred gallons of waste depending upon the details of the process used."

The committee adds: "It has been estimated that about five cubic miles of water would be required just to dilute the waste from one ton of fuel to the maximum permissible concentration (MPC). The time required for its longest-lived components, strontium 90 and samarium 151, to reach the MPC by natural decay is from 1000 to 1500 years."

The AEC, when it is cozily closeted with a Congressional committee, is ready to disclose that at Hanford (Washington) alone, there are 83 storage tanks, with capacities of up to a million gallons each, for the storage of radioactive wastes. Other radioactive waste "graveyards"—very appropriately named—are scattered around the country.

Are they safe? The AEC casually informs members of Congress that at Hanford, the "useful storage" is 46.2 million gallons. But F. P. Baranowski, the AEC's director of the Division of Production, says: "That number is arrived at after you take a look at those tanks which are *currently leaking*, subtracting that from the total . . . For example, at Hanford, 10 tanks out of the total number are leakers . . . of highly radioactive materials."

Turn again to the Scientists' Institute for Public Information: "If there are only a few large processing plants in the 'developed' nuclear economy of the year 2000, large amounts of irradiated fuel will have to be transported for processing, with the attendant danger of accidents in transport"—and the need for local disposal of radioactive waste. "If there are many sites, for example, one or more at each population center, then the likelihood of compromises in siting, ready access of leakage to groundwater and individual peculiarities of design is increased."

"Finally," the Institute warns, "the sort of minor accident that occasionally occurs in our present industrial technology due, for example, to natural gas leakage from pipe lines, vandalism, and simple human error could be disastrous in a neighborhood nuclear waste plant." That kind of "simple human error" at the West Valley, New York, reprocessing facility led to the dumping of millions of gallons of radioactive waste into surrounding waters.

This is why W. A. Boyle, president of the United Mine Workers Union, in his Labor Day speech, calls radioactive waste "a threat to every man, woman, and child in our nation." That is why he has warned that "trucks and railroad cars are transporting radioactive waste materials at night through urban centers across the states to dump it." One overturned truck, one derailed freight car, could scatter a lethal load on the landscape.

In aid of what? At a cost of how many billions? To bring death into America's cities? To perpetuate the AEC? Or to pour more billions down atomic rat-holes?

September 1967

HERBERT HOOVER AT 90–
A SMALL TRIBUTE

Mr. Hoover, an obvious hero to Toledano, was, reciprocally, a great fan of Toledano. Ralph has, said The Chief, "one of the keenest political minds in the nation." I feel that this small garland proves them both quite right.

It seems incredible that Herbert Hoover is 90 years old today. For in this gently witty, deeply religious, and enormously compassionate man, there is a quality of spirit that is detached from time. We think of time as break-neck or stiff-gaited, but always as an impersonal force which seizes us as we are placed in this wonderful, tragic world, and never allows us to forget that at some point we shall be snatched away.

Time is cold, but Herbert Hoover—to those who have known and loved him—is a warm man, sharing that warmth with all who approach him. This, too, is a little incredible, for there is a shyness about him which a world given to extroversion once considered aloofness.

I cannot claim to any long-standing intimacy with Mr. Hoover. His circle of friends, all fiercely loyal, deserves not to have comelately interlopers holding themselves up for credit they do not deserve. But I have known Herbert Hoover and, like all of his friends and acquaintances, I am deeply in his debt. This is a personal matter and perhaps of no consequence. The debt that others owe him—men and women throughout the world who have never spoken to him and perhaps seen him only in newspaper photos, newsreels, or on the television tube—is far greater than what the direct recipients of his giving heart must acknowledge.

By this, I do not mean the people who owe their lives to his labors in feeding the starving after two great wars. I do not refer to the people at the receiving end of his secret charities. I go back to the root of that word, to *caritas*—and I say that in Herbert Hoover this *caritas* has shone like a good deed in a naughty world.

But this, too, is only part of the story. You can read the details of that story in Eugene Lyons' biography, *Herbert Hoover*, which Doubleday has just published. It is a book to read and to ponder, for Mr. Lyons has known the Chief well and has caught him in motion with quick skill and perceptiveness. Mr. Hoover's life as a private and a public man, as a President who took the brunt of unmerciful attack with a calm that transcends stoicism, as a leader of men and a servant of his country—these are the stuff of this book and should be known by every American.

But I think of my debt to Herbert Hoover in terms which could have been enunciated had I never met him or joined however briefly in his conversations. I refer specifically to Herbert

Hoover as an example in his life and his works, in his aspirations and his ideals. In our time, there have been men who have won the shouting adulation of the multitude—and it is sad to remember how many of these idols served evil and betrayed their idolaters.

The cheering stopped for Herbert Hoover in the dark days of a Depression he could have ended had the country given him the opportunity. Like patience on a monument, he watched the fabric of American life being rewoven to a pattern he could not conscience. But in time, and in an accretion almost imperceptible, he found himself surrounded by affection, by love, by respect, and by gratitude. History will assess his role, but it does not require the verdict of ages to say that Herbert Hoover will be written in the books as this nation's most loved President.

This love, this respect, this gratitude derives from an instinctive and infallible knowledge among his countrymen of Mr. Hoover's rich patriotism—extreme to some in its sweeping search for what is just and best for the United States, for the American soil, but moderate when it is measured against this country's needs.

It requires no campaign in public relations for Americans to sense this and to respond to it. They can match Herbert Hoover's patriotism against his devotion to honor—a trait which is individual and cannot be served in the mass. This is a little about what Herbert Hoover is, what his example has been and continues to be, and what the nation's debt to him approximates.

We can look to Herbert Hoover, quietly celebrating his 90th birthday—a man full of years and full of wisdom. He has seen the world's sorrows; he has never flinched from the realization that life is pain. It is a world he has never turned away from, in fear or rejection. For his wisdom, born of courage, has smiled in joy or in pity at man's fate—but it has smiled. For this, too, I am grateful.

Happy birthday, Chief.

August 1964

THE GUERRILLA MENACE IN SOUTH AMERICA

Once again, while the popular view of trouble in Latin America continued to be sociological, the view from Toledano's headlines kept in sharp focus the fact that, to the despair of those who seek simple textbook answers, there were other stirrings, other ferments, other knives than the pangs of poverty.

In order to focus destruction on imperialism, we have to aim at the head—the United States of America." Those words were written by Ernesto "Che" Guevara, the tough guerrilla fighter and chief ideologue of Castro's Cuba until he disappeared many months ago.

"Che" was thought to be dead, but there are recurrent signs that he is very much alive and active in the guerrilla uprisings now plaguing Latin America. As a hard-line Communist, he is an implacable foe of everything American. And he firmly believes that this country can be so badly embroiled in resisting subversion and terror south of the border that it will collapse from over-extension.

He may be right. Failure by the Kennedy-Johnson Administration to crush Castro-brand Communism in Cuba, or to contain it within the island's borders, has allowed Fidel Castro to turn his country into a Soviet military base as well as a staging area for the most widespread attack on Latin America since the landing of the Conquistadors.

The longer the penetration of Latin America continues, the harder it will be for the United States to counter it. At present Castro-trained forces are fighting in Guatemala, Venezuela, Bolivia, Colombia, Brazil—to name the major areas now under fire. Castro-trained subversion units are active in every one of the Latin republics, with varying degrees of success.

In Cuba itself, there are more than 45 training camps, turning out guerrilla fighters and saboteurs who infiltrate Central and

South America. The island has become a vast Soviet arsenal. Everything from handguns to explosives, from mortars to missiles, is stored in Cuba's great complex of large caves. Underground roads have been carved out of soil and stone to prevent American air surveillance from photographing movements in and out of these caves.

To protect the cave complex from possible attack by the small anti-Castro underground, Soviet army units have been deployed on the island. Other units are manning the underground missile storage sites. Some of these missiles are of the SAM (surface to air) type. But there is a growing body of documentation, such as American Intelligence operatives gathered for months prior to the 1962 missile crisis, substantiating charges that the Kremlin has not given up its plans for pointing IRBM (intermediate range) missiles at the heart of the United States.

The parallels between the spring and summer of 1962 and the present time are frightening. Five years ago the then Senator Kenneth Keating (R.-N.Y.) began warning of the missile build-up. This writer, without the access to Intelligence reports that Mr. Keating had, was able to gather sufficient evidence on his own to repeat those warnings and to spell them out in considerable detail. The Kennedy Administration, through Secretary of Defense Robert Strange McNamara and other spokesmen, had harsh words to say about those who were attempting to alert the American people to the Cuban missile peril. When it was almost too late, President Kennedy acted.

Today, warnings from the best-informed experts on Cuban activities are again being brushed aside. They are being told that their information is faulty, that U-2 surveillance would have turned up signs of missile units if they existed. Forgotten is the fact that the actual emplacements, during the 1962 crisis, were the last act in what could have been a disaster for America.

President Johnson is much too preoccupied with his Vietnamese problems to pay careful attention to Latin America. And Secretary of State Dean Rusk, re-reading his 1962 script, has cozily informed the American people that the Soviet-Cuban threat "is subsiding." As he spoke, four Latin American republics were under martial law as a direct result of Castroite guerrilla operations.

This is what the United States faces now—and the situation grows graver with each passing day. What could have been stopped by one division of Marines five years ago has become a Pan America-wide threat to the security of all the republics making up the Organization of American States.

This escalation of Castroite warfare and subversion can be stopped now only by multiple intervention in Latin America—and with the United States so heavily committed in Vietnam, the question looms: If large-scale warfare breaks out in any one of a half dozen Latin American countries, where shall we get the troops to help?

May 1967

CHE GUEVARA'S ADMIRERS

In all of the reams of coverage of Che Guevara, alive and dead, I can recall no other attempt, except this modest one, to put him into some sort of perspective as a revolutionary leader. Yet, unless some perspective is achieved, it is troublesome to think that many youngsters with decent 'revolutionary' impulses will be misled into accepting the Che as a folk hero rather than as just another storm trooper.

Che Guevara, the murderer of thousands, has been dead for less than two weeks, but already the male sob-sisters of the Liberal Establishment are working overtime to make a legend of him. In one Washington newspaper, a leading columnist places Guevara in the ranks of "heroic revolutionaries" and praises him as "a patriot and an anti-colonialist, ready at all times and in all places to take up the cudgels for peoples submerged by foreign powers"—a "romantic, a guerrilla fighter specializing in daring thrusts against top-heavy military machines."

This rewriting of history is typical of organized punditry. There is no record that Che Guevara ever took up the cudgels for the Hungarian Freedom Fighters when they were being crushed by the top-heavy Soviet military machine—or that he fought for any of the peoples submerged by the Soviet imperialists in Western Europe. Nor did he call out for help when the people of Tibet suffered what amounts to genocide at the hands of Red China.

Guevara, a hard-bitten and doctrinaire Communist, was killed when he tried to bring chaos to Bolivia in the hope that American forces would become involved and bog down in another costly and bitter military operation. Had the Bolivian adventure succeeded, other Latin American countries would have had the benefit of Che's "anti-colonialism" and men and governments would have bled under the scourge of his "romantic" approach.

Even Che's reputation as a skillful and daring guerrilla is a myth. The Castro-Communist forces which he helped to lead were hopelessly on the run until the State Department and some of the men around President Eisenhower cut off the Batista government at the knees. Only when the United States turned thumbs down on Fulgencio Batista—and not until then—did the Castro-Communist forces move, and they took over the island with almost no opposition.

Once Fidel Castro and Che Guevara had seized power, Cuba was subjected to a blood-bath such as no other Latin American country had known since the slaughters of Haiti's early history. Repression and murder became the order of the day and prisoners were left to die in dungeons, or exposed to the elements without food or water until they went mad. For them, death was a release.

The Washington columnist, since he has covered the events of the last decade, knew that Che Guevara was the gauleiter in Cuba for the Soviet and Chinese Communists, that he was the strong man who set up the Cuban version of Leninism on the island, and that he worked hand-in-glove with the Kremlin to build an advanced Soviet missile base 90 miles from the American coast. Had Nikita Khrushchev and Che Guevara succeeded in their plans, devastation would have been visited on American cities and millions who live might now be dead. Had the government not acted with dispatch and energy, the United States would now be caught between the upper and nether millstones of a Vietnamese war and a Latin America in bloody revolution.

Like the Washington columnist I have been quoting, a few writers deplore the "disposition among some Americans to crow over the collapse" of Che's Bolivian putsch and of Communist-oriented governments like those of Nkrumah in Ghana and Sukarno in Indonesia.

The outcry over the Vietnamese War derives from these attitudes. Even as the sob sisters mourn for Che Guevara, ignoring his crimes against humanity, the Vietniks shout only of American bombers and loss of life, never of the terrorism against the Vietnamese peasant by the Communists, the barbarous tortures, and the premeditated attacks on innocent bystanders in the streets of Saigon.

There must be a reason for this sickness. Karl Marx wrote in the Communist Manifesto that when the Revolution came, it would be aided and abetted by the very people it was aimed against—the very people, as Lenin demonstrated, who would be liquidated first. But history has taught little to men who would rather weep than think. The world is better off for the death of a Che Guevara. Because of it, lives will be saved and the peoples of Latin America will be able to go on with the admittedly slow and painstaking work of making a better society for themselves. In this endeavor, they need no "patriots" and "heroic revolutionaries" like Che.

October 1967

WASHINGTON AND CAIRO—
A PARALLEL?

This particular point, it seems, eluded most of the
supposedly acute diplomatic reporters during the after-
math of the Six Day War and the continuing ordeal of
the Vietnamese war. It is a singularly provocative piece
of reporting and, one suspects, it will hold up long
after the collapse of most of the other interpretive
items written at the time.

It is being ironically noted along Embassy Row that the problems faced by President Johnson and President Nasser bear some
striking similarities. Both of the countries that they presumably
lead are involved and inflamed in war—of different kinds, granted,
but with all the dislocations, exacerbations, stresses, and strains
that belligerency causes or magnifies.

Mr. Johnson would like peace in Southeast Asia. And Mr.
Nasser, according to reliable diplomatic reports, is slowly moving
behind the scenes toward a real desire to bring quiet to the Middle East. Both presidents are deterred by the extremists within
their governments and countries. In Egypt's case, there are those
who still believe that to bring about peace, Israel must be ex-
terminated. In the United States, the extremists argue that the
solution to Vietnam is American surrender—however they may
disguise the sentiment.

The nature of the opposition in each instance delimits what
can be done with political safety in the two countries. President
Nasser, who is ruthless but not stupid, realizes that without all-
out Soviet help, he cannot mount another offensive against the
Israelis. And the Kremlin has made it very clear to him that, at
present, international Communism has other fish to fry—that a
semblance of cooperation with the United States is temporarily
necessary.

Mr. Nasser is aware that to recover the American aid he so
badly needs, and to restore to Egypt the critically important

income from the Suez Canal, he must resolve the conflict in the Middle East. The Israeli government has manifested its willingness to sit down with its Arab neighbors and to work out peace terms which would benefit those stubbornly backward countries in economic and technological aid. This could well be the answer to the problems of progress and poverty that afflict Egypt.

According to reliable sources, Mr. Nasser has confessed privately that if he were to sit down at the negotiating table with the Israelis, fanatical extremists would attempt to topple his government. They are not strong enough to do so, but they could throw Egypt into even further internal difficulties. (King Hussein of Jordan is seated on the points of the same dilemma.)

To worsen matters for the Egyptian dictator, each passing week makes it more difficult to arrive at a settlement with the Israelis. The Tel Aviv government cannot wait indefinitely, so it has begun to incorporate the lands it captured from the Arabs in last summer's war into its own national territory. So far, Mr. Nasser has drifted—attempting to find a compromise solution that would keep the extremists quiet yet lead to a viable settlement in the Middle East. He has yet to use the tremendous powers at his disposal to neutralize the extremists to the point where he would have a free hand.

President Johnson, by his indecisions and by his insistence on compromise as a method of political action, has allowed the Vietnamese War to deteriorate into a costlier and costlier struggle, with no end in view. A minority in Congress and in the country has convinced him that it would be death to his chances of re-election if he should move firmly toward a military solution. As a result, he has indirectly encouraged the North Vietnamese and the Viet Cong to continue fighting. He has also deprived our forces in Southeast Asia of any independence of maneuver. Worst of all, he has signaled his every move, thereby giving the Communists an incalculable advantage.

Had Mr. Johnson moved with the firmness and dispatch that marked President Truman's action in the early days of the Korean War, he would be the most popular President in recent history. But his fear of the Vietnik assault and of what the loud and braggart "peace" movement can do to him has restrained his hand and led him to piecemeal actions that have solved little. He has also been beset by the foot-dragging of his Secretary of Defense, failing to use his great powers to exact support within his Administration for such forceful policies as he has now and then enunciated.

In both cases, those of President Johnson and President Nasser, vacillation and timidity may bring about the very outcome that these two chiefs of state have tried to prevent. Unless Mr. Nasser comes to grips realistically with the Middle East problem, the extremists will eventually tear him down. Unless Mr. Johnson firmly grasps the nettle, the "peace" movement will create such political and emotional disarray in this country that his chances of re-election in November, 1968 may well be seriously jeopardized.

These are the parallels which Embassy Row sees in Cairo and in Washington. The circumstances in each capital are different, but the basic errors are the same.

October 1967

REAPING THE WHIRLWIND– OR HOW CONGRESS CONVENED

If ever there was a view of a troubled future in a single event, it is sharply etched in this report of one day on Capitol Hill.

What happened on Capitol Hill, on the day Adam Clayton Powell was not seated, was a disgrace to the spirit of American democracy. But in this day of unlaw and disorder, of pressure groups which claim special privileges, what really happened was not news.

A half-dozen busses had left Harlem early in the day, full of "civil rights" demonstrators who believed that due process meant an organized pillage of the taxpayer's dollar. In Washington, they were joined by others, white and black, who had nothing better to do than to disrupt the opening of the 90th Congress. Before the day was up, they had been exhorted by Adam Clayton Powell, a man of the cloth who spends weeks in the British West Indies with his girl friend, to break the law, to refuse to pay taxes.

Capitol Hill is a beautiful enclave of government, but the empty whiskey bottles littered the pavement. The Capitol police, whose major duty normally is to check passes and direct visitors, found themselves on riot duty—while a detachment of Marines waited on the alert in case things got completely out of hand. The whiskey bottles that had been emptied in the service of civil rights did not remain as litter. Some of them were brandished and some thrown, finding their targets on the heads of the police.

The rhetoric of the occasion was not the kind that will grace the annals of the Republic. "White cop bastard" was among the milder terms heard. And Mister Powell, the Representative from Harlem who had been forced to stand aside until his fitness for office was determined, in accordance with Constitutional fiat, stood on the Capitol steps taking the name of the Lord in vain.

This was the net result after years of sober and principled work to give the Negro status and dignity. The responsible leaders—the men who had worked hard and successfully in their cause—were either elbowed aside by the demagogues or joined the mob. And that mob was manipulated in the hope that it would break loose and add bloodshed to disorder. Stokeley Carmichael, the ranting extremist who hopes to obliterate the white man, was cheek by jowl with Mister Powell. "How permissive can you get?" said a horrified correspondent for a British newspaper.

What saved the day was the appearance of President Lyndon Johnson. His protection was in the hands of the Secret Service, and they were having no Dallas in reverse on Capitol Hill. The rules are strict. When the President addresses a joint session of Congress, the crowds are cleared. No one can get into the Capitol without proper credentials. So the drunks were steered away and the entrances protected.

But what was achieved in this destruction of the decorum which must surround the legislative process if mobocracy is not to rule? Those who demonstrated for Mister Powell were telling the nation and the world that no matter what his crimes, he should not be held accountable because a small part of his racial line was Negro. In the long run, the Reverend Adam Clayton Powell was hurt all the more, and so were the Negro people. He had hurt them in the past when he played footsie with one left-wing group after another. But now he was acting in the glare of the television lights, so the damage would be greater.

How, in this spirit of attempted intimidation, could the Congress act otherwise than it did? House investigators had pleaded with Mister Powell to return to Washington during the autumn to answer the charges against him. But he had lolled in the Bimini sun and mocked his colleagues. The evidence remained there, with no denials and only the threat that if the Congress acted against him he would expose other members of Congress. He was sure that this would frighten his colleagues. And frightened they were. Only the overwhelming pressure from the voters had changed their minds.

On the floor of the House, reason and logic prevailed. But the vituperation that filled the air on the broad plaza in front of the Capitol steps hung over the building like a cloud. It left the Congress soiled. Whatever happens to Adam Clayton Powell, he is finished as a power in the House of Representatives. But the House, too, was sadly wounded. In a democratic society, its law-making institutions must be like Caesar's wife—above reproach and above suspicion.

What happened on the opening day of this 90th Congress left it open to the attack of those who would destroy the Constitutional principles on which it was founded. The day will not be soon forgotten, no matter how much whitewash the propagandists daub over its sordid record.

January 1967

DISLOYALTY–NEW STYLE

It is unfortunate the President of the United States, rather than Ralph de Toledano, did not write this. For it contains very sharply the point at which, for instance, a President could turn the full weight of his powers and office properly against "dissent." When dissent becomes advocacy of crime, as in giving aid and comfort to an enemy, then even the most staunch advocate of dissent–and I number myself there–would have to say that a line could and should be drawn. When a man advocates military defeat of the soldiers of his country he has surely passed beyond dissent. And yet, oddly, while the President of the United States reserved at this particular time most of his wrath for such men as Senator Fulbright–engaging in dissent–he seemed completely to overlook the existence of these men who, as this Toledano column points out, are guilty not of dissent but of disloyalty.

Once upon a time, disloyal men met in dark cellars to plot the downfall of their countries. Today, they write letters to newspapers. But the stigma that should have been visited upon them never arrives. Foul-thinking students organize to send blood to Viet Cong troops that are killing Americans, and Senator Robert F. Kennedy says that what they are doing is in the "oldest tradition of this country." A professor calls for the defeat of this country in the Vietnamese War, and the governor of a great state defends him.

Comes now John Raymond to add himself to the ranks of the disloyal, stating his mission clearly. Mr. Raymond is a newspaperman who has worked for several reputable daily papers. In a letter to the National Guardian, a newspaper cited by at least one Congressional committee for its devotion to the extreme left, Mr. Raymond wrote that "I can offer my sincere wishes for a decisive victory by Ho Chi Minh and the people of North Vietnam.

Further, I disavow any personal loyalty or support to the present government of the United States."

At another time, this assertion of disloyalty would have placed Mr. Raymond in the category of a "man without a country"—a pariah in his profession. Today, however, patriotism is dead in certain quarters and Mr. Raymond is being rewarded for his disloyalty by an assignment from Fact magazine and the tacit cooperation of the State Department. For Fact, he will journey to Red China and North Vietnam to report the fighting from the enemy's point of view. From the State Department, he has received a passport to speed him on his way. The Communists have already said that they will welcome him with open arms.

It would be an easy formulation to say that Fact and John Raymond deserve each other. The publisher of the magazine is Ralph Ginzburg, whose conviction for publishing and disseminating obscenity has been upheld by the Supreme Court. The magazine inself is being sued for libel by Barry Goldwater in a litigation that should make publishing history.

The Raymond-Ginzburg editorial marriage is something to be contemplated more with irony than with anger. But the State Department's complacent approval, manifested by the granting of a passport to a newspaperman of confessed disloyalty, is something else again.

Other newspapermen have tried to get visas from the Red Chinese to visit and report on what Communism has brought to Asia, but they have all been refused. In the national interest, the State Department should have refused to be an accessory to this propaganda scheme. It has the power to withhold a passport under circumstances of this nature, and this power has been employed in the past.

There has been no public outcry against Mr. Raymond's blunt disavowal of loyalty to his country. Years of left-liberal indoctrination have eroded the fabric of national pride and national interest. The boundaries of political indecency have been pushed back to the point where the academic and journalistic communities fail to respond to a provocation of this kind.

But disloyalty, when tolerated, encourages disloyalty. Those students who burned their draft cards were proclaimed by many of their elders as brave dissenters whose actions parallel those of George Washington rather than Benedict Arnold or Aaron Burr. "Permissiveness" is today's shibboleth. Neither Sigma Dela Chi nor any other of those journalistic organizations which speak in the name of editorial honor have drummed Mr. Raymond out of the profession. They have not even expressed their repugnance by any resolution or manifesto.

The "new disloyalty" has, in fact, become somewhat fashionable, and it is predictable that Mr. Raymond's "reportage" will receive respectful comment from pundits who dominate our ideological thinking. This is both tragic and frightening. For it raises the most pertinent of all questions for our times: Does a nation that fails to protect itself deserve to be saved?

June 1966

THE FRENCH ARE STILL LOOKING UNDER AMERICAN BEDS

There is an unfortunate portion of the political right, or whatever you call the anti-leftists, that accepts any-thing Charles de Gaulle does to France or the world simply because, at one time way back when, they felt that he was an anti-Communist, or regal, or something. This column happily exempts Toledano from that un-discriminating idiocy.

PARIS—Very little that is friendly is being said by the French left and right of President de Gaulle. But on one point, Parisians are in complete agreement. He has taken their beautiful and ancient city and, by edict, ordered its face scrubbed. The grime of centuries has been washed off buildings which knew not the touch of refurbishing. Today they present the light and warm yellow tones of stone quarried from caves under the streets of Paris.

But if the French have restored to Paris and its innumerable historic buildings their original color—softened by age but still alive—they have retained the suspicious nature which is so typically a part of the national character. To sit over the post-prandial coffee with a group of influential Frenchmen is like attending a meeting of the John Birch Society. Everything is a conspiracy, a plot, the work of malign minds seeking to undermine what this newspaper editor or that government official believes is the ordained way—*his* way.

For an American newspaperman, with some small reputation even in France as a political analyst, it is a little weird to be told, in firm and uncompromising words, just what is going on in the United States—and frequently by people whose entire knowledge of the country derives from a reading of the flimsy and sensational American news which fills most of the French press. After all these years, even informed Frenchmen see these United States in the more garish terms of a James Cagney gangster movie. And this carries over to their views on our national political scene.

The FBI, CIA, the Dallas police force, the U. S. Narcotics Bureau, and the Secret Service are all lumped together into a vague but sinister conglomerate called "the American police." And this "American police" is credited with a stranglehold on all of the political and economic life—in partnerships with "les gangsters" and other malodorous types. Chief Justice Warren, to cite but one example, is widely believed to be an agent of these netherworld forces. If you explain the American system of three-way stretch between legislative, judicial, and executive—and then describe the growing dominance over the national legislature by the Supreme Court—you are met with sly or condescending smiles.

Perhaps the most shocking evidence of this is the almost universal belief among informed and influential Frenchmen that the Warren Commission report on the assassination of President Kennedy is fiction from beginning to end—dictated by "les gangsters," the politicians, and the secret government of America.

Those somewhat more charitable will argue that the fiction was imposed by a tender concern on Chief Justice Warren's part for the American image abroad.

The most widespread theory—and one that it is impossible to budge—is that President Kennedy was murdered for political reasons by very important people in the Administration—and the imputation is made very clear as to who those people are. In the telling, the facts get garbled, the sequence is rearranged, and important details are omitted. But it all adds up to the conviction that Lee Harvey Oswald was framed, that the Dallas police connived with Jack Ruby to allow him to murder Oswald, and that the motivation for the crime cannot be discovered in the disorderly thought processes of a semi-insane American renegade.

In the *roman policier*, France's version of the detective story, motive is very important. "And who," a French diplomat asked me, "profited most from the assassination of M. Kennedy?" I laughed, but he was serious. Then he laughed when he saw how genuinely horrified I was at the implications of his question.

In this context, I wondered sadly what was done with the millions spent to maintain the United States Information Agency. Its job was to promote a truthful report of the American scene. But it obviously did nothing to counter the vicious myth, conceived by the European left and its Communist activist allies. Hundreds of thousands of copies of the Warren Report—abridged, translated, and in paperback—should have been distributed in France or sold on an at-cost basis. Every means available in the mass media should have been employed by U.S.I.A. to present the facts to the French people.

More important than this, the U.S.I.A. should have devoted its efforts, from the time of its first multi-million appropriation, to the education of the European public in the essentials of the American system—of how our government operates, of how the currents and cross-currents of our society affect the body politic. What U.S.I.A. has been doing remains a mystery to me—and to most Frenchmen. Perhaps the wonderful ways and by-ways of Paris have seduced those on the scene.

February 1966

LORD RUSSELL: "GIVE UNCLE SAM A FAIR TRIAL AND HANG HIM"

It is just possible that this column, happily, was over-stated. The mock trial, by Lord Russell and Sartre, actually provoked some healthy revulsions on the Left, so arrogantly unfair was it. Also, it would be difficult to say which came first, Lord Russell's egg or Bobby Kennedy's cackling in terms of transmitting the full litany of anti-Vietnamese sloganizing to the halls of Congress. Frankly, I feel that Toledano was unduly exercised by this one. But, in compensation, the fact that he was exercised puts him in a far better position, no matter what, than those who excused the whole nasty incident simply because, for instance, at one time Lord Russell had had a fine, rational mind.

Bertrand Russell, a once-brilliant philosopher now making a headlong rush into senility, has set up a "tribunal" to try President Johnson, Secretary of State Dean Rusk, and Defense Secretary Robert Strange McNamara as "war criminals." Heading this "tribunal" will be Jean-Paul Sartre and his longtime mistress, Simone de Beauvoir. Both are known for their uncompromising repugnance to all things American.

The "trial" will start in November, and its purpose will be to show that America's leaders are guilty of cruelty, aggression, and inhumanity. So far, everyone chosen to participate in the activities of the "court" has already declared himself against the United States and uttered a belief that we are guilty of unspeakable crimes against the Vietnamese Communists. Lord Russell, who has made himself a spokesman for the point of view that the free world is hellish, and he himself all-knowing, has frequently expressed the belief that America's role in Vietnam is "aggressive and unjustifiable."

But the kangaroo court, a perverted version of the Nuremberg tribunal, protests that "we don't want to be accused of being unfair in this." Though it is scheduling only anti-American testimony, it has generously declared that it will "allow" any witness for the defense who wishes to speak up—if he volunteers to run the gauntlet.

That Lord Russell and the New Left should engage in this farce comes as no surprise. That Americans will add their voices to the outcry is a little harder to understand, but what can be heard on the floor of the Senate these days has prepared me for it. Some of those voices have grown old in the disservice to their country, preaching a one-sided pacifism which sees only the alleged sins of America, never those of the Soviet Union.

The tendency among sensible people is to ignore these manifestations of leftwing madness. But you may be sure that the "evidence" presented by the tribunal, in their roles of judge, prosecutor, and jury, will be spread far and wide. The sponsors plan to tape-record the proceedings and to publish them as a book. Throughout the world, there will be demonstrations of protest against "American fascism" which will allow our pundits to warn that this nation's image is being destroyed by the Vietnamese conflict.

Forty years from now, the innocent and the duped will learn that the big show was stage managed, right down to the smallest rock thrown through a U.S. Information Library window—just as it took an equal amount of time for Americans to learn just how the Sacco-Vanzetti riots that convulsed Europe in the Twenties were organized by trained Communist agents.

There is no way of stopping the "tribunal" from doing its dirty work. But a strategy of rebuttal, effective and conclusive, must be devised. To sit back and do nothing is to court serious trouble. But no strategy will be worth a second thought unless the White House begins an agonizing reappraisal of its permissive attitude toward Communist activity and its present article of faith that the Kremlin is "maturing" and seeking a modus vivendi with the United States.

The campaign against America's role in Vietnam began with the beatniks, but their slogans are being repeated in the halls of Congress today. The "findings" of the "tribunal" will find their way into the folklore of an antagonistic world. This is how the Kremlin has planned it, though Lord Russell will be the last to know. The Communists have learned that they can do us far more damage in this manner than they could with warlike statements and provocations. In the past, the cat's-paw has been a favorite Communist weapon, and so it is today.

August 1966

ADMINISTRATION'S 'DATA BANK' CAN DESTROY AMERICA'S PERSONAL PRIVACY

Perhaps the most pointed comment one can make about this column is that it was not until exactly one year later that such a supposedly liberal and concerned magazine as The Atlantic finally got around to soberly appraising the meaning of this particular bureaucratic menace. One of these days the editors of such journals will closely examine their consciences as to whom the true liberals have been over the past years. No one will appreciate the shock of recognition more than Toledano.

If the Johnson Administration has its way, a central "data bank" run by the Federal government will pool every scrap of information known about every American. Through the use of computers, these dossiers will be instantly available to any bureaucrat who pushes the right buttons.

What this means, in effect, is that the day when a man's business was his own, when he was entitled to the privacy of his personal life, will be over. For every detail of an individual's activities—as garnered from income tax returns, personnel forms, investigative agencies, armed forces records, or you name it—will be fed into the huge computers for the use of the government.

This, of course, is what the totalitarian governments have practiced for decades. Lacking the wizardry of the computer, they nevertheless were able to compile dossiers on every individual, his acts as well as his thoughts and hopes. And these dossiers were used repeatedly to keep the people in line. Nazi Germany and the Soviet Union made the dossier an integral part of their systems for keeping opposition down and holding a nation in the grip of a repressive bureaucracy.

Plans for this centralized Federal Data Center have been prepared by a Committee of "social scientists" headed by Professor Carl Kaysen of Princeton's Institute for Advanced Studies, a think factory developed by Dr. J. Robert Oppenheimer. Behind this committee was its sponsoring body, the Bureau of the Budget, which works directly out of the White House.

The report of the Kaysen Committee indicates that the data bank is already being organized, without the sanction of Congress or any broad debate by the American people. In fact, the report speaks of a "sufficient beginning" in creating the bank to give it a "running start." How much has been done remains secret, as so much does in these days of runaway big government.

Nothing would be known of this totalitarian computerization of every man's private life except for the determined efforts of one Congressman to make the facts known. He is Chairman Cornelius E. Gallagher of the House Special Subcommittee on the Invasion of Privacy, part of the House Government Operations Committee. Mr. Gallagher has carried the ball against further government encroachments. His work has not been popular with the Johnson Administration, which feels that this New Jersey Democrat is creating trouble and giving opponents valuable ammunition.

The Federal Communications Commission has already warned that any centralized and governmental data center might "erode fundamental values" and lend itself to "unauthorized invasion or disclosure" of confidential information. The Kaysen Committee

and its sponsoring Budget Bureau, however, imply that "the
Federal government should get on with building a data bank and
worry about such matters as possible invasions of privacy later,"
to quote Representative Gallagher. He is aware that even the
present private and decentralized data banks, lacking the power
to probe of the Federal government, are already making inroads
in the rights of individuals.

For example, the credit bureaus, now operating as a means of
protecting the business community from deadbeats in a credit
card society, have gotten out of hand. These credit bureaus compile information without checking its accuracy and then distrib-
ute it to anyone who inquires about an individual's rating or
trustworthiness. This derogatory information has done considerable damage to people who, unaware of its dissemination,
have no opportunity to defend themselves. They suddenly see
their credit drying up, but have no recourse to due process of law
to clear their names. It is all done quietly, secretly, and with
deadly effect. Try to find out what your standing is with the local
credit bureau and you will understand the peril the average
citizen would be in if a Federal Data Center took over the business of preparing dossiers on the entire country.

Mr. Gallagher believes that the Federal government has no
right to become a computerized snooper. Through his special
subcommittee, he will fight to the bitter end to prevent this
destruction of the Constitutional right to privacy. But without an
aroused public opinion, he will be defeated by those who so crave
"efficiency" that they are willing to sacrifice the American system to get it.

December 1966

UNDER-STRENGTH AND UNDER-EQUIPPED: WHY AMERICANS DIE IN VIETNAM

This is about a real problem in a real war. There is no comment necessary. The dead, as Toledano suggests, have completely clear voices in such an instance.

Let the dead speak. A reader, Mrs. John Breda of California, has sent me the last letter she received from her son. It was written on March 13, 1967. Six days later, Lieutenant Dennis Breda was killed in action in Vietnam. His words to his parents are a posthumous document, expressing eloquently the plight of our fighting men in the Vietnamese War. Vietnik propaganda has restrained the hand of our government and contributed to the deaths of Americans who find themselves without adequate support in a war that must be won.

"Now we are still on the Cambodian border, right in the middle of the Ho Chi Minh Trail. We have been here for about a month and a half. We take our tracks through even the thickest jungle. There are all types of missions: search and destroy, ambushes, blocking forces, convoy security. Most of the time the VC (Vietcong) avoid contact with us . . . General Westmoreland says we are the best mechanized infantry unit in Vietnam today . . .

"We have been kept pretty busy. After being in the field for so long, we are tired and dirty. I have been wounded twice. Once from a command detonated mine, detonated from Cambodia. Another time from a VC machine gun. The day I was wounded from a VC machine gun, I lost 14 of my men.

"My biggest gripe is that my platoon is so under-strength. It is a rare day that I go into the field with 30 men . . . I'm getting tired of being under-strength. It is hard on the men because they have to pull twice their normal duty. These things can kill us all . . . We need a lot of fighting units here, not people who sit in Saigon with stockpiles of equipment we need and never see, who don't even know that a war is going on . . .

"We are losing too many good soldiers clearing an area, then moving out only to let the VC move back in. That is what happened to the Iron Triangle. When a truce comes . . . the VC move back in and resupply. After that we have to go back and do the job again, only this time we run into the mines and booby traps that the VC put in.

"On my latest combat mission, my men and I were without a radio in our track because none were available . . .

"I think that when one man dies in a war there should be no half-way effort to end the killing. When anyone dies it is a war and should be crushed with all the ability we have to do so. People, soldiers' lives should cost a hell of a price. With our country's great strength, it is a face-losing thing when we must take so long to crush a weak, poorly-equipped enemy. Well, I've put my two cents in your ears. I guess I'll stop screaming into the mighty winds that just blow."

A Vietcong command detonated mine put an end to Lieutenant Breda's plea for men and equipment, and for the all-out support of a government made timid by the smears and distortions of a reckless minority.

Did this American fighting man die in vain?

"Yes," says his mother. "As long as we, the United States, do not voice our inner feelings and convictions, our sons and husbands will continue to go into this war under-strength, with insufficient supplies, fighting a war with many restrictions, fighting Communism overseas while it flourishes on our shore. Become aware of the facts, form your opinions, speak out, and let every voice be heard. Only then can we say a life given in this conflict was with cause."

In this hour of sorrow and travail, Mrs. John Breda has spoken out the way the mothers and wives have always spoken out in times of American crisis. And crisis it is, as the President has come to learn. The people of this country are not intimidated by the propaganda horrors invoked by the Vietniks and their cynical advisers.

The voice of America is not the voice of Martin Luther King, of Robert F. Kennedy, or of Stokely Carmichael. The men of action are not the draft-card and flag burners. Americans know what appeasement and unilateral withdrawal mean. They oppose the Vietnamese War because it is being fought with half-measures under a double-think strategy. They want an end to the fighting, but with honor and in victory.

That is what Lieutenant Breda's letter means. That is what the Mrs. Bredas of America know. They make me feel humble.

May 1967

ROBERT STRANGE McNAMARA

The fact that Robert Strange McNamara was relieved of his duties, or permitted to resign, or whatever did happen, in December, 1967, in no way dates or makes obsolete these perceptive columns about the most significant American public official of the mid-Twentieth Century. He was the most significant quite simply because, unlike President Johnson, who simply put the nation in danger of bankruptcy, fiscal and moral—Secretary McNamara put us all in danger of actual destruction. He did this, through motives I shall not even hazard to guess, to serve a firm belief that this nation should not initiate any innovations in weapons until after the Communists had begun something. This appalling decision, more than any other of which I can think, may in the 1970's place the Soviet in command of weapons which will give it a clear balance of power over everyone else in the world. At such a time, all the pious talk of ideologies and rights and wrongs, or rights and lefts, may be tossed right out the window. They will be meaningless. The Soviet bureaucracy will have power and everyone else on earth will have simply their sufferance to do whatever they want us to. And that, as they say, will be that for some unhappy time to come. The question that hangs like a sword over us all,

even with McNamara gone, is whether his decision
actually can be reversed in time. In matters of tech-
nology there comes a point at which even crash pro-
grams cannot compensate for a very bad decision. In
reading these columns, this cruicial importance of the
McNamara era should be kept in mind always.

PROJECT 60: McNAMARA'S MOST DANGEROUS MOVE

Very hush-hush, Defense Secretary McNamara has asked his
assistants to make up plans for a new and, I believe, dangerous
method of procurement. There is much grumbling and head-
shaking at the Pentagon over the projected move but as one
veteran official put it, "In this administration, you do as you're
told."

What Mr. McNamara hopes to put into effect is grandiosely
called countercyclical procurement. What it means is chilling to
the blood. The Pentagon, if Secretary McNamara has his way, will
buy military hardware not as it is needed but as the economy
calls for massive pump-priming.

In other words, if there is prosperity in the land, then military
procurement will be drastically reduced—no matter what the international situation. If unemployment begins to rise, the Pentagon will rush through orders for new weapons or reorders for old
ones. If missiles are in short supply, the Pentagon will ignore the
fact—just so long as the Nation's economy is on the rise.

Thus, countercyclical procurement—or procurement that runs
against the economic cycle.

Secretary McNamara's Pentagon is being organized to employ
this countercyclical procurement as soon as possible on a regional
level and in political fashion. The Office of the Secretary of Defense is highly elated over its Project 60 which divides the
country into 15 regions. Each region is under a special procurement officer who reports directly to the Secretary ignoring responsible civilian and military officials.

If the regional chief feels that things aren't going to well in his area, he is expected to let Mr. McNamara know so that defense funds can be siphoned off into the district. Here again, this is a new wrinkle. In the past, the Pentagon was expected to favor to some degree depressed areas in allocating defense contracts. But under Project 60, need (political or economic) rather than efficiency or low cost is the major criterion.

Under "counter-cyclical procurement" the Nation's military power will decline when we are prosperous and rise when we are having economic troubles. Or so it would seem. But since the lead time on weapons is so great—and adversely affected by stop-and-go procurement—the monies necessary to prime the economic pump would be a long time going into the pipeline of production—and larger sums would be needed. Designers of new weapons systems—if this administration ever gets around to such matters—would never know whether or not their blueprints are ever to be used. The chaos in procurement would be fantastic.

Under Project 60, there would be another dangerous factor. If regional economic needs are to be the guideline for procurement, who is to say if political considerations are supreme. Already this administration is penalizing States which happen to be Republican, and tossing the juicy contracts to those presumed to be Democratic.

Most frightening of all is the consequence of these new forms of procurement. The Pentagon is the Nation's biggest customer, spending well over $53 billion a year. If it is to pick and choose the time for making this or that weapon, guiding itself (however conscientiously) by its reading of economic signs, then it will in effect begin to control the economy. Its experts, moreover, will have to keep a grip on a variety of raw material sources. This can only lead to a repressive effect on the free market which—to work at all—will have to succumb to wage-price manipulation.

All of this explains why civilian and military officials at the Pentagon look so worriedly at Secretary McNamara. They do not know what he will do next—or what area of the national life will fall into his grasp.

September 1963

AMERICAN DEFENSE–AND McNAMARA'S FOLLY

Like all totalitarian countries, the Soviet Union has its own "Mein Kampf." In it, Soviet generals say precisely what they want and what they intend to do. And so they have made it clear that if the United States loses its preponderant strength in nuclear weapons and delivery, they will strike hard and fast.

Against this, Defense Secretary McNamara and his computer-happy "whiz kids" have set up a bargain basement strategy which may find us all burned to an atomic crisp–simply to save a dollar here and a buck there. The statistics are so frightening that few have wanted to publish them.

Mr. McNamara, taking advantage of the literary efforts of those who write blithely of "overkill," has been steadily reducing the potential of American arms. In this he has relied not on the experience of military experts but on the mathematics of computers, which fail to take into account the imponderables of war.

During the Second World War, our generals knew that the greater amount of "overkill" they had–and this is a highly mis-understood term–the greater the chances of victory at a minimal cost in American lives. To quote Representative Craig Hosmer–and he knows more about this than all of the Pentagon crew–"During World War II we manufactured a quantity of bullets 65 times that of the entire population of the Axis powers and 2,000 depth charges for every enemy submarine. For every enemy submarine "killed" an average of 1,500 depth charges were expended."

With no irony, but a deep concern for the safety of this nation, Mr. Hosmer adds: "Compare this 1,500 to one ratio with the Secretary's two or three to one ratio," which is now our margin of deterrence.

This reduction is being justified as an "economy" by Mr. McNamara and his "whiz kids"–but the question arises: What good will economy do us if we are all dead?

Secretary McNamara and President Johnson have announced cut-backs in our retaliatory power which would shake most

Americans if they gave them any real thought. At the present time, our 680 B-52 and B-58 bombers, which average a nuclear bomb-load of 40 megatons each, could deliver 27,200 megatons to the enemy. Our 1,350 strategic missiles, averaging warheads of one megaton each, could drop an additional 1,350 megatons on the enemy. This totals a counter-punch of 28,550 megatons, or enough to make war against the United States a suicidal venture for the Soviet Union.

But the Administration has announced that it will scrap 425 manned bombers. This means that we are cutting down our retaliatory megatonnage by 59.5 percent. To offset this, the Pentagon will produce 210 new bombers and 360 new missiles by 1971. This will still leave us at 71 percent of our present strength.

Even this is an optimistic figure. The new bombers are still on the drawing boards. No one knows whether these new FB-111 bombers can do the job. In fact, experts seriously doubt it. General Curtis LeMay, now retired and able to speak his mind without fear of Administration reprisal, says that they will be "inadequate to do the job for several reasons . . . insufficient ranges, insufficient size."

Secretary McNamara, with the backing of the President, insists that he is right and everybody else is wrong. The computers tell him so—and this is enough for the Administration. But Mr. McNamara has been so consistently wrong on military matters that his reliance on computers is open to serious question.

Just eight months ago, Mr. McNamara proclaimed that according to his figures, it would cost an additional $700 million to carry on the war in Vietnam. Today he concedes that the final tab will run into the multi-billions. In 1963, Mr. McNamara was citing his superior knowledge to back up the promise that by Christmas of 1965 the troops would be coming home from Vietnam. Instead, the number of troops in Vietnam has been steadily increasing. Today, we have roughly the same amount of men in combat as the Joint Chiefs of Staff, who are treated like messenger boys by the "whiz kids," said would be there.

The computers have been winning the fighting in Vietnam for years, but somehow the Communists don't pay any attention to

Mr. McNamara's "scientific" findings. As he moves to cut down the Strategic Air Command and to give us less military muscle every year, one statistic which even his "whiz kids" don't deny lives to haunt us: If the Soviet Union launches a nuclear attack on the United States, 149 million Americans will be killed. Only overwhelming superiority—"overkill"—will prevent this horror from descending upon us. If this happens, few of us will be around to tell Mr. McNamara and the President, "I told you so."

January 1966

McNAMARA PLAYS NUMBERS GAME WITH AMERICAN DEFENSE

When Defense Secretary Robert McNamara is caught in one of his massive blunders, he snows you under with statistics. The figures he cites may have nothing to do with the case, but they sound impressive. Reporters quote them without correlating them to the problem at hand—and everybody is satisfied. Everybody, that is, except the men fighting a bitter war in Vietnam without adequate arms and munitions.

This is precisely what has been happening. Secretary McNamara has tried to hide the fact that there is a serious shortage of certain key munitions, a shortage brought about by his "economy" drive. Since the military budget is full of boondoggles—and fancy profits for a chosen few, as this column has repeatedly disclosed—Mr. McNamara has had to save money somewhere. The "Whiz Kids" told him he didn't need things like 750-pound bombs and other munitions. The Secretary decided to "show" that the nation's spendingest defense establishment of all time was really "economizing."

But the Whiz Kids have been dreadfully wrong, as the Joint Chiefs of Staff predicted. As a result, two-thirds of our divisions are not in combat readiness because weapons were taken from them to give to the boys in Vietnam. Mr. McNamara at first denied this, making big headlines, then admitted it later in the fine print.

There is a shortage of 750-pound bombs—the most effective for the Vietnam fighting—and in other sizes. The Pentagon has been forced to buy back World War II bombs that had been sold as surplus. You can bet that someone will make a profit in that deal, and it won't be Uncle Sam. The bombs now being taken out of storage to prop up Mr. McNamara's fancy statistics are types that force bombers to remain longer over their targets, making each run more hazardous. But like the man with a slightly beat-up car who "makes do," Mr. McNamara is willing to take second best if only he can save a buck.

It is also true that a shortage of bombs has slowed down the pace of the air war in Vietnam during the past weeks. Mr. McNamara's very disingenuous answer to this charge from the fighting fronts is to give the press figures for February and March—interesting but hardly relevant. What of the first two weeks in April, Mr. Secretary?

Mr. McNamara also fuzzes up the picture by citing figures for the entire year of 1966, also interesting, but merely projections. His projection for the Vietnamese war in mid-1963 had American troops out by Christmas of that year, with the fighting done and victory in our pockets.

When you get down to the hard facts, the shortages of first-class arms and materiel will continue for a long time. This is obvious from the figures Mr. McNamara himself will grudgingly give, once he has made his optimistic headline. Factories will not begin to produce the new 750-pounders until July. Over-all bomb production, moreover, will reach only 80 percent of what the fighting forces need by next month. What it is today is a secret that will remain classified until the Defense Secretary can make a point with it.

The Republicans have sat quietly by and seen this happening. They have taken the advice of the "moderate" group in Congress whose arguments always seem to reflect Democratic thinking. In this, Representative Gerald Ford, the House Republican leader, has not been entirely blameless. But he has finally seen the light, and his attack on Mr. McNamara should be the beginning of a series. That is, unless the immoderate "moderates" again convince him that support of the Vietnamese war means support of Mr. McNamara, his Whiz Kids, their computers, and their grievous errors and miscalculations.

There were others on the Hill who were somehow intimidated by those computers, as if all wisdom began and ended with them in this technological age. Congress is learning the hard way—and much too slowly—that the old quip about "figures can't lie, but liars can figure" has taken a new form. Computers can't goof, but goofers can compute. An electronic marvel is not smarter than the man who programs it, no more reliable than its data.

The war will go badly in Vietnam just as long as Mr. McNamara's figures are deemed more important than the training, experience, and know-how of men who have devoted more years than the Whiz Kids have whiskers to the science of defense and the art of war. Mr. McNamara should be questioned closely before the nation by a Congressional committee. In the past, he has told his story in secret session, claiming that to do otherwise would violate security. His latest performance, in which he quoted classified data in order to defend himself, destroys his old excuse.

April 1966

THE TFX RETURNS TO HAUNT McNAMARA

The TFX, that "wonder plane" of Defense Secretary Mc-Namara's hopes is still around, still making trouble for the Armed Forces. The facts remain the same—only the name has been changed. It is now officially the F-111, although the more acid wits refer to it as the "Flying Edsel." How many hundreds of millions have been poured into making the prototypes of this albatross the Pentagon isn't saying.

But you may be sure that Congress will get around to asking the question, and the prime asker will be that downy bird of investigators the very capable Senator John J. McClellan (D.-Ark.)

The TFX, or F-111 was the brain child of the "whiz kids" and their computers. There was opposition all along the line from the Joint Chiefs of Staff, but Secretary McNamara, with a persistence that might better have been elsewhere employed, beat it down. He insisted, against the pleading arguments of the Air Force and the Navy, that money could be saved by producing a plane able to serve both services. It was to be a swing-wing job of supersonic speed. At low speeds, the wings would jut out almost at right angles from the fuselage. At supersonic speeds, the wings would be pulled back.

Two companies worked on the development of the TFX—General Dynamics in Texas and Boeing in the State of Washington. The Joint Chiefs recommended the Boeing version as cheaper by billions of dollars and better from an aerodynamic standpoint. Mr. McNamara overruled them—and Texas won out. The Joint Chiefs were told that they didn't know what they were talking about and warned to mind their manners.

Well, the Navy has received three of the TFX-F-111 fighter-bombers, and finds that they weigh seven tons too much to be used on aircraft carriers, as they were planned to be used. They are also afflicted with "aerodynamic drag" and trouble with their jet afterburners. The Navy, therefore, has refused to let the planes go into assembly line production yet. Designers are working feverishly to make the proper modifications.

Making matters just that much more embarrassing for Secretary McNamara, private industry has come up with plans for a swing-wing version of the present F-4, now doing yeoman service in Vietnam. Several hundred of the Swing-wing F-4, could be in the hands of the Navy and operational in about two years. The TFX-F-111 could match that production record, though not the performance, if the Navy ordered them without further testing. But that would mean putting its eggs in the basket of a so-far inferior plane—and Congress has no desire to make that gamble.

Before authorization of any such purchases is made, the Navy wants to test the new and presumably improved prototypes for several months. Once those tests have been made, the TFX controversy will be reopened. Senator McClellan bowed to the Administration's decision to go ahead with the TFX. But he was never happy about it and resented the heat put on him, as chairman of the Senate Government Operations Committee which looked into charges that politics rather than sound military thinking was responsible for the Pentagon's choice of the more expensive, less suitable version of the TFX.

Secretary McNamara was able to impress Capitol Hill when the TFX question came up a couple of years ago because his prestige and reputation as an administrative and financial whiz was high. There are, however, a number of Senators waiting for the opportunity to put him on the stand and quote back at him the glowing statements he made about the Texas version of the TFX.

This could make headlines and lead to more of the fun-and-games which an investigation of the kind now planned involves. Meanwhile, however, the Navy will be awaiting the type of modern fighter-bomber it needs in Vietnam, as well as on its far-ranging carriers. From the American point of view, the national security must always be rated higher than the temperamental stubbornness of a public official who takes the position that he is always right—and that those who oppose him are either fools or rogues.

And it will give little solace to those of us who called out in anguish when the TFX was being rammed down the throats of the Air Force and Navy to know that we were right. Secretary McNamara owes the Congress and the nation an explanation—and himself just a little humility.

July 1966

WHILE McNAMARA SLEEPS: SOVIETS PREPARE FOR NUCLEAR BLACKMAIL

Defense Secretary Robert Strange McNamara is very clever at figures. He has systematically convinced two Presidents and the Congress that the United States is ahead of the Soviet Union in military strength and nuclear power. To do this, he has been forced to do some careful juggling, eliminating 700 Soviet heavy bombers from his tally, or arguing that IRBMs pointed at the cities of NATO allies were not part of the Kremlin's strategic forces.

But the facts cannot be statistically erased. One fact that Mr. McNamara cannot talk out of existence, in his ceaseless effort to justify his steady cutbacks in production and research, is that during his period of tenure as Defense Secretary—and as one of the most influential men in the Kennedy-Johnson Cabinets—the Soviets and the United States have begun to switch positions. By 1971, they will be up where we were in 1962—and we shall be down where they were.

Let me quote from a frightening and heavily-documented study prepared by the American Security Council for the House Armed Services Committee:

"In 1962, the United States had a total megatonnage delivery capability ranging between 25,000 megatons and 50,000 megatons. The corresponding figures for the Soviet Union ranged between 6,000 megatons and 12,000 megatons.

"The year 1967 falls in a crossover period with the U.S.S.R. estimates ranging between 16,000 and 37,000 megatons, to equal or exceed the U.S. estimated range between 8,000 and 27,000 megatons . . .

"For 1971, it appears that a massive megatonnage gap will have developed. U.S. delivery capability is estimated to range between 6,000 megatons and 15,000 megatons, whereas the estimated high for the Soviet delivery capability is 50,000 megatons, (with) a low figure for the Soviets of 30,000 tons."

This is the record of an Administration that came into power in 1961 on the cry of a "missile gap"—a scare phrase that was taken back after the ballots had been counted.

Lagging behind the Soviets in offensive capabilities, Secretary McNamara, with the full compliance of the Johnson Administration, has refused to move rapidly ahead with any Anti-Ballistic Missile (ABM) system. The administration has said that a Soviet first-strike would cost the United States 120 million lives. But a $40 billion ABM system (of which $20 billion would be in related programs not having anything to do with missile defense) is too expensive. Mr. McNamara concedes that $20 billion spent, over a period of years, on ABM systems would save 70 million to 90 million lives. But he has fought strenuously against it.

Mr. McNamara, let's face it, is a great one at saying, No! In 1962, he killed the Skybolt program, which would have given our heavy bombers a stand-off missile with a 1,000-mile range. He told the Congress then that this was a waste of money because the Soviets had no such air-to-surface missile—a weird kind of logic. Well, the Soviets have now unveiled their version of Skybolt. And since they now have 1,110 such bombers, to our 680—thanks to Mr. McNamara's "success" in phasing out the Strategic Air Command—they are this much ahead of us.

In the Intermediate Range (IRBM) and Medium Range (MRBM) ballistics missile field, the Soviets have come from behind dramatically. While the United States was closing down IRBM and MRBM launching sites in Europe and the Middle East, the Soviets were building and deploying their own systems.

The figures tell the story. Today, the Soviets have 750 IRBMs and MRBM missiles deployed against us, including a completely mobile system, with a roving firing platform. The United States has none.

It should be noted that the main defense of the Pentagon for this cutback in ICBM, IRBM, and MRBM systems is that the Polaris, firing from nuclear and other submarines, can take care of United States defense. But the Soviets are taking long strides in that direction, and also developing "hunter-killer" submarines which can seek out the American Polaris fleet and sink it under water before it has a chance to launch its missiles.

In short, America's nuclear "deterrent" deters less and less. The Soviets, in a few years, will have such a preponderance of power that it will not need to worry about American retaliatory power. Then it can deliver an ultimatum to the United States. It will come as a shock to Robert Strange McNamara, but this will afford America little comfort.

July 1967

TFX: THE SCANDAL THAT WON'T DIE

Back in the early days of the Johnson Administration, Defense Secretary Robert Strange McNamara was the fair-haired boy of Washington. He was the favorite of the President. Congress listened with rapt attention when he promised to bring sound management practices to the Pentagon. His promises of economy and policy streamlining were widely quoted.

Since then, Secretary McNamara has fallen on evil days. His repeated statements that all was going well in Vietnam, that the boys would be home by Christmas (1963, that is), and his way of suppressing information and double-talking his legislative questioners—these have made him one of the more unpopular men on Capitol Hill. If the three Stennis Committee reports are ever published, McNamara will be hard put to explain the dangerous shortages in arms and other military materiel that have resulted from his handling of the Defense Establishment.

At present, Mr. McNamara and Senator John L. McClellan (D.-Ark.) are at sword's point over the release of testimony about the TFX, one of Mr. McNamara's pet projects—and one of the larger disasters of his tenure as Defense Secretary. It will be recalled that Mr. McNamara gave the contract for the swing-wing fighter-bomber to General Dynamics of Texas, even though many of his military advisers argued that a Boeing version of the plane would cost less and be a better plane.

Mr. McNamara, of course, had his way. The TFX has been flight-tested, both in its now designated Army F-111A and Navy F-111B versions. It is a plane that no one really wants, either in the Army or the Navy. It was to cost $2.9 million, but the bill has sadly gone up to a unit cost of $8 million. And the Navy, which had planned to use the TFX as a carrier-based fighter-bomber, is now planning to substitute another plane for this purpose—with Mr. McNamara's "Flying Edsel" as an auxiliary. This decision, according to the Chief of Naval Operations, Admiral David L. McDonald, "eased the minds of a lot of people"—namely those men who command and fly the Navy's planes. In fact, the men who have flown the TFX describe its performance as "marginal"—which is hardly reassuring.*

The TFX is heavier than it was supposed to be. It does not accelerate as rapidly as the contract called for. Its maneuverability makes it a sitting duck for fighter planes in a dogfight. In fact, Navy test pilots, in their formal but unreleased report, stated flatly: "The F-111B (Navy version) remains unfit for service use as previously reported and was found to be incapable of carrier-based operations."

These pilots spelled out 100 deficiencies in the plane where correction was mandatory and 15 other deficiencies which they would have liked to see eliminated. The Naval Air Systems Command has said that 23 of those 100 deficiencies would be difficult, if not impossible, to correct. In test flights, moreover, the engines of the TFX have partially stalled. Changes in design to prevent this would further slow down the plane.

Senator McClellan, who has followed the course of the TFX fiasco, is pressing for a full public report on the plane. He wants Mr. McNamara to prove conclusively to the Senate Armed Services Committee that the TFX is worth the $287 additional millions that the Secretary of Defense wants to pour into its production. And the committee sides with Senator McClellan. Though the TFX program is already two years behind schedule, the committee has recommended that only six planes be purchased. Mr. McNamara is pressing for 20 planes. The Senate recommendation, as seconded by the House, will prevent Mr. McNamara from acquiring any more planes until he has conclusively demonstrated that the TFX can be carrier-based.

Among Pentagon-watchers, the question remains: Why does Robert Strange McNamara persist in demanding a plane which has been rejected by the men who must fly it? At this point, good sense would dictate that the Defense Department cut its losses. Even better sense would urge that the Secretary and his "whiz-kid" advisers pay some heed to the advice of career officers and

*The first two to go into action in Vietnam (March 1968) were shot down.

civilians rather than resort to the petulant tactics which have characterized Mr. McNamara's relations with the military.

But Secretary McNamara decided a long time ago that he was a law unto himself and that Congress must be disciplined into accepting his judgments and dictates as infallible. The TFX is but one example of this. His juggling of the figures on aircraft losses in Vietnam is also indicative of his attitude towards the Congress and the people. That he seems to retain President Johnson's respect and admiration, even though he increasingly becomes a political liability, is one of the mysteries of Washington.

August 1967

McNAMARA'S $70 BILLION

The movement through Congress of the $70 billion military appropriation bill has so far succeeded in intensifying criticism of Defense Secretary McNamara and of his Pentagon policies. Though the press plays up Mr. McNamara's difference with the Joint Chiefs over tactics and strategy in Vietnam, this is but a small part of Congress' quarrel with the Johnson Administration's Svengali. Escalation, limitation of bombing targets, and the interference in ways and means to defeat the Communists make the headlines. The real opposition to Mr. McNamara's stewardship of the Defense establishment goes far deeper.

By rigorous censorship, this story has been suppressed. But three reports, locked up in the safe of the Stennis Committee, document the case against Secretary McNamara, his "whiz kid" advisors, and the policies which they and their computers have imposed on U.S. armed forces. So far, efforts to force publication of these documents have failed. Bit by bit, the contents have begun to leak.

This is what Robert Strange McNamara and the Defense establishment do not want the American people to know:

● Two-thirds of America's combat forces are not combat-ready. It would take at least 30 days to make these combat-effective, an impossibly long period under today's conditions of warfare.

● Because of McNamara "economies," U.S. combat divisions are short of vital military hardware and of adequately trained officers and men.

● To supply U.S. forces in Vietnam, divisions in Europe and in the continental United States have been "cannibalized"—that is, weapons and men have been drawn off.

● Because of Secretary McNamara's refusal to keep the nation's aircraft production lines moving, losses in planes exceed the number of aircraft being turned out each month.

● A shortage of 2,430 trained pilots has placed a cruel burden on crews fighting the war in Vietnam by increasing their workloads. Nevertheless, Secretary McNamara has refused to authorize pilot training at the levels requested by the armed services. He has also refused to call up reserve pilots and, in fact, has turned down requests for active service of pilots who served in the Korean War.

How is the $70 billion being spent? Since 1961, members of Congress have complained, to no avail, over procurement practices—sole source, rather than competitive—which have raised the price of the items purchased by the Pentagon by as much as 2,000 percent. In some instances, exorbitant prices were paid for items easily available at a fraction of the present cost to the taxpayer. In other cases, as Representative Otis G. Pike (D.-N.Y.) has demonstrated, items "for which excess prices of 500 to 2,500 percent were paid by the taxpayers need not have been purchased . . . because the government already had them in storage bins."

Mr. McNamara has been reversed in his veto of an anti-missile defense system. In his opposition to this elementary form of protection for the U.S., he was sustained by the support of the State Department, which argued that it would irritate the Kremlin if this country raised its military guard.

But McNamara has been able to overrun military opposition to his Little Maginot Line in Vietnam. In public statements, field commanders have said that they can "live with it." But off-the-record, strategists warn that it may shift the tide of battle, negating American victories and putting the war effort in serious jeopardy. Any kind of static defense line, they argue, violates the primary principle of counter-insurgency and anti-guerrilla warfare: Mobility. By tying down large numbers of troops, it will expose U.S. forces to the same kind of attrition that defeated the French at Dienbienphu.

September 1967

THE WRONG APPROACH: BOMBS ARE ONLY PART OF THE ANSWER

A diligent researcher, months ago, picked up paper and pencil to do some military arithmetic. It didn't take him very long to discover that the United States has dumped more bombs on Vietnam than all the combatants on both sides dropped during World War II. This simple statistic opens the door to interesting conjecture.

One Washington wit suggested that the bombs were being jettisoned over special targets in North Vietnam marked "bomb disposal areas—for U.S. Air Force use only." Obviously, the strategy developed by Defense Secretary Robert Strange McNamara was a little more sophisticated than that—like risking precious lives and million-dollar aircraft to blow up ox-carts on dirt roads that sop up high explosives.

Given the ridiculous restrictions on targets imposed by the Napoleonic Mr. McNamara, the debate on escalation—on bombing or not bombing—merely plays into the enemy's hands. For bombs alone cannot win, nor have they ever won, a war. As long as the controversy rages over the number of targets not restricted to American pilots—or to the number and density of the sorties by U.S. planes—the real problem is forgotten.

The purpose of any strategy is to destroy the enemy's war-making ability, and on this point, Mr. McNamara and the Administration remain strangely silent.

To end the war in Vietnam on American terms, or even to bring the Communists to the negotiating table, Mr. McNamara will have to put aside his computers and start thinking in terms of logistics. He will have to admit that North Vietnam's war materiel is almost exclusively imported and must be interdicted by U.S. naval forces. This means closing the harbor of Haiphong by mining its approaches and blockading the North Vietnamese coast.

This has not been done, for fear, we are told, that a Soviet vessel will be inconvenienced by running into one of those mines and sinking. The answer to this objection, raised repeatedly at the Defense and State Departments, is a flat assertion that if Communist bloc ships enter a war zone, they are accepting the rules of war.

But if the Administration cannot see this, certainly it must realize that there are other means to slow down the flow of military goods to the Communists in Vietnam and to impose logistic starvation on the enemy. This strikes at the root problem, not only of Vietnam but of any future "small" wars that the Soviet Union encourages. The answer is to put a stop to the shipment of potentially strategic goods to the Communist bloc.

Recently, Senator Karl Mundt protested bitterly because the Defense Department had authorized the shipment to the Soviet Union of equipment for stabilizing missiles, thereby giving the Communist war machine a military boost it badly needs. That Mr. McNamara should have sanctioned these exports is one of the more puzzling aspects of his present rule.

But the shipment that Senator Mundt protested, though more dramatic than most, is a small part of what the United States is giving the Communist bloc, strengthening its hand and permitting it to bolster the North Vietnam Communists. Young Americans for Freedom recently compiled what is only a partial list of goods licensed for shipment to the Communist bloc. For example:

Gear manufacturing machinery; precision-grinding machines; copper cable; diesel engines; precision-boring machines; rocket engines; turbines and generators; technical data for the design and construction of a chemical plant; valves, pistons, and exhaust manifolds; data on radar devices; electronic computers and parts, which permit the Soviets to miniaturize their old-fashioned computers; ship stablization systems, badly needed for the growing Soviet navy; rifle-cleaning compounds; airborne navigation equipment; diamond core bits; tungsten carbide bits; radio receivers and parts; petroleum drilling and production equipment.

According to the Administration, no one of these items is strategic. As Young Americans for Freedom asked: who is kidding whom? YAF called for passage of HR 67, introduced by Representative Glen Lipscomb of California for the re-establishment of a House Select Committee on Export Control. But this is the slow way. The initial effort to stop the flow of war and war-potential materials must come from the President. Only Mr. Johnson can stop Secretary McNamara's stubborn drive to make the Soviets happy—at American expense, and at the cost of American lives in Vietnam.

September 1967

The Soft Underbelly
of the U. S. A.

*Note carefully the date of this article. It is February,
1953. In all of the years since then, every year has
proven beyond a doubt, the truth of what Toledano
was reporting way back then—and also each year has
proven the absolute ability of the bureaucracy in Washington, Republican and Democrat alike, to ignore those
facts. It has now become an annual tragi-comedic farce
of the Organization of American States to receive fully
documented evidence of Communist subversion, to
deplore and explore it, and then to adjourn without
having done a damn thing about it.*

In the early morning of January 25, 1945, a plane crashed as it
took off from the Mexico City Airport. The body of Soviet
Ambassador Constantine Oumansky lay in the burning wreckage.
The crash was no accident. NKVD agents had planned it metic-
ulously to send Oumansky—and the other members of his party—
to that particular circle of Hell reserved for Communists.

The method of liquidation—a time bomb planted in the hold
of the plane—was ironic. For Oumansky and his agents had
labored mightily to place another time bomb against the soft
underbelly of the U.S.A., in Central and South America, and the
Caribbean. Protected by the immunity of his diplomatic status,
he had helped to assemble it. When he was murdered, that other
bomb had already begun to tick.

That bomb is still ticking today, loudly and ominously.
Despite cold-war setbacks, the apparatus which Oumansky per-
fected and coordinated continues to operate. It threatens
American security and the Panama Canal. It threatens the liveli-
hood, and the lives, of millions of Latin Americans. It already has
endangered the small degree of trust and cooperation between the
Latin nations and "el coloso del norte"—their name for the
United States.

For Oumansky's work—and the work of important Soviet
agents who came before and after him—has already resulted in the
virtual capture of Guatemala, a country strategically located in
Central America. The Communist conspiracy has set up shop
there. From Guatemala, a great espionage, sabotage, and propaganda organization works day and night for the Soviet Union,
against the United States and the other countries of the hemisphere.

"A full-fledged Soviet beachhead is established on our flanks,"
Representative John W. McCormack said last February. "The
penetration by Soviet Communism in Guatemala has developed
into a position of great peril."

"Beachhead" is an understatement, for a beachhead can be
contained. Guatemala has become a plague spot. As in Czecho-
slovakia before the Iron Curtain was rung down, Communists
have taken over the key posts in the government. Government-
owned radio stations and newspapers pour out propaganda in an
incessant stream of vilification against the United States. It is
couched in the delicate rhetoric of Herr Goebbels and Tovarisch
Vishinsky, and it has one theme: "el imperialismo Yanqui."

The Foreign Office is a tool in the hands of the Communists.
Its consulates and embassies are centers of espionage, its world-
wide diplomatic network is Stalin's post office. Anti-American
propaganda is shipped out by the ton, under diplomatic seal. In
New York, Guatemala's United Nations delegation votes cozily
with the Soviet bloc against her sister nations.

Within the country itself, activists are trained and armed for
sabotage and subversion in El Salvador, Honduras, Panama, the
Canal Zone—or in any trouble spot where Spanish is spoken.

Anti-Communists are beaten on the streets and in police stations. American movies often are barred, but Soviet propaganda films, such as those peddling the discredited charge that bacteriological warfare is being employed by the UN against the North Koreans, get a wide showing with the government's blessing.

In the Guatemalan Congress, labor and agrarian legislation is rammed through by a Popular Front coalition which, as usual, is dominated by the Communists. Documentary proof exists that this legislation is consciously planned to bring about a slow strangulation of the economy, to create economic chaos, and to drive out the foreign investors who have given Guatameltecos a sound currency and one of the most prosperous economies in Central America.

The Communists are moving slowly; they know that Moscow was not built in a day. They are playing not for Guatemala but for all of Latin America. Like the Nazis, their slogan is, "Tomorrow the world." The Communist assault on Latin America began two decades ago. The Communist International made gargantuan mistakes of strategy and tactics; it profited by these mistakes.

Guatemala is the result.

The Guatemala pattern is the one the Communists hope to follow in every Latin Republic, eventually. At the moment they are concentrating their efforts on the Central American and Caribbean countries which straddle our lifeline of the critical supplies we must import from South America in increasing quantities, both in peace and in war.

The pattern was painfully developed after a series of reverses in Brazil, in Mexico, in Chile, in Peru, Cuba and other southern countries.

In Brazil, in the summer of 1935, a young Army officer by the name of Luis Carlos Prestes led a few regiments of soldiers and the tiny Communist Party in an armed revolt against the government. It had no chance of success and was savagely repressed.

In Mexico, during the middle 1930's, they gained a dominant position in the regime of President Lázaro Cárdenas, principally by taking advantage of Cárdenas' deep-seated antipathy for the United States. It was during his regime that Vicente Lombardo

Toledano—now regarded as the spearhead of the Communist conspiracy in Latin America—gained control of the Mexican labor
movement, and expanded it by organizing the Confederation de
Trabajadores de America Latina (CTAL), a Moscow-controlled federation of Latin American trade unions with tentacles reaching
into every country south of the Rio Grande.

During the latter months of his presidency, however, Cardenas
turned on the Communists, gradually stripping them of control of
the larger unions, and forcing their members out of government
jobs. Communist prestige in Mexico dwindled even more during
the presidency of Alemán, who broke the last vestiges of control
that Lombardo once enjoyed over the Mexican labor movement.
Similar setbacks, following temporary successes, were suffered by
the Communists in Chile, Peru, and later in Cuba.

From their reverses, however, the Communists learned an important lesson; politics in Latin America is governed by a shifting
balance between the military and the professional politicos. To
gain power, it was neither possible nor necessary to attempt a
frontal assault.

From Moscow, new instructions went to the Latin American
Communist parties. According to the paraphrase of a one-time
high Kremlin functionary, the orders were "not revolution, but
participation in power be it ever so small. The pressure groups are
advised to utilize all means that will serve the purpose, to enter
into any combination with political or military groups, be they
democratic, fascist or socialist." The only thing exacted of these
Latin American parties was a "common minimum program of
direct or indirect support of Russia's acts and activities." Moscow
even allowed a few key agents to join anti-Communist groups, in
order to use them for anti-U.S. purposes.

There was also a slight shift of objectives. The long-range
objective in Latin America, as in all parts of the world, remains
the complete seizure of power. However, with the increasing
intensity of the cold war, the Kremlin placed more and more
emphasis on an immediate, or short-range objective—to create
situations throughout Latin America, and particularly in Central
America, that can be exploited to the advantage of the Soviet

Union in the event of all-out war with the United States. To
achieve this the Communists developed the following program:

1. To gain control of the labor and agrarian movements.

2. To aggravate to the maximum degree the deep-seated ani-
mosity that exists in all those countries toward the United States
and especially toward U.S. private investment.

3. To drive U.S. private investment out of Latin America.

4. To disrupt slowly local economies to the point that political and social chaos can be quickly and easily created.

This was the pattern they followed so successfully in
Guatemala.

Guatemala lies just below the Yucatan bulge of the Caribbean
coast, straddling Central America from Atlantic to Pacific. On its
45,452 square miles of lowland, upland and mountain live some
three million people. Its principal crops are coffee and bananas.

Its principal emotion is hatred of the United States.

In the 1930's and early 1940's, Guatemala was ruled by a
dictatorship under General Jorge Ubico. His policies leaned
toward the U. S.; his government was no more corrupt or ruthless
than that of any one of a dozen Latin American countries. If he
did not look after the welfare of his people, at least he did not
consciously seek to destroy the economy which sustained them.

In 1944, a coalition of garden-variety revolutionists, idealists,
young military officers, leftists, and Communists overthrew the
Ubico regime. A military-civilian junta took over the government.
It promised free elections and, *mirabile dictu,* kept the promise.
The newly formed revolutionary parties united to elect Juan José
Arévalo to the presidency. Arévalo, a school teacher who had
spent years of exile in Argentina, preached a vague political and
economic doctrine of "spiritual socialism." Probably, he was no
more a Communist than Henry Wallace in his Progressive Party
phase. But, like Wallace, he was a complete tool of the Communists, worth more to them out of the party than in it.

His first important act as president was to push through the
Guatemalan Congress a labor reform law. Then he invited
Lombardo Toledano and the Communist-dominated CTAL to
come to Guatemala and organize the workers into unions. Within

months, 50,000 Guatemaltecos were strait-jacketed into labor groups, headed and controlled by Communists. The Mexican experience was duplicated, with one critical difference. Unlike Cárdenas, Arévalo was not the leader but the puppet. Lombardo saw to it that the new unions were organized along strictly political lines. The Communist labor leaders quickly consolidated their power by demanding, and obtaining, seats in the councils of the major political parties.

To cement control of the unions, Lombardo turned them over to two of Guatemala's leading Communists—Victor Manuel Gutierrez and Manuel Pinto Usaga. Of these, the more important is Gutierrez, a brilliant young Marxist intellectual, member of Congress, history professor, and power in the strongest political party, Partido Acción Revolucionaria (PAR). He has made his pilgrimage to Moscow and said his litany: "Communism is one of the highest revolutionary ideals of humanity."

Two years ago, Communist labor power was further consolidated when Lombardo and the Communist high command for Latin America ordered Blas Roca, the Cuban Red leader, to Guatemala City. With his help, the unions were brought together into a federation, the Confederación General de Trabajadores de Guatemala (CGTG), headed by Gutierrez, with Pinto Usaga as the second in command. (Since then, Pinto has been appointed Consul General to Mexico, a post which allows him to maintain direct contact with the large Mexican underground and particularly with the Russian and Polish embassies in Mexico City, through which are channelled the instructions from the Kremlin to their Latin American stooges.)

The labor movement was only the first of Arévalo's gifts to the Communists. From the very beginning, he opened Guatemala's doors to Communists from other Latin American countries: José Zamora of El Salvador, Virginia Bravo Letilier of Chile, Vicente Saenz of Costa Rica, and Cesar Gody Urritia of Chile—Communists all, devoted to the subversion of Guatemala and their own countries.

The president made Zamora his publicity chief, a post which enabled him to supervise the thorough infiltration by Com-

munists and reliable fellow travelers of all government propaganda agencies. Under Zamora, the government-owned newspapers and its radio station (TGWA) became effective propaganda
outlets for Guatemalan Communists. (The present director of
TGWA is Carlos Alvarado Jerez, an avowed Communist who
attended the recent International Peace Conference in Peiping as
an official Guatemalan delegate.) Free radio time was given to
Communist organizations on the government station to attack the
United States.

Newscasts and educational programs followed the party line—
and still do—as faithfully as *Octubre,* the official Guatemalan
Communist newspaper. The *Diario de Centro America*, the
government-owned daily, under the editorial direction of
Leopoldo Castillo Saenz, is virtually a carbon copy of *Octubre.*
The path toward Communist domination of the press taken under
Arévalo has been followed ever since. *Nuestro Diario*, a slightly
leftish paper, turned strongly Red about two years ago. When a
political writer slipped in an article criticizing the government's
pro-Communist policies, he was fired. The entire editorial staff
resigned in protest and set up a financially weak but vigorously
independent daily, *Prensa Libre. Nuestro Diario* was restaffed
with "reliable" elements, became forthrightly Communist, and is
now receiving a substantial government subsidy.

Arévalo also turned over to the Communists the Institute of
Social Security, the nation's welfare agency, and opened the
doors of the Ministries of Public Health, Foreign Affairs, and
Education.

Toward the end of Arévalo's six-year term, two candidates
emerged to seek his office: Colonel Jacobo Arbenz, the Minister
of Defense, and Colonel Arana, the Army Chief of Staff—both
members of the junta which overthrew Ubico in 1944. Arévalo,
the Communists, and the extreme leftists supported Arbenz.
Arana, however, not only had the support of the Army and the
conservatives, but he was widely popular with the people.

A few months before the election, Arana learned of an arms
cache near Lake Amatitlan, about 35 miles from Guatemala City.
He informed Arbenz that he was investigating personally. On the

road to Amatitlan, Arana's car was ambushed and he was murdered by two men with submachine guns. His chauffeur escaped and identified the assassins as an army captain and a member of the notorious Caribbean Legion.

The murder of Arana left Arbenz virtually unopposed. When he assumed the Presidency, one of his first acts was to appoint the two alleged assassins of Arana to influential government posts.

Despite the scandal surrounding Arana's assassination, many conservatives felt that Arbenz would make a good president. He was an Army man, of considerable wealth, and they felt that his alliance with the Communists was motivated by political expediency rather than ideological sympathy. This view persists, though Arbenz' administration has in no way strayed from Red orthodoxy. A brief catalogue of his acts show this clearly:

1. He has continued in office the Communists and fellow travelers appointed by Arévalo or replaced them with other Communists or fellow travelers.

2. He named as one of the three judges of the Elections Board, Jaime Diaz Rozzotto, who helped organize the Moscow-inspired Partisans for Peace Committee in Guatemala and served as its first general secretary. One of the other judges is Alfonso Orantes, co-chairman of the Partisans for Peace Committee. Thus the Communists have control of the politically powerful three-man board, which has final jurisdiction in all election disputes.

3. He later made Rozzotto secretary of the Presidency of the Republic, where he acts as a sort of *chef de cabinet* and wields strong influence in the formation of administration policies. Rozzotto is also Secretary General of Renovacion Nacional (RN), one of the five government political parties. He has been replaced on the Elections Board by another fellow traveler.

4. He has publicly proclaimed that anti-Communist activities in Guatemala are "subversive."

5. He has received personally at the Palace a steady stream of visiting Communists.

6. He reviewed, with his entire cabinet, the last May Day parade, a Communist demonstration in which platoon after platoon of

marchers passed the reviewing stand carrying banners with such slogans as "Yankees, Hands Off Korea" and "UN is the Vile Instrument of Financial Forces of U. S."

7. He ignored a section of the Guatemalan Constitution which prohibits the existence of any political party that owes allegiance to a foreign power or international movement. Shortly after Arbenz' inauguration the Communists came out into the open and proclaimed themselves a Communist Party. Under Arévalo they had stayed strictly in the background. Acting on direct orders from Moscow, José Manuel Fortuny was named secretary general of the Guatemalan Communist Party, and *Octubre* now carries the slogan, "Official organ of the Communist Party of Guatemala," on its masthead. For the first time the Communist Party put up its own slate of candidates. But, despite numerous petitions from citizen groups, Arbenz refused to act. He even ignored the petitions, one of which bears 100,000 signatures, although Guatemalan law says a formal petition must be answered by the President within a stipulated period of time.

8. He has threatened to use force to suppress anti-Communist meetings. On March 23 a huge demonstration was held in Guatemala City under the auspices of the Joint Anti-Communist Coordinating Committee and the Comite Civito Nacional, an anti-Red group headed by a lawyer, Jorge Adan Serrano. An estimated 75,000 to 100,000 people attended (this figure is probably a bit exaggerated). The meeting was held to protest Arbenz' failure to answer formal petitions challenging the legality of the Communist Party. At the meeting new petitions were drafted demanding enforcement of the Constitution and the expulsion of Communists from the government. Arbenz ignored the demands and the next day announced that any new unauthorized demonstrations would be broken up by force.

9. He allowed a government official, the director of the radio station, to head the Guatemalan delegation to the International Peace Conference at Peiping. Other delegates to this Communist-inspired and Communist-controlled conference were José Alberto Cardoza, member of Congress; Juan Autorio Cruz Franco, co-chairman of the local "peace" committee; Carmen Moran, head

of the Committee for Protection of Children, in Guatemala; and
Francisco Caligia del Valle, of *El Imparcial,* leading independent
daily.

10. He threw the full support of his government behind the
unions in the persistent "squeeze" of the United Fruit Company, the
International Railways, Empressa Electrica (the American-owned
power company), and Pan American Airways. Arbenz publicly
supported a recent strike against the railroad, although it was
clearly in violation of Guatemalan law, and congratulated the
workers when the strike was settled to their satisfaction. An
important aspect of the recent strike against Pan American was
that one of the few issues which delayed the settlement was the
demand of the union for complete control over who is employed
and discharged. This would have given the Communist leaders
control over the PAA radio communications facilities, which
could be dangerous to the security of the United States in event
of full-scale war.

11. He continued to allow the government propaganda facilities
to be used to spread pro-Communist and anti-United States
progaganda.

At one time Arbenz seemed on the verge of breaking with the
Communists. Last year he vetoed a set of labor code amendments, which were sponsored by Gutierrez. The amendments
were so extreme that it would have been virtually impossible for
an employer to discharge an employee—for any reason whatsoever. They set up a scale of severance and sick leave pay which
would have bankrupted private business.

But the real story behind the veto is that Gutierrez, himself,
wanted the amendments killed. He had just received new orders
from Moscow that he should avoid any action which might create
widespread resentment, either in Guatemala or among neighboring Central American republics. In the Party's parlance, this
was the "Go Slow" order. So Gutierrez simply worked out a deal
with Arbenz, "granting" to the President the authority to veto
the labor amendments and allowing him to take full credit among
the conservatives. But the President's end of the deal was a

pledge—which he kept—to push through Congress an agrarian reform program which the Communists had drafted.

The author of the Agrarian Reform legislation, passed by the Congress after minor amendment, was Gutierrez. It was a bulky, unwieldy, and explosive piece of legislation, aimed at the ex-' propriation of land, the reversion of agriculture to uneconomic methods, the bankruptcy of the agricultural economy, and the creation of a threat to be held over all landholders. Under its terms, disputes over expropriation were taken out of the hands of the courts and turned over to a special set of committees— Communist-dominated, of course—which could set indemnification of owners of expropriated property and parcel it out to any persons it chose. In other words, it was "reform" which fostered patronage, uncertainty, and economic trouble.

Guatemalan Communists have openly boasted that the goal of their labor and agrarian policies is to drive out North American enterprises and U. S. capital. This has a wide appeal among Guatemaltecos whose residual antagonism to the "Yanqui" has been stirred up by persistent government propaganda. But the Communists are faced with a problem. Direct expropriation of foreign business might result in complete economic collapse of the nation, and would leave them holding a big and very unpopular bag. It is their hope to do the job by making things so difficult for the United Fruit Company, for Pan American Airways, the railroad and the power company that they will pull out. Then the Reds can blame the "Wall Street imperialists" for the economic misery of the country. The instrument for this policy is, of course, repressive labor and agrarian legislation.

But the Communist camarilla, which has carefully refrained from open seizure of power, for fear of reactions among other Latin American states, has been less shy in its external affairs. Arévalo gave them the Foreign Office, and Arbenz permitted them to keep it. Arévalo's Foreign Minister, Dr. Enrique Muñoz Meany, was completely subservient to Moscow.

Muñoz sent the Costa Rican Communist, Saenz, to the important Bogota Conference where the constitution of the Organization of American States was drafted and plans for hemisphere defense mapped out. At this conference, Guatemala was a close second to Argentina in efforts to obstruct the agreement. An economic agreement among the American nations was shelved, primarily as a result of Guatemalan maneuvers.

At a more recent OAS conference, called to formulate plans for hemisphere defense against Communist infiltration, Foreign Minister Galich played the same role. When he returned to Guatemala, he publicly boasted that he had inserted so many qualifications, and so forced the U. S. to weaken the proposed program that it was virtually meaningless. No Communist, he said, need have any fears of the OAS program.

Under Muñoz and Galich, the Guatemalan diplomatic corps has been honeycombed with Communists. Diplomatic immunity allows them to carry out subversive work with minimum risk. The diplomatic pouch—as it moves from Paris to the other capitals of the world—gives them a first-class, foolproof courier service. In the past years, three Guatemalan diplomats have been expelled from their posts in friendly countries for Communist activities:

The Guatemalan Ambassador to Panama recently was given 48 hours to leave the country or be declared *persona non grata*. He left.

The first secretary to the Embassy in Nicaragua, Alfred Chocano, was seized on his arrival there. His "diplomatic" luggage was crammed with Communist literature. Chocano was permitted to assume his post, but six months later he was declared *persona non grata* because of activities against the Nicaraguan government. The Guatemalan government rewarded its diplomat by appointing him *chargé d'affaires* to the Embassy in Washington. He is now its first secretary.

Carlos Manuel Pellecer was expelled from France, where he was secretary to the Embassy, when two cases of Communist propaganda were found in his luggage. While working in Paris, Pellecer had granted visas to some three hundred Spanish Communists, mostly veterans of the Loyalist Army. Some of these men turned up in the Caribbean Legion, which attempted to overthrow the governments of Costa Rica and the Dominican Republic.

In the foreign field, dozens of professional agitators on the Guatemalan civil service payroll move back and forth to Honduras, El Salvador, and other Latin American countries, distributing propaganda, organizing and agitating against friendly neighbors, and engaging in other Communist activities. El Salvador was forced to revoke its tourist card agreement with Guatemala. It now insists on visas and carefully screens all visa applications. When the El Salvadoran President, Oscar Osorio, recently declared a state of siege to prevent a Communist coup, his first act was to seal the border. Though it has since been reopened, Guatemalans entering the country are subjected to an intensive search.

Perhaps the most important Communist in the Foreign Office is one Castaneda, an avowed Party member. Strategically, though humbly, placed, he holds the job of official translator. Castaneda participates in all important conferences and diplomatic discussions. He has access to all diplomatic correspondence. One of his unofficial duties was to keep an eye on Galich, whom the Communists suspected of being restive—though no U. S. diplomat found any outward evidence to support this suspicion.

This penetration of the foreign service is dramatically visible at the United Nations. Guatemala's delegates often have either voted with the Soviet bloc, of which Guatemala is a covert member, or abstained. They were the only Latin American delegation, for example, which sided with Russia in a vote on a resolution condemning the Mutual Security Act of 1951. When the Soviet Union sought to block UN attempts at bringing about conciliation between Israel and Iraq, all the nations voted against it with the exception of the Iron Curtain countries—and Guatemala.

For its propaganda effect, moreover, 21 members of the Congress signed a Communist proclamation last June, aimed at the United Nations and particularly the United States. It congratulated the "heroic defenders of North Korea" for standing up against the "imperialist invaders"—namely the UN, of which Guatemala is presumably a member in good standing—and their "bacteriological warfare." The signers included the President of the Congress, its First Vice President, and other prominent deputies.

An apologist for the Communists might well say at this point: "All of these considerations are extraneous. What has the so-called Communist-dominated government done for the people of Guatemala?" The answer would not reassure him. Only the continuing high price of coffee on the world market, and the excellent market conditions for the Guatemalan product in the United States, have prevented economic catastrophe since the Communists took over.

Despite this, the potentially wealthy economy has begun to show serious signs of stress. The adoption of the Agrarian Reform Law in June, 1952, caused a sharp business recession. The steady flight of domestic capital to foreign banks, begun under the Arévalo regime, increased suddenly and markedly. It has been estimated that between $50 million and $60 million of Guatemalan capital is on deposit in U. S., Cuban, and Swiss banks, or invested abroad, where it does the country no good.

The once lucrative tourist trade began to dwindle as a result of adverse publicity and the abortive revolt which followed the assassination of Colonel Arana. It has been literally throttled recently by the unnecessary strike against Pan American Airways—a strike called for political rather than economic reasons. Hotels, shops, and native industries in Guatemala City, Antigua, and Chichicastenango are suffering heavy losses. Although PAA service has been resumed, Guatemaltecos see little prospect of a return of the tourist.

The operations of the United Fruit Company, which had already been hampered by restrictive government policies and the Communist-packed Labor Courts, were further affected by a series of "blow downs" which badly hurt the banana industry. Banana exports were $18 million in 1947. They fell to $6 million in 1951. Because of prolonged labor disputes, they will be even lower in 1952.

Living costs have increased almost 30 percent since 1946. The cost of food has increased over 50 percent. Even these figures do

not fully reflect the inflation; they come from official Guatemalan sources which have steadily rigged statistics to minimize
adverse trends.

Under Arévalo and Arbenz, a treasury surplus has been dis-
sipated and a national debt incurred. It is estimated to be in
excess of $27 million—although even the Guatemalan government
itself does not know the exact figure. The estimate is based on a
partial investigation made by a government commission.

Meanwhile, the budget has multiplied more than five-fold—
from $11,800,000 in 1944 to $63,400,000 in the current fiscal
year. Over 30 percent of this money is not subject to public
accounting, and much of it goes toward the financing of Communist activities in Guatemala and in neighboring Latin countries.

Geologists believe that Guatemala has at least enough petroleum under its soil to supply all domestic needs. The government
has not permitted any development of these oil resources by U. S.
companies—the only ones willing to risk the necessary capital. As
a result, the country is forced to import gasoline and oil to keep
its internal combustion engines going.

Aviateca, the government-owned airline, has been suffering a
steady loss of revenue. It operates now at a substantial deficit.
The government railways have deteriorated, principally because
of inefficient management. The motor road system has been
neglected, primary highways have been allowed to run down, and
new highways have not been constructed.

This is what eight years of Communist domination have done.

Guatemala is a problem. It is also an example of what may
happen—is already happening—in other Latin American countries.
The pattern is being repeated in Costa Rica where the Communists have reportedly made a deal with the leading candidate
for the presidency, José Figueres. In return for their support,
Figueres is said to be willing to give them control of the labor
movement and to allow them an important place in his government.

Figueres has already made it clear that he will conduct business on a strictly anti–U.S. basis. He has promised to drive out
the United Fruit Company, and other U.S. investors, a move

which would bring economic collapse to his country. The conservatives are divided, but even if they form a united front, they can hardly muster enough strength to defeat him.

In Honduras and El Salvador, anti-Communist governments are struggling with adept Communist agitators who are exploiting the poverty and social unrest prevalent in those countries. President Osorio of El Salvador recently rounded up 1,200 Communists and other left-wingers and threw them into prison for conspiring to overthrow his government.

Panama has its own problems. The Canal Zone, an easy bomber's flight from Guatemala, has a sizable Fifth Column equipped with plans of all installations. The plans were stolen by Soviet agents.

Communist success in Latin America has been achieved thus far by a small group of skilled and energetic men who have been able to enlist in their conspiracy a conglomeration of bemused idealists, fanatical nationalists, and venal politicians interested solely in the "mordita" (the little bite of graft). With these—and playing on generations of anti-Yanqui antagonism—they have been able to draw in the workers and peons and to capitalize on their hopes by making the loudest and most lavish promises. That local nationalists parrot Communist propaganda has given it a kind of credibility which the Communists alone could never have achieved.

On the other hand, the very fact that the Communists have to depend so heavily on the non-Communists, presents to American diplomacy an opportunity to drive a wedge between them. This opportunity has been summed up by one diplomat:

"Through persistent, patient, and tactful employment of the art of persuasion, to convince Latin Americans in general and Latin American officials in particular, first of the true character of the Communist conspiracy, and second of the genuine good will felt toward all of their countries by the U. S. government and the vast majority of U. S. citizens."

This strategy has already produced results in Mexico and Cuba, where the governments have ousted Communist leaders—at least temporarily—from key labor unions.

The same strategy apparently is now being followed by Ambassador Schoenfeld in Guatemala, though with no visible results as yet. On the official level at least, it has produced results in El Salvador and Honduras, whose governments seem fully alert to Communist methods and Communist tactics.

However favorable these developments may be in comparison, they should not be overemphasized. They have resulted principally from convincing a few key officials of the nature of the Communist conspiracy. Thus far, the Voice of America program and the State Department's other propaganda efforts have failed to produce any tangible results among the restless, impoverished masses.

The effects of thirty years of Communist propaganda directed against U. S. investment, most of it unchallenged, are evident among all classes in Central America, even those most hostile to Communism, and in all countries, even those in which the Communists themselves have never been able to gain a foothold.

"The time has long since passed," one American remarked, "when all we had to do when a U. S. firm got in trouble down here was to walk into the office of some politico, bang our fist on his desk, and, if he seemed obdurate, threaten to call a regiment of Marines."

It has been strongly recommended that firms with large stakes in that area immediately undertake long-range public relations programs, designed:

1. To counteract the Communist propaganda against them.
2. To build up good will for U.S. investors, generally.
3. To convince all segments of the local populations that the firm is genuinely interested in the economic development of their country and in improving the living standards of the people.

The need of private firms to undertake their own programs to build up public and official good will in Central America is increased by the fact that the one overriding responsibility of the embassy staffs today is the preservation of our national security.

The United States government regards the presence of an aggressive, well-organized, Communist-influenced conspiracy in Central America as the greatest threat existing in this hemisphere to our security. As long as our relations with the Soviet Union continue at anything approaching current tensions, Embassy officials will subordinate all other problems to their efforts to woo influential Central American politicos away from the Communists. While nobody puts it in so many words, it is obvious that, if making strong representations in behalf of a U. S. private investor might ruffle the feelings of the officials they are trying to win, the interests of the investor will be shunted aside in favor of the national interest.

The picture is hardly a cheerful one. State Department officials in Washington and those in the Embassy at Guatemala City are convinced that as long as the present coalition of Communists and politicians holds together, it cannot be upset by a free election. They are also convinced that as long as the army remains complacent, there is little possibility of a successful coup. They draw back from any suggestion that tough talk is the answer. Economic sanctions, too, are out of the question. Such a course might topple the Communists, but it would also topple Guatemala, with a resultant increase in anti-Yanqui sentiment.

American diplomats are also hampered by the heavy albatross they wear around their necks. It was the State Department which virtually forced many Latin American states to recognize the Soviet Union in the 1930's. This is one fact which Latin nationalists do not forget.

The State Department, while it waits for the dust to settle in Latin America, is counting on two eventualities. The United States has anti-Communist allies in the Organization of American States and in the Organization of Central American States. Little El Salvador has been working mightily to put Guatemala's Red regime on the spot in the OCAS. There are some indications that this pressure from fellow Latin Americans is having some effect on President Arbenz. Rumors are plentiful that the Communists are beginning to distrust him.

The power of the Guatemalan army is recognized by the State Department. It has been established beyond doubt that the junior officers are becoming restive. They do not approve of their Red gauleiters. They have, it is said, begun to wonder what will happen to them on the day the Communists decide to stage an open coup. So they are being wooed by the large military and air missions assigned to the U. S. Embassy.

Ever present in State Department thinking is the hope that we can bribe the Guatemalan non-Communists with large loans. An offer of $3 million to help Guatemala complete its stretch of the Pan American Highway was ignored by Arbenz two years ago. The Guatemalan ambassador to Washington has suddenly shown reawakened interest. Guatemala has graciously decided to accept our dollars. If the money is advanced without substantial concession to the United States, however, American prestige will tumble. Without demanding a *quid pro quo*, we will become the laughing stock of Latin America. Politicians, even greedy ones, don't admire patsies.

From time to time, there is talk of an effective counterbarrage which will answer Communist propaganda. Such talk is easy, but the job is complex. It must be carried out by people who believe in American principles—and respect Latin Americans; by Americans who believe in free enterprise and political democracy—but who realize that the road to both of them is sometimes arduous; by Americans who do not spend their evenings denigrating the government they serve during the day. The key words: Good will at all times; patience when it is called for; obduracy when it is required.

There are no cheap solutions. But the price of failure, for the United States and Latin America, will be higher than the costliest success. For failure will mean that the ticking bomb planted by Constantine Oumansky, by Lombardo Toledano, and by Stalin's other busy men, will explode.

The roar will drown out the sound of all the gunfire in Korea.

The American Mercury
February 1953

Operation Storm!

If memory serves me, this was the very first mass-circulation, popularized, full-scale accounting of Communist sabotage and subversion planning in this country.

L ast July, the FBI launched a great man hunt for four Communist bosses who had jumped bail while awaiting imprisonment for conspiring to advocate the violent overthrow of the United States government. Seven other Red leaders, convicted on the same charge, were on hand when the prison van called, but Gus Hall, Robert Thompson, Gilbert Green and Henry Winston had a special reason for skipping out:

They were the general staff of "Operation Storm," the Communist code name for an incredible anti-American campaign of subversion, espionage, treason and sabotage, culminating in revolution—and American Communist participation in a Soviet invasion!

From high-level leaks within the Communist party, from the life records of these four men, and from secret party records which this writer has in his possession, the plot can be pieced together. A close study shows why these particular men were chosen; although professional Communists leave no telltale traces behind, there are enough facts to develop the significant background. From them emerges a clear and frightening picture of Operation Storm and the men named to command it.

Hand-picked by Moscow's espionage headquarters (generally referred to as the "Center") from among the 11 top American Communists, the members of this quartet are, in Stalin's words, "people of a special mold," tough, reliable, and undeviating professional revolutionaries. Their disappearance cost the Communists $80,000 in confiscated bail, but for the party's purposes it was money well spent.

For, like the old Comintern (Communist International) crew which dug underground until the time to emerge was ripe—Tito of Yugoslavia, Pauker of Romania, Eisler and Pieck of Eastern Germany—the fugitive four could be counted on to bide their time in hiding or in exile until the bloody chaos the Kremlin hopes for had come to this country. The plan even provided safeguards in the event of their capture by the FBI; lieutenants now in the field have orders to take up the mission of destruction.

The decision which made fugitives of Hall, Thompson, Green and Winston, and which gave them command of the clandestine Communist apparatus in the United States, was carefully weighed. Ever since 1945, when the American party discarded the compromise tactics of Earl Browder and returned to its earlier rigid Marxism-Leninism, the four men had been marked for big things by the Center. They had been carefully trained, their lives placed under continual and close scrutiny. They were, in a sense, the revolutionary elite of American Communism.

The Communist Manual on Organization decrees that "if the class struggle demands it, the professional revolutionary will leave his family for months, even years." The four bail-jumpers were men of this caliber; the Center was not so certain it could extract the same devotion from the bumbling Eugene Dennis, nominal head of the party (because of the illness and semiretirement of Chairman William Z. Foster). Its counterespionage had warned that Jack Stachel, the party's propaganda chief and once "Stalin's man" in the U.S., was becoming disillusioned beyond the usual cynicism of the old Communist functionary.

During secret meetings of the American Politburo last April 7th, 8th and 17th, at a hotel in downtown New York, these suspicions against Stachel, the shrewdest and most experienced conspirator in the group, were crystallized.

At these sessions, Thompson and Green called for immediate sabotage work, in line with Operation Storm. The party was ready, they said. "A prerevolutionary condition" existed. Trouble in Korea and the Middle East was rocking the U.S. At any moment, the Soviet Union might move. In the argument, Benjamin J. Davis, former New York City Council member, called for increased efforts in provoking police violence against his fellow Negroes.

Stachel forgot all caution. "The party's hands on the Negro question aren't clean," he exploded. "Most of our heart bleeding is phony and the Negroes know it. We gab and gab, but what do we ever accomplish but collect nickels and dimes to pay for insurance for Ben Davis' limousine?"

Revolutionary talk was nonsense, he insisted, and called for moderate tactics instead. Bitterly, he accused Thompson, the party's New York State chairman, and John Gates, editor of the Daily Worker, of being *agents provocateurs* on the FBI payroll.

This was heresy, and only Stachel's personal ties to Moscow, and the fact, useful for propaganda purposes, that he was slated to go to federal prison, saved him from expulsion. The Red powers-that-be wrote him off as an underground leader. Hall, Thompson, Green and Winston got the nod.

Late in June, the highest individual Communist authority in the U.S.—a shadowy figure known only to top echelons of the Soviet secret police, to the Red Army's Fourth Bureau (Intelligence), and to a handful of American Reds—issued the command that the quisling quartet was to skip bail and go underground. Transmitted to them circuitously by a series of trusted couriers, this order was accompanied by money, papers and passports establishing new identities. The four men were instructed to disclose their instructions to none of their colleagues.

They kept the secret faithfully. On July 2d, when the other seven of the "top eleven" surrendered themselves at federal court in New York to begin serving their five-year sentences, they were as surprised as the Justice Department to learn that comrades Hall, Thompson, Green and Winston had disappeared.

Yet the fact is that these men have been training themselves for years for just such a project as Operation Storm. The fugitives are more than four "activists" (as opposed to mere party dues payers) ready to do or die for dear old Lenin U.; they are a team in which every man fills a specific need. Within the neurotic framework of their fanaticism, they are nerveless men. They are all alumni of the Lenin School in Moscow; in the world Communist movement, this is both a caste mark and a prerequisite for high office.

For, at this top-level military academy, the strategy and tactics of armed revolt have been developed to an exact science. Much as West Point studies the wars of the past, the Lenin School takes as its text the armed insurrections of other eras.

Picked men receive instruction in strike strategy, weapons familiarization, military science, espionage and counterespionage methods, civil warfare, sabotage, street fighting and the organization of the Red Army. They are taught to manufacture homemade explosives, antipersonnel and demolition bombs, slow fuses and the like. Industrial sabotage—everything from short-circuiting a power line to spiking heavy machinery—is taken up. When a man graduates from the Lenin School, his strength and weaknesses have been assessed, his potentialities as an activist weighed.

Gus Hall attended the Lenin School in 1931, Gil Green and Henry Winston in 1933, Robert Thompson in 1935. Each one offered some important prerequisite for leadership in underground operations.

Gus Hall was to become national secretary of the U.S. Communist party, simply because the Comintern so directed. A big, husky man with rather vague, watery-blue eyes, he had none of the qualities which make a popular leader of a mass movement. He was both a bad speaker and a sloppy writer. The more sophisticated among the comrades have always been wryly amused at Hall's pretentious boast that he was born in a log cabin in Iron, Minnesota.

Yet to Moscow, it was important that—unlike most other American Communists—Hall is really a proletarian, the son of an old Wobbly miner (a member of the old-line radical Industrial

Workers of the World). At the age of sixteen (he is now forty-one) he had completed grade school and was ready to begin life as lumberjack, hobo, railroad worker, steelworker and, almost from the first, member of the Communist party.

After two years in Russia, he turned up as leader of a Minneapolis Young Communist League riot in 1934, boasting to a local court that "when the time comes" he would proudly fight against the American government. Active in the bloody Minneapolis Teamsters strike the same year, he was to reminisce later: "Never saw such a shellacking of police in my life. They were running all over the city, throwing away their badges."

By 1937, still using his union affiliations for the cause of Communism, he had shifted his operations to Ohio. In the CIO's "Little Steel" strikes that year, he put his Lenin School training to good use when he organized a "dynamite squad" in Youngstown and set up a paramilitary crew to terrorize nonstrikers and Republic Steel. When he was arrested for possession of dynamite and nitroglycerin, Hall shouted, "Frame-up!" But he pleaded guilty to the lesser charge of malicious destruction of property. The CIO paid his $500 fine and, within the year, he was running for governor of Ohio on the Communist ticket under his real name, Arvo Halberg. In 1941, he tangled with the law again—90 days in the Youngstown pokey for election fraud.

Hall enlisted in the Navy in 1943 and was honorably discharged in 1945, just in time to re-create the American party in Stalin's image following the ouster of Browder. For it was Hall who became the party's actual leader, although others outranked him technically. For the changing times, he was the perfect No. 1 man—steady, emotionless, a stickler for detail, a perfect sabotage machine. From the relative obscurity of the Ohio party he pushed ever higher into the hierachy on East Twelfth Street, which until recently was the Communists' national headquarters in New York.

Where Hall supplied the organizational brawn, Gil Green furnished, presumably, the theoretical stability and cunning for the apparatus-to-be. At eighteen, a member of the Young Communist League and a high school graduate, the city boy from Chicago began holding a series of small jobs: shipping clerk, drill press operator, substitute letter carrier.

But party activities were his main work. In 1927, the twenty-one-year-old careerist, fired from his post-office job for absenteeism, stepped on to the party payroll as district organizer of the Chicago YCL. He was to make this "youth" organization his main work for many years.

After doing party work in 1928 during the New Bedford textile strike, he turned up in New York as editor of the Young Worker—YCL official organ—and as New York State YCL organizer.

In 1932, Green was summoned to Moscow for additional training. Thereafter, he made frequent trips to Russia, meanwhile setting up such fronts in this country as the American Youth Congress. By 1934, he was advising YCLers: "Military science is indispensable to proletarians. You must learn how to fight the *bourgeoisie* of your own country." In 1935, as a delegate to the Seventh World Congress of the Communist International in Moscow, he was elected to the Comintern's important Executive Committee.

Increasingly, Green's job in the Comintern was to spy on other Communist leaders. In time, he put this function to official use in this country, when he became the American party's thought-control boss and a terror to those comrades who were brought up on charges before the so-called National Review Commission. Like many other hand-picked Communist functionaries, in the late thirties Green turned up in Spain to further his training in heresy hunting in the civil war there, but he himself never fired a shot in anger.

By 1939, Green held a seat on the National Committee of the American Communist party. In 1945, with the expulsion of Browder, he moved up into the highest echelon, the American Politburo. Here he began to rival Stachel, both as a guardian of Communist morals and as an agit-prop (party lingo for agitation and propaganda) agent. Younger (he's now forty-five to Stachel's tired fifty-one), more ambitious as a schemer, and less tinged with Browderism, Green began to nose out the saturnine Stachel.

Under other circumstances, forty-year-old Henry Winston, the third man in the command team, might have been a home-loving suburbanite. Even as a Communist functionary—unlike other top Reds—he tried for a time to live a normal life with his wife and two children. Yet once he had joined the Communist party in 1931, his break away from this was almost inevitable (1) he was a Negro, (2) he came from the South, (3) he was a trustworthy, responsible executive. For Communist purposes, all three were essential. A Negro Communist like Benjamin J. Davis was valuable as a front man in New York. But Davis came from a wealthy family, he had gone to a fancy Eastern college, and he was given to a wild neuroticism which made him unreliable as a conspirator.

The party used Davis, but it slowly groomed Winston for leadership. After grammar and high school in Hattiesburg, Mississippi, and Kansas City, Missouri, he had joined the party in 1931. In the 1930s, his record was typical: arrested for vagrancy (often a police cover-all term for Communist activity); a YCL delegate to the national hunger march on Washington in 1932; a job with the Young Worker publication; and a YCL organizer in the New York slum areas of Red Hook and Harlem.

After attending the Lenin School in 1933, he was ready for more important party posts in the U.S. In 1937, he turned up in Moscow for two months of postgraduate training, then went back to New York to run the YCL's "action school" at Camp Beacon, where deserving young Communists formerly were trained for future responsibilities. (The camp is now privately owned, and highly respectable.) He was elected to the National Committee in 1940, drafted into the Army two years later.

Like Hall, Winston received his honorable discharge from the service just in time for the critical Browder shake-up. He emerged from it a powerful man in the American Politburo. His title, National Organizational Secretary, was innocuous, but his function was important: to supervise the party's finances and treasury, and somehow to yank the movement away from the intellectuals who were largely in control and steer it back to a working-class base. This task of "industrial concentration"—the Leninist term—was the most important the party faced, a vital prelude to Winston's role in Operation Storm, and to his eventual move underground.

In startling contrast to these three is Robert George Thompson. Slick-haired, sallow, puffy, he is a dead ringer for a Broadway hard guy. At thirty-six, he is also the youngest of the fugitives. Like most Communists of the Stalin era, Thompson has had little formal education: grammar school and one year of high school in Portland, Oregon. After quitting his textbooks in 1929, he went on the bum, working as a lumberjack, wheat harvester, canner, and railroad hand on the Sante Fe, till the depression lured him into the party in 1933.

By the time he made the inevitable trip to Moscow in 1935, he had a record of two arrests for labor agitation. Ostensibly working at the Kaganovich Ball Bearing Works in the Russian capital, he was actually attending seminars at the Lenin School. When the big opportunity, the Spanish war, came along, he had already begun his meanderings under false names (Robert Johnson, Bob Condon, Roberto Tomes) and false passports.

Spain offered the perfect life for him—violence, danger, brutality—and he quickly rose to command the MacKenzie-Papineau brigade, the Canadian unit in the famous International Brigade. Wounded in action, he was back in the States by late 1937. In the summer of 1941, he made a trip to Mexico, reportedly to take instruction from Carlos Contreras (alias Sormenti, alias Vidale), one of Stalin's most sadistic hatchet men, who had earned a fearsome reputation in Spain as a purger of suspected weaklings in the party.

Nine days before Pearl Harbor, Thompson was again in uniform—this time of GI cut. His record was excellent: staff sergeant in the Red Arrow Division, awarded the Distinguished Service Cross for bravery during the Buna campaign, wounded in the left knee. He came out of the war with a limp, a mild case of malaria, and a $150-a-month total disability pension which he collected until he disappeared in July.

Back in the party, nominally as the New York State chairman, Thompson was surly and overbearing. His home life foundered and he took to drinking heavily. At top-level meetings, he quarreled with the other U.S. Politburo members. But he was a valuable man to Moscow, and the American party knew it. As an expert on street fighting and guerrilla tactics, he lectured frequently to Communist activists. He served another function. Where Green was the party's secret police, judge and jury, Thompson was fitted for the job of carrying out the sentences Green imposed.

These, then, are the four men to whom Stalin has entrusted the fate of the "second American revolution." They are not men of heroic cast, but instruments in a conscious strategy, based on three decades of intrigue, infiltration and treason. Above all, they meet the requirements laid down by Stalin himself in the homily from which the name Operation Storm was taken. Discussing Communist behavior in times of prerevolutionary stress, the Soviet leader said: "In the face of a storm that has broken out, a group of fishermen mobilize all their energies, spur on their people, and boldly steer the boat into the storm."

"Storm" was a fit word. The party waters were being whipped by a cold wind from Russia (via France). A letter by French Communist Jacques Duclos in an obscure party paper—obviously written at Moscow's command—had sharply rapped Earl Browder's theory that capitalism and Communism could live side by side. Taking the hint, the American Politburo summarily expelled Browder. The older slogan, "To the Revolution," had been raised.

It was a hard slogan to carry out. For, although the party had loyal friends in government, business, the arts and professions, the college campuses, its base in the factories, mills and shops was almost nonexistent. In 1945, a party leader could lament that of the 8,000 party members in Brooklyn, only 201 were bona fide proletarians.

The party, in short, had got soft. It had battened on the goodness and wealth of the American people. By 1944, when Browder "disbanded" the Communist party and set up the Communist Political Association, its political activity had almost ceased, although it had a large membership; fellow travelers brought the tally to about 1,000,000 by FBI estimates.

With the ouster of Browder, reorganization of a revolutionary "party of a new type" began. The Communists started to think in terms of direct action. Back in 1935–'36, Reds in a WPA writers' project in New York had used their time to prepare an encyclopedic report and map of every underground passage, subway tunnel, sewer and water main in the city—a package neatly delivered to Moscow. This was how a Leninist party acted, and the aim was to return to that status.

Taking stock of the party's postwar resources at a series of secret meetings, the Communist leadership sketched out a plan of action. The new blood—Thompson, Green, Winston and Hall—thought in grandiose terms. Jack Stachel predicted that the party's store of good will was going to dwindle rapidly; that there were hungry days ahead, and—with Soviet-American relations worsening—this was the time to retrench. The party, however, was riding a wave of self-confidence (which would not be dashed until the Progressive party under Henry Wallace—non-Communist, but preaching a soft attitude toward Russia—foundered in the 1948 election).

Even as the Communists hoped in manic generalities, they were plotting in depressive particulars, re-examining the old framework of Operation Storm. Its program was no real secret, having been published in the world-wide party's organ, the Communist International, in the more Spartan year of 1931. Written by B. Vassiliev, an outline called Organisational Problems in Underground Revolutionary Work spelled it out cogently:

"The question of an illegal organization must now receive the closest attention . . . In proportion as the legal apparatus of the Party is liquidated, the directing functions will inevitably pass more and more to the illegal apparatus."

To form such an apparatus, Vassiliev directed, the party must find hiding places for vital archives; organize illegal printing plants at which to print a party organ, once legal party papers had been suppressed; form an apparatus for the distribution of party literature and propaganda; set up a corps of activists who could quickly disappear into the underground; acquire houses, some for mail drops and others in which underground leaders could meet and hide; establish a plan for liaison between legal and illegal functionaries; and train a minimum number of party workers in underground work to run illegal presses, handle codes and organize the defense of Communists who ran afoul of the law.

One sentence in Vassiliev's treatise is especially significant: " . . . Preparation for the struggles for power are impossible unless the whole system of Party work is reorganized and the whole Party apparatus reconstructed on the basis of factory nuclei." *Today, every one of these instructions has been put into practice.* This process of building secret factory nuclei, "industrial concentration," has been the chief chore of Henry Winston.

Behind the posturing and speeches, the Communist party got down to solid work in 1946. First it conducted a careful security check of all members. A questionnaire was issued by the control commissions of all Communist districts. Designed to probe a member's past, his party connections, family, the seamy side of his life, this form served a multiple purpose. It gave the control commissions insights into the respondent's reliability and his underground potential, afforded a handle for blackmail, and offered a possible means for identifying government spies. Every one of these questionnaires was microfilmed and shipped to the Comintern in Moscow.

The party's defense forces were also discussed at U.S. Politburo meetings, along with the question of Red Front combat squads. Such units had been organized in 1934, and had held regular training sessions at a summer camp in upstate New York, receiving everything from judo instruction to female hatpin drill (for use against police mounts in street riots). But the combat squads had declined in the prewar years, as the party made greater and greater use of goon squads from captive unions.

Now, with the growing defection of once pro-Red labor groups, the party decided to reconstitute the squads. They made their first combat appearance in September, 1949, in Peekskill, New York, at the second of two riots involving the appearance of

pro-Communist baritone Paul Robeson. According to the West-
chester County grand jury which investigated the melee, a
"security guard" of 2,500 was on hand well before the hour
scheduled for Robeson's provocative appearance. Says the report:

"Their leader wore the uniform of a United States Army
lieutenant. They were stationed in military formation, shoulder
to shoulder," forming a perimeter about the concert grounds.
"This force remained in position for eight to ten hours. They
were armed with baseball bats, bottles, pepper and can
openers . . . The security guard was a disciplined force and conducted itself in a military manner under the direction of leaders."

In its postwar stocktaking, the party also made a survey of its
industrial strength. Mournfully, the National Committee learned
in March, 1946, that "in plant after plant in the main cities we
have little or no organization. For instance, in General Motors
plants totaling 20,000 workers we have only 122 members." The
survey urged that "in the auto industry, our concentration work
must be aimed at sinking strong roots among the workers in such
key spots as Flint and Ford Motors." That could be achieved only
"if we assign forces, leadership, money, literature, press and
schooling facilities to these areas." This was done.

By 1947, "industrial concentration" was going into gear. The
party had learned during the Hitler-Stalin pact, in the days before
Germany attacked Russia, that strikes at key points, sparked by a
handful of Communists, could accomplish more for Stalin than
thousands of mass meetings in New York. (In January, 1941, 50
party members at Allis Chalmers had engineered a wildcat strike
which held up $45,000,000 in defense contracts, blocked produc-
tion on 25 destroyers, virtually shut down Ford Motor's aircraft
engine plant, and slowed down vital production all along the
line.)

With this in mind, the party issued a secret directive to its
western Pennsylvania district. Headed, "Concentration Plan of
Work for the Homestead Shop Club for 1947," it bluntly proclaimed:

"Political decision resolved that Homestead shall be one of the
two district wide concentration points in steelwork for the whole

Party in western Pennsylvania. Political reason is that Homestead is one of the two links in the whole chain that makes up the steel industry . . . Through its strategic position politically, economically, and working-class organization, it can influence the whole body of links that makes up the chain in steel . . . "

The shop clubs being set up in Homestead, and in every industry where the Communists had a foothold, were not to be like ordinary party cells. Members were to meet in complete secrecy, to hide their Communist affiliation at all costs, and to agitate merely as union members. They were to operate in the lower echelons, among union rank-and-filers, gain their confidence, and utilize this trust to bring about slowdowns and wildcat strikes.

In some areas, according to a confidential dues check in 1950, this campaign to infiltrate into industry came within 73 percent of meeting the party's goal (which was not low). For example, the CIO United Auto Worker's Ford Local 600 (which claims to be the world's largest, with almost 60,000 members), is now considered by the party as a "sphere of influence" of inestimable value, although not entirely in the Communist camp. Red leaders cite this as an example of what industrial concentration can do for the party.

In April, 1949, Gus Hall was happily endorsing the effectiveness of Henry Winston's campaign to infiltrate into industry under the slogan, "Face the Factories." "The party is all the stronger as a result," he confided to the National Committee. And he ordered that young Communist, regardless of any personal plans, "must get a job in industry wherever possible."

In November, 1950, Winston was exhorting his cohorts: "It is in the shops, at the point of production, that the class struggle originates and rages unceasingly." A party directive spelled it out more clearly:

"It is important to advance the struggle against imperialist war by effectively linking it with the struggle on issues the workers understand more clearly, against wage freezes, controls . . . Even workers who mistakenly support Truman in Korea can many times be won to support action on one or another of these partial demands . . . "

Meanwhile, with U.S.-Soviet relations growing steadily worse, steps were taken to insure the party's future effectiveness. In June, 1947, the direct order from Moscow had come: Go underground. Following the 1948 convention, the entire party was put on a war footing. It was split up into roughly 3,500 fragments, the base being the cell of no more than 10 members.

Leaders of cells now maintained secret liaison with sections leaders, who in turn passed messages along through one set of couriers to another set of couriers, who then carried the ball to the district leadership. This security-conscious system of lower-echelon leadership-to-courier-to-courier-to-higher-echelon leadership is called a "cutoff"—a term right out of the Soviet espionage handbook. Cutoffs were to maintain liaison between the district leadership and the American Politburo. Secret directives went down this chain of command from the U.S. Politburo to the lowest party members.

The wisdom of these precautions became apparent when the entire American Politburo was indicted on July 20, 1948, under the Smith antisubversive act. The trial was held in 1949, and panic hit the ranks when Angela Calomiris, Herbert Philbrick, and other duty-driven Americans who had infiltrated the Communist movement at FBI request took the stand as witnesses for the prosecution.

A secret directive was sent out to every party district, entitled: "Regarding the Need for Increased Vigilance in Combating the Attacks of the FBI . . . " It warned against the "enemy" (the U.S. government), insisted on a close check of new members, and gave a list of do's and don't's for members approached by the FBI or arrested. Calling attention to the party's legal arm, patterned according to Vassiliev's instructions, it ordered members to "contact the Civil Rights Congress and its lawyers" the moment there was a stirring of the law. "It is imperative that the rights accorded citizens under the Constitution be rigidly insisted upon," the directive stated, warning against "loose talk" and the "bandying about of names."

At the 1948 convention, the party already had ordered the destruction of all party cards, placed a ban on dues receipts, cautioned against the use of telephones for confidential messages, devised codes and provided for more couriers. The use of mail drops—postal addresses of unsuspected Communists—became standard operating procedure where mail communications were employed.

The party's financial structure was overhauled. By the use of "front" organizations, the Communist party had siphoned off huge sums over the years from its great campaigns. Millions of dollars—ostensibly collected for Spanish Relief, the defense of the nine Negroes tried in the famous Scottsboro, Alabama, rape case, and hundreds of other causes (many of them also espoused by sincere liberals)—went into party coffers. Much of it was shipped to Russia, which has always attempted to finance its espionage operations with American dollars, because they are negotiable anywhere.

But the larger portion of this money had been invested in legitimate capitalist enterprises—real estate, record companies, a perfume house, a small mail-order firm, a machine tool establishment which handled World War II defense orders, several night clubs, bookshops, even a doll factory. Dummy corporations controlled by trusted Communists have operated these businesses. Among the investments were several large printing firms, through which the party bought presses, mimeograph machines and large stocks of paper and newsprint, all stored away secretly against the day when an illegal press might be necessary. (Unfortunately for the Communists, FBI "plants" have supplied the bureau with the locations of many of these "secret" storage places.)

With the acceleration of underground plans, the party began to liquidate some of these holdings, converting them into ready cash. At the party's last convention in December, 1950—closed to everyone but hand-picked delegates—Henry Winston announced at a secret session attended by several of the top state chairmen that the party had "a reserve fund of several million dollars to carry on our work no matter what course events take." As part of the party's fluid funds, one fellow traveler has close to $500,000 in his bank account. A Communist employed in the bank reports all withdrawals to the party.

Coincident with launching Operation Storm, the party's growing industrial and water-front cells were instructed to begin a survey of sabotage "potentials." In a New York Herald Tribune series, Ogden R. Reid and Fendall Yerxa reported that the first of these surveys—begun in 1947 and repeated in 1948—included painstaking studies of defense plants, as well as transportation and industrial facilities, food life lines and water supply in the large urban areas. This writer is convinced that a third survey was begun in 1950 to gather information made available by the deeper penetration of secret cells in the automotive and electronics industries.

Some idea of the degree of control the party exercises over such cells can be obtained from the secret directives continuing to pour forth. Here's a sampling from among those in this writer's possession:

For a demonstration in Times Square in 1951, over the controversial rape convictions of Mississippi Negro Willie McGee: "Comrades are to come in groups no larger than three," circulate in a given "assembly area," and await "a signal from several comrades who will be visible from the balcony of the Hotel Astor."

For picketing at the American Safety Razor Company strike in Brooklyn this year: "Comrades . . . are to be as militant as possible, even to courting arrest."

On President Truman's recall of General Douglas MacArthur: "Where possible, members whose political affiliations are not known are to contact anti-MacArthur forces and work with them on the basis of mutual opposition to MacArthur's advocacy of full-scale war against New China . . . This tactic can win scores of people of importance . . . to support our position . . . It is not necessary for these members to divulge their opposition to Truman's policies."

By the end of that year, Gus Hall felt that the time had come to put Operation Storm into second gear. To delegates carefully picked by the party's security experts he announced that the party had the "machinery and forces to intiate and lead" a movement to sabotage U.S. defense mobilization. The keynote: prepare for "militant strikes and carefully executed slowdowns, particularly in war industries."

A new line on revolution was also being promulgated by Moscow. Where Communists had once stressed "armed uprisings of the workers against the *bourgeoisie*," agitprop directors were to talk now in terms of "armed descent" by the Red Army itself!

The strength of capitalism and the "backwardness" of American workers was responsible for the change in thinking. Communist cells, henceforth, were to prepare not for outright revolution but for sabotage, guerrilla tactics and subversion of the U.S. armed forces, timed to the "breakdown" of Wall Street and an attack by the Red Army. Just when this was to occur was not made clear.

Through late April, May and June, as the U.S. Politburo waited for the Supreme Court decision which ultimately ordered it to prison, the secret directives continued to tighten security and carry out Operation Storm. Marked "Fl. N."—the ninth-floor sanctum at the then party headquarters at 35 East Twelfth Street, New York (now at 29 West 125th Street)—the orders prepared party members for further FBI action. On April 30, 1951, a detailed directive stated:

" . . . Leaders elected to replace those imprisoned are to work as secretly as possible from places already designated . . . Presses and newsprint . . . are to be well secluded and should be known only to those charged with the printing of literature." (There are 31 such printing caches.)

On May 8th: "Shop cadres whose political affiliations are not known in their shops are not to reveal them under any circumstances . . . Measures should be taken immediately to discredit the reliability of members under suspicion . . . The type of measures . . . should be of such a nature as to arouse the members' shopmates and neighbors against them."

On June 5th: " . . . It is imperative that [labor] unrest [over wages, prices, rent control] be channeled into action as soon as possible. . . . Once the workers are won to fighting for a wage increase, the peace issue can be raised."

By June 6th, it became apparent that something big was about to pop: the party had ordered the equivalent of radio silence. A verbal order from the highest leadership to all districts stated that, from then on, communications were to be in code with *absolutely no exceptions;* mail drops were to be changed weekly; incoming mail eventually destined for national headquarters was to be in triplicate and addressed to separate drops; couriers were to be changed frequently.

Late in June, an FBI roundup of the alternate party leaders— replacements for those about to enter prison—disclosed that four of them had vanished. On July 2d, the American public learned that Winston, Hall, Thompson and Green were nowhere to be found. Where had they gone? The FBI had no way of knowing. To have maintained 24-hour surveillance of the convicted 11 would have taken eight agents per Communist; the shorthanded bureau had no such man power available.

As federal agents began the difficult task of tracking down the four bail-jumpers, it was clear that the important thing was not where they were holed up—whether in some secret American hiding place, or behind the Iron Curtain—but that somewhere a hard-working, ruthless top command, armed with hate and fanaticism, is coolly plotting sabotage, violence and, when the time comes, American Communist participation in the "armed descent" of Stalin's soldiers.

Already their efforts are bearing fruit, as evidenced by the recent Justice Department disclosure that reports of sabotage in U.S. defense plants are on the up-swing. Will the situation grow worse? The American Communist general staff, in its secret lair, is planning it that way.

When the day the Reds dream about comes true—when the Soviets are ready to attack—the leaders of Operation Storm will emerge, just as Tito, Pauker and Pieck emerged behind the Red Army to subjugate eastern Europe. The fugitives will then be fugitives no longer, but Stalin's gauleiters in the war against freedom and civilization.

Collier's
October 1951

It's Still the Soviet Party

Many a tide has tossed the old CPUSA since this was written, but the general ground rules still apply. Or should we say, the general ground swell still applies?

The Communist Party USA is down in membership, torn by dissension, and beset by the ideological long knives of its leaders. The proliferation of Party fronts has slowed down. The Jefferson School (of subversive sciences) has shut its doors. The *Daily Worker* occasionally paints Khrushchev with his halo askew.

These facts, the result of the downgrading of Stalin and the Soviet terror in the satellites, are all very true. But they do not warrant the complacent conclusions of the pundits that the Communist Party, as an arm of the Kremlin and a force for evil, is ready for the undertaker. The CPUSA is far from dead. Despite the febrile rhetoric of its current controversies, disciplined activity still continues where it really counts—in the underground apparatus, in the Party's industrial concentrations, and on the infiltration front.

What the pundits see are the surface manifestations of a *malaise* which has struck the Communist world, moving out from the Muscovite center to the smallest cell in Timbuctu. Problems of vast importance occupy the men of the Kremlin, and they are reflected in microcosm in the American Communist Party. When the Soviet Politburo has resolved its differences and arrived at its answers, the CPUSA will fall into line as it always has. The passionate debates will be forgotten, no matter who wins the current struggle—just as they were in 1929 when Stalin ousted the Lovestonite majority and remade the American Party in his own image. Today, the Kremlin representative may stand behind the arras, but he is no forgotten man.

That the factional fight will decide nothing, however, does not detract from its bitterness. At the moment, the CPUSA is involved in a three-way stretch. Pulling one way is John Gates, editor of the *Daily Worker* and Spanish war commissar—aided and abetted by such sterling idealists as Steve Nelson, also a Spanish war hatchet-man and more lately the head of the atomic espionage operations at Berkeley, California, and Los Alamos. The Gates group represents what might be called the Titoist wing, although this is something of a simplification. It is plumping for an "independent" Marxist party—to include Earl Browder, deposed but yearning *Fuehrer* of the CPUSA, Norman Thomas (if he can be seduced), and any stray leftists it can gather up, a "mass" party.

Gates is motivated by ambition. He remembers the day when Browder was the darling of the intellectuals and a blast from the Communist Party brought the State Department to heel. His wife has been supplying him with other motive power. She has been saying to some of the stalwarts that she "will be no party to any support of the Soviet butchery of unarmed Hungarian workers."

Tugging against Gates is William Z. Foster's Stalinist faction. Its program, however disguised by jargon, calls for close and submissive relations with Moscow, a monolithic party whose "centralism" eschews free debate, and an end to the dangerous nonsense of "democratization." Somewhere between Gates and Foster, though allied tactically with the Fosterites, is Eugene Dennis, timeserver and hack, who sees the wave of the future in the dimpled Khrushchev.

So far, Foster has blustered at top echelon meetings, calling Gates a "social democrat" and Browder a "stool pigeon." (Behind his back, Foster's enemies charge that his Stalinism and his support of Egypt against Israel is the result of anti-Semitism, a not unknown quality among Communists.) Gates on the other hand, has been busily winning over delegates to the Party's national convention. His slogan, lifted from the bourgeoisie, is "Time for a change."

The battles of the leadership have found their counterpart on the unit, section, and district levels, where the hair-pulling and name-calling (with cries of "Drop dead, comrade!") hark back to the early 1920's. This has led to some defections, but not enough to shake the structure of the Party. The cold war, the Smith Act trials, and the fear of FBI penetration has reduced the CPUSA to a hard core of the dedicated, stubborn, or cynical. The Party's strength is somewhere between 18,000 and 20,000—and likely to stay at that figure.

But if the Communists can mourn the decline from the days when they could manipulate one million members and fellow travelers, they can also take a bow for the efficacy with which the reduced membership carries out the Party's mission. In labor, in civic and political organizations, and in the movie-theater-television complex, the comrades are back in force, bringing money and prestige to their cause. Here is how an important trade union official, strategically placed to observe the Communist at work puts it:

"Sure, there is ideological chaos in the Communist Party. But that's only in the so-called open Party. Recent events have distressed many of the rank-and-file members. But the real Party is still intact. You've got to remember that the CP is a paramilitary organization. It's under attack, so it has resorted to the military doctrine of dispersal. It's harder to put your finger on the Party today. But I'll tell you this much:

"Whole groups from the Commie-controlled U.E. have moved into the 'anti-Communist' I.U.E. and the Machinists union. The Farm Equipment workers have been taken into the U.A.W. by Walter Reuther. Ben Gold, who made no bones about his Party membership, got out of the Fur Workers, but he's still running it from the sidelines. I'd say the Commies in the labor movement are back almost as strong as when their unions were kicked out of the CIO in 1949. They're not in the top echelons, that's true, but on a shop level they still retain a firm and dangerous hold. As for the political picture—well, everybody said it was a sign of CP weakness when they disbanded the American Labor Party. But they just moved into the Liberal Party, where they're giving us trouble, into the Democratic Party and—don't start looking so smug about it—into the Republican Party."

Assets of about $6.5 million, taken from the International Workers Order when it was dissolved by New York State courts, have been poured into children's and adult camps which serve as indoctrination centers and also help to keep Communist and fellow-traveling entertainers employed. The entertainment world, moreover, remains a key source of infection. A leader and active participant in several Liberal groups complained:

"When it comes to Communist infiltration, we're back in the 1930's—or worse. Identified Party members, clear-cut Fifth Amendment cases, and the Party faithful are back in force—on Broadway and specially in the off-Broadway theater. You keep hearing about 'blacklists' of 'dissenters,' of terrorized 'noncon- formists,' of actors and directors being prevented from making a living because of some minor political indiscretion. But I keep looking over the casts of plays as they open, and I keep finding the Party names. As a matter of fact, the comrades are strong enough now to force out those with anti-Communist reputations. Worse than that, they have begun to use their influence, as they did in the thirties, to push the uncommitted over to their side.

"Those of us who see this going on are helpless to act or speak up. No matter how liberal we've been, how much we've fought for civil liberties, we lay ourselves open to the charge of McCarthyism. You know, there's an anti-Communist play, a terrific job, which has been kicking around from producer to producer. They all praise its qualities, but they say that frankly they can't afford to touch it. One producer who tried to go ahead couldn't find a director or actors. Maybe we can get the Fund for the Republic to produce it, like hell!"

The Party felt confident enough to discuss, at a very high level, the possibility of setting up an Alger Hiss Defense Committee. On second, and more canny thought, the Party decided that this might hurt—rather than help—Hiss. But now that Alfred A. Knopf is publishing Hiss' apologia for treason, perhaps the CPUSA will take heart.

National Review
January 1957

The Walter Reuther Story

Part of the mythology of the day is that critics of Walter Reuther base their attacks on old-hat rehashing of Mr. Reuther's brief days in the Soviet Union. Nothing could be farther from the truth, as this classic of the genre clearly shows. To attack Mr. Reuther simply because of some youthful pro-Communism would be like attacking yellow fever simply for its color scheme.

Walter Reuther has been called a "Twentieth Century Moses," a fascist, a Communist, "the most dangerous man in the United States," a genius, a "young man in a hurry," and a "disingenuous opportunist."

His longtime friend, James A. Wechsler, has summed him up as "labor's most radical leader." Reuther, never one to indulge in false modesty, thinks of himself as an "architect of the future." He has made it clear that he carries the blueprint in his back pocket, ready to be whipped out if and when he becomes President of the United States—an ambition which his friends are uttering in ever broader hints.

How faithfully does the 45-year-old president of the CIO live up to his billing? The answer lies in Reuther himself, or in a rounded portrait of the man. The full-time press agents of the United Auto Workers have created a glowing Reuther myth. This study of the man who has captured the imagination of millions is filed as a minority report, to place on the record a side of

Reuther which has studiously been ignored by his typewriter-wielding adulators.

Reuther is a complex and fascinating character. As the leader of his chosen people, he has been, in the words ascribed to Lenin, ready to "use any ruse, cunning, unlawful method, evasion" to gain his ends. From the Communists, he borrowed and put into effective practice the theory of the strategic minority. His ideas on a controlled economy could have been yanked out of Mussolini's notebooks. An outspoken anti-Communist, he nevertheless clutched the party so tightly to his bosom, in the formative UAW years, that a rank-and-file member would have had difficulty slipping a knife between the party and Reuther.

A prim moralist, he abolished by fiat the time-honored postlude to UAW executive board meetings—the all-night poker game. But in 1937, when he was president of the booming Local 174, he was not above signing the equivalent of a pauper's oath in order to get free medical attention. An energetic drumbeater for U.S. intervention in World War II, he grabbed a deferment from military service—because he was "essential" or, reportedly, on the ground that his wife, then working as his private secretary, would lose her means of support were he drafted.

"Probably no American outside the government has made a greater contribution to the war effort than Walter Reuther," an official UAW biography stated. It ignored that his much-touted first Reuther Plan, which was rejected by the "reactionary" auto companies and the Washington "brass hats," was a dangerous dud. It would have set the assembly lines to producing 500 fighter planes a day, but what the ignorant military planners needed, and got, were the bombers which plastered Germany and Japan.

But the Reuther Plan is significant. Like Stalin's Five Year Plan, it was first class salesmanship and and it helped catapult the stocky, barrel-chested redhead into the national picture. And it has been salesmanship, perhaps more than any other single factor, which has put Reuther where he is today. William Knudsen, a shrewd appraiser of men, recognized this when, after a heated collective bargaining session with Reuther, he said:

"Young man, I wish you were selling used cars for us."

"Used cars?" Reuther wondered.

"Used cars," Knudsen repeated. "Anybody can sell new cars."

Salesmanship made a prime commodity of Reuther's agile mind, his ability to make platitudes sound profound, his superb skill at both ax-handle and stiletto politics, and his disregard for the legal amenities. Unremitting publicity and unremitting energy, the combination which made Tom Dewey, compensated for his cold personality and his distaste for the masses—in a field where social drinking and hearty backslapping had heretofore been prerequisites for success. Like Lifebuoy, Reuther made good despite a slightly carbolic scent.

If Reuther is a packaged product, the article within is real enough. His doctrinaire beliefs and the demagogic phrases which express them are as much a part of his heritage as the red hair, baby face, and steely blue eyes which his parents' chromosomes decreed for him.

Walter Philip Reuther was brought up in a household which took the Gospel According to Marx very seriously. His father, Valentine Reuther, was a social democrat, subscribing to the more humanistic doctrines of German Socialism—*Freiheit und Brüderlichkeit*. The indoctrination of Walter and his brothers Victor and Roy—they were later to become the operating triumvirate of the UAW—was conscious and thorough. The three learned much from their father, but they somehow failed to absorb that sense of responsible unionism which so many Germans brought to this country.

At sixteen, Walter quit high school to become an apprentice tool-and-die maker at the Wheeling Steel plant. The Reuther legend says that he was fired from his job for organizing a one-day stay-at-home strike. In any case, he moved on to Detroit, where the wages were higher. There, by parlaying an important skill and his ability to sell himself, he began to push ahead. Had he remained in the productive end of the automotive world, he would undoubtedly have risen to managerial rank. Others with no more on the ball have done it, and Walter was no slouch.

Working nights and going to school days, Reuther completed his high school education in two years. He continued his studies at Wayne University, still holding down a full-time job. In the 1930's, he was joined in Detroit by Victor and Roy. In those depression-ridden times, the three gravitated into the League for Industrial Democracy, an arm of the socialist movement, and later into the Socialist Party itself. Thoroughly infiltrated by Stalinist and Trotskyites, the S.P.'s left-wing faction was then taking its first steps into the alliance with the totalitarian left which later destroyed it.

At Wayne, the Reuthers plunged into Socialist activities with characteristic vigor. When ROTC was introduced, they organized agitation and succeeded in driving military training off the campus. Strikes at auto plants found the Reuther boys and their fellow students on picket lines. In the 1932 presidential election, they stumped Detroit for Norman Thomas. Campaigning and the insidious thrill of hurly-burly speech-making put ideas into their heads. Walter and Victor didn't know precisely what those ideas were or where they were going. All they knew was that they wanted to go. In 1933, they took their savings out of the bank and set out for Europe.

Stopping in New York *en route,* they had dinner with Paul Porter, Mary Hillyer (now Mrs. Paul Blanshard), Ruth Shallcross, and J. B. Matthews. That evening, they made no secret that their ultimate destination was the Soviet Union. Another architect was blueprinting the future; they were eager to see how he worked. It took them close to a year to get a visa. But if their letters to friends were any indication, the wait had been worth it; their enthusiasm over what they found in the Soviet Union was unqualified.

On February 20, 1935, J. B. Matthews, who was lecturing in Flint, Mich., ran into Roy Reuther. Walter and Victor, Roy reported glumly, had "gone completely Stalinist." He also showed Matthews a copy of a letter written by his brothers to two good friends—Melvin and Gladys Bishop.

In recent years, the Reuthers and the UAW publicity machine have worked mightily to discredit its authenticity. The Reuthers have created a myth that the visit to Russia soured them on Communism and on the Soviet system, that they returned to the U.S. "disillusioned by the workings of bureaucracy" and confirmed anti-Communists.

The text of the letter, however, has been incorporated into the printed record of the House Un-American Activities Committee. Walter Reuther tacitly admits its authenticity by disclaiming it as a "burst of adolescent enthusiasm," but insists that the version in House committee files added phrases and distorted its sense. The Reuthers have so far refused requests for examples of these distortions.

Dated January 21, 1934, the letter reads:

> ... What you have written concerning the strikes [in Detroit] plus what we have learned from other sources of the rising discontent of the American workers, makes us long for the moment to be back with you in the front lines of the struggle; however ... the thought that we are actually helping to build a society that will forever end the exploitation of man by man ... is the compensation we receive for our temporary absence ... And let no one tell you that we are not on the road to socialism in the Soviet Union. Let no one say that the workers in the Union of Soviet Socialist Republics are not on the road to security, enlightenment, and happiness.

> ... You know Wal and I were always strong for the Soviet Union. You know that we were always ready to defend it against the lies of the reactionaries. But let me tell you now that ... we have already experienced the thrill, the satisfaction of participating in genuine proletarian democracy ... we are ready to fight for it and its ideals. And why not? Here the workers, through their militant leadership, the proletarian dictatorship ... have maintained power, they have won over the masses ... They have transformed the Soviet Union into one of the greatest industrial nations in the world. They have laid the economic foundation for socialism, for a classless society ... This is what the outside world calls the "ruthless dictatorship in Russia." I tell you, Mel, in all the countries we have thus far been in, we have never found such genuine proletarian workers' democracy in every respect....

> Mel, we are witnessing and experiencing great things in the Union of Soviet Socialist Republics. We are seeing the most backward nation in the world being rapidly transformed into the most modern and scientific.... We are watching daily socialism being taken down from

the books on the shelves and put into actual application. Who would
not be inspired by such events?

Carry on the fight for a Soviet America.   Vic and Wal

Even if the Reuther contention that tampering hands revised
the letter is true, the official account that Walter and Victor were
disgusted by their view of Communism collapses under the weight
of the evidence. After his return from Russia, Walter Reuther
spoke at a Masonic Temple under the auspices of the Young
People's Socialist League. Enthusiastically, he lauded the Soviet
Union and incidentally put himself on record on another matter.
"We do not believe in God," he said grandly.

The next years in the lives of Walter and Victor Reuther,
moreover, marked their most active collaboration with the Communist Party in Michigan—a collaboration so close that many
people were honestly, though erroneously, convinced that they
were party members. In August 1938, for example, President
John P. Frey of the AFL's Metal Trades Department testified
concerning a meeting of the pro-Communist "unity caucus" of
the United Auto Workers, before the union's second convention
in Milwaukee:

> There were present at this caucus Wyndham Mortimer [who led
> wildcat strikes during the Hitler-Stalin Pact period, to halt the manufac-
> ture of planes for the Allies], Ed Hall, Walter Reuther, and about 90
> delegates to the convention who were actually Communist Party
> members. Also present were William Weinstone, Michigan secretary of
> the Communist Party; Jack Stachel, of New York, a member of the
> central committee of the Communist Party; Morris Childs, of Chicago,
> secretary of the Communist Party . . . Jack Johnstone, of Chicago, a
> member of the central committee . . . and Louis Budenz . . . a member
> of the staff of the *Daily Worker*. . . .

Walter Reuther was a young man in those days—and to many
the Communist Party did not seem then what we know it to be
now. This past record would be relatively unimportant were not
Reuther and his press agents so desperately anxious to make it
seem that he was and had always been an undeviating anti-
Communist. It is not the act itself, but the deception, which
makes the act significant.

By 1936, Reuther had discovered that his talents lay in organization, his field in the trade union movement. In the mewling UAW of the day, he was able to weld several tiny Flint, Mich. locals into West Side Local 174, where he easily rose to the presidency. But his entire domain consisted of 78 members. It was then that he first brought into play the Leninist theory of the strategic minority. Half of his membership worked for the Kelsey-Hayes wheel plant, and Reuther made that his target. At a "strategy bull session" in his home, attended by a handful of Helsey-Hayes employees, Reuther worked out the plans which parlayed his 78 members to 30,000—within days.

"We had a big Polish gal at the meeting who had fainted at the assembly line once before," Reuther has since said. "We assigned her to 'faint' again and showed her how to do it. That was to be the signal. When she 'fainted,' someone else was to shut down the assembly line. We trained a couple of men in pulling the right switches." Then the Local 174 members were to shout, "Strike!" Victor Reuther was to begin a harangue of the workers.

The plan was carried out with precision. All activity ceased at the plant and Walter was admitted on the pretext that he would tell the men to go back to work. Once in, however, Reuther made an organizing speech. He refused to desist until permitted to sign up hundreds of the members. But when the workers returned to work the next morning, they found the Kelsey-Hayes plant locked up. Led by Reuther, they broke in and settled down for a siege. For ten days, while a Local 174 quartermaster corps supplied food, the local held the fort. Then management capitulated.

The Kelsey-Hayes sitdown was the turning point in Reuther's life. He emerged from it as the natural leader of the wave of sitdowns—some spontaneous, some planned—which seized the automotive industry. In the turmoil and violence which followed, the United Auto Workers grew into a vast, broiling union. And Reuther saw to it that for the rank-and-file members, as for the public, he was always identified with this stormy adolescence. In setting off sitdowns, Reuther took a big gamble—for he was working at cross purposes with John L. Lewis, the CIO chieftain, who wanted to give priority to the organization of the steel industry. He took what seemed like another gamble in threatening the sovereign authority of the State of Michigan.

But he had an ace in the hole which prevented the sitdowns from developing into bloody failures: a one-man strategic minority named Governor Frank Murphy. In violation of his oath of office, Murphy refused to impose either law or order until Reuther had broken the back of public opposition, dragooned many reluctant workers into his union by threats of violence, and forced the auto companies into settling with the UAW. The need for organizing the auto industry is not being questioned—but Reuther's means, particularly in a New Deal era which gave labor a free franchise, cannot be justified except in terms of totalitarian logic.

Time, and the soothing lotion of captive historians, have softened the picture of the sitdown strikes. But the record is there, in the sworn testimony of those who lived through them. They were a vast military operation in which Socialist and Communists served as the *cadres* and the shock troops. There was a general staff under Walter Reuther, a system of political commissars under Victor Reuther, a regular army, and a horde of semi-organized guerrillas. Lines of communication were maintained; supplies, both food and ammunition (stones and bolts and acid) were sent to threatened points. Assembly lines were set up in some of the seized plants to manufacture blackjacks made of metal encased in leather. A sound truck, manned by Victor Reuther, moved from one trouble spot to another, exhorting the strikers with words and with "Internationale"—the Communist anthem.

Throughout the trouble, John Barringer, the city manager of Flint, called in vain for intervention by the State Police to restore order. He could not reach Governor Murphy, and other State officials refused to act. When the State Police finally came in, they had strict orders from Murphy not to intervene. During several riots, they stood by watching. Barringer's testimony summed up the situation tersely:

About 8:30 [of January 11, 1936] word came to the police department . . . that a mob was storming the entrance to the first floor

of the Fisher Plant No. 2, and requested immediate help. The riot squad
of the Flint police . . . was ordered immediately to the scene . . . By the
time they arrived a first-class fight had started, and the police immediately endeavored to restore order . . . They were greeted by the
mob with missiles of all sorts . . . pieces of steel, iron brickbats, milk
bottles, and bottles containing acid . . . Victor Reuther was talking
from a loudspeaker wagon and was inciting the men to further violence
and to combat the police . . . The fight developed into serious proportions . . .

Knowing that I could not send any additional reserves . . . I phoned
immediately to the State Police headquarters . . . I finally located
Governor Murphy by phone and told him the story. He would
authorize no help but told us to meet him later at midnight at the
Durant Hotel. When the Governor finally arrived at the hotel and
started up the elevator to his rooms, he was followed immediately by
Roy and Victor Reuther . . . The Governor conferred with these men
for more than three-quarters of an hour before he would talk to the
mayor and myself and other city officials . . .

After a three-hour conference . . . he still refused to order the 70 or
75 State Police which were in Flint at the time to help our Flint police
department to restore order . . . I told him that our men . . . were
virtually surrounded and outnumbered many times . . . and that if they
were not allowed to withdraw by the mob . . . they would have to use
solid shot and machine guns. This seemed to have no effect on the
Governor.

The only interference came from the LaFollette Committee—
later denounced by the Senator himself for its Communist
personnel—which demanded the names of deputies sworn in to
help maintain order. "They did not seem a bit concerned as to
what was going on," Barringer said of the committee investigators. "Their main object or purpose there was to demand of me
the names of those men we had signed up as police reserves."
Would the UAW have access to the list?—Barringer asked. The
investigators said yes. The city manager refused.

It was during this period, when Walter Reuther was defying
the forces of law in Michigan, that he appeared at the office of a
Dr. Shafarman in Detroit to get a tuberculin test. Reuther signed
his name to a green Board of Health card, attesting that he could
"not afford to pay," and the $5 fee was charged to the city of
Detroit. An interesting sidelight to this incident was the fact that

Shafarman was serving then as a one-man medical board screening young Communists who were being sent by the Communist Party to fight in Spain.*

The sitdown strikes made Reuther a big man in the UAW. But he was not ready to make a bid for the presidency of the union. Combining with the Communist faction of George Addes, however, he was able to pry loose the well-meaning but bumbling UAW president, Homer Martin. The manipulatable R. J. Thomas took over that office and Addes succeeded to the key post of secretary-treasurer. Reuther remained snugly on the executive board and continued to enlarge his domain—the General Motors department of the union. He had been able to unionize only seventeen of the close-to-100 GM plants. He bided his time until GM was tooling up for its 1940 models and then applied his strategic-minority tactic: He called out the tool-and-die makers whom he controlled. GM was faced with the alternatives of capitulation to Reuther or loss of the 1940 car market to its competitors. It capitulated and Reuther won his first corporation-wide contract.

The first Reuther Plan gave Walter his labor-statesman reputation. He began offering new plans at the drop of a hat on practically every problem, including the one of righting the *Normandie,* lying on its side at a New York pier. The war, and the need for labor cooperation, gave him a handle. As a consultant to the War Production Board, he had *entrée* into high government offices.

"When I was having a hard time putting over an idea," he told the *Saturday Evening Post's* Jack Alexander in 1948, "I could always go to Mrs. Roosevelt or [Harold] Ickes and in that way get to see the President." He and Roosevelt had much in common.

Reuther's strength was, and has been, his ability to turn defeat into propaganda victory. In 1945, he demanded—and struck for—a 30 percent increase in wages, to be tied to a guarantee from

*This episode is detailed in sworn testimony before the House Un-American Activities Committee, Vol. 2.

GM that it would not raise the prices of cars. The strike lasted for 113 days, Reuther got 18½ cents for his men, and the company raised the price of cars. But in the accounts of labor publicists this was somehow converted into a resounding victory for forward-looking unionism.

As the war drew to a close, Reuther began painting grim pictures of postwar depression, mass unemployment, and economic chaos. His solution, embodied in another "plan," was characteristic of his thinking. Wartime control of the national economy and the freedom of the citizen were pallid compared with Reuther's prescription for social health. He envisaged—and tried to sell to the government and the public—a Peace Production Board which would serve as an "economic high command" with "full authority to enforce its decisions." Its scope would be total and totalitarian.

The PPB, as Reuther saw it, would have "full control" over materials, allocation of manpower, prices, tooling facilities, new patents, the migration of farm workers, and the distribution of goods under a system of "social priorities," manufacturing quotas, types of goods manufactured. Over the PPB would be industrial councils composed of labor, management, and government, which would make overall plans. Reuther's dream was terrifying but not original. An ex-Socialist named Benito Mussolini had thought of it first, as a means of ending Italy's postwar chaos in the early 1920's. It had ended the chaos—and Italy with it.

But before Reuther could bring the dictatorship of a corporate state to America, he had to subdue his union first. Whatever its faults, the UAW was, until 1946, the freest union in the country. Brawling factions and an independent membership prevented the leadership from assuming the iron control which obtained in most other unions. In 1946, Reuther made his bid for the presidency of the UAW—and the situation began to change. Reuther campaigned as an anti-Communist against the Communist faction of George Addes. He won, but only by a tenuous margin. Following the voting, he told the convention which elected him:

"I want now to extend my hand to George Addes . . . and tell him that together we can unite this organization."

In 1947, Reuther had sufficiently "united" the UAW so that his election was a shoo-in. With him he swept in an executive board which he dominated. His victory was followed by a ruthless purge of all those who had opposed him. His lieutenants did not work haphazardly; they had already prepared lists of all those slated to go, and the job was accomplished smoothly though not painlessly. From that moment on, the UAW's independence began slipping away. The Reuther machine, well oiled by Victor and Roy Reuther, rolled ahead implacably.

With the UAW safely in his pocket, Reuther set his sights on the presidency of the CIO, a goal he has reached, and—if Arthur Schlesinger, Jr., the Goebbels of Americans for Democratic Action, and Abe Raskin, the *New York Times* top labor reporter, are to be accepted as fair analysts—on the Presidency of the United States.

Reuther has been building steadily to achieve this goal. He has never given up the idea of an American labor party or, failing that, the domination of the Democratic Party. As one of the powers in Americans for Democratic Action—an illegitimate offspring of the New Deal made up of anti-anti-Communists, labor leaders with intellectual pretentions, fuzzy liberals, and the *New York Post*—he has forced rule-or-ruin decisions on a traditional American political organism which had won elections by effecting coalitions rather than by imposing rigid orthodoxy. It was the ADA which planned the showdown over "civil rights" at the 1952 Democratic convention—a showdown which delivered a sizable hunk of the South's electorial votes to General Eisenhower.

The ADA's demand for recognition of Red China, its opposition to loyalty oaths and security measures in the government, and its cynical propagation of the canard that "thought control" and "hysteria" are the current characteristics of American life, were all part of an overall battle plan. Had Adlai Stevenson won the 1952 election, Reuther would have had his strategic minority at the fountainhead of government—in the form of the ADA.

As a demagogue, Reuther bows to no man, with the possible exception of Harry S. Truman. At a time when industry accepts collective bargaining as an established fact of life, Reuther continues to raise specters of "union-busting." In a capitalist economy which has created the greatest productive mechanism in the world, he still warns that industry is plotting a planned scarcity—and this from a man who grew up in Detroit, a city which must continually feed its assembly lines or perish. ("You have to be a millionaire to be sick in America" he tells his followers.) An expert on production, he speaks glowingly of a society in which the number of cars manufactured each year will be decided by popular vote.

Reuther is a compiler of statistics, a student of contemporary history, and an astute analyst of the Roosevelt years. As such, he must know that the "recession" of 1937 created more unemployment than the bust of 1929, that the Roosevelt administration failed miserably in its economic policies until it put the country on a war production basis, that the Roosevelt-Hopkins answer to mass unemployment was WPA—period. Yet he offers as a slogan, "Not *back* to the New Deal but forward *from* the New Deal.

This, then, is Walter Reuther, the public man. The private man doesn't smoke or drink, dresses like a middle-rank executive, seldom unbuttons his shirt or loosens his tie, loves Strauss waltzes, holds his colleagues aloof—privately they complain that he is "inhuman"—and carries on his back the monkey of clawing ambition. The magazine writers may say of him—as one did—that "in intellect and personál appearance, he combines the most engaging qualities of Albert Einstein and Van Johnson," but elsewhere the story is different.

Even at death's door, he keeps his life's blueprint in mind. In 1949, a would-be assassin blasted him with a shotgun. The instigators and plotters of the attempt on his life were well known—if not by name, by affiliation. The Communists and the numbers racketeers had worked together, and the plans were made in the office of a Communist labor leader. The Communists wanted Reuther out of the way because they could have regained control of the UAW. The racketeers wanted him dead because he was seeking to drive them out of the auto plants where their take was reportedly $150,000,000 anually in numbers money.

But when the story of this unholy alliance and its role in the Reuther assualt was published, Reuther and other UAW officials knocked it down. It was so much more expedient, in the long run, to hint darkly that the auto manufacturers, grown desperate, were responsible.

The American Mercury
May 1953

DEFENSE OF REUTHER
by Father George Higgins

President Walter Reuther of the CIO is the hapless subject of a very unfriendly and rather venomous article by Ralph de Toledano in the May issue of *American Mercury*. The article is shockingly out of character for a respectable and hitherto responsible journalist whose earlier articles, in such diverse periodicals as *Newsweek* and *The Commonweal,* have been anything but Pegleresque either in style or content. The harm it will do to Mr. Reuther's reputation in certain quarters is relatively minor as compared to what it will do to lower the reputation of a writer who previously has enjoyed the professional respect of his colleagues in the field of labor reporting—even when they happened to disagree with his conclusions.

Walter Reuther has admittedly made mistakes—some of them very serious—in the course of his meteoric rise to national prominence as president of the UAW and, latterly, of the CIO. Nor is it any secret that he was a rather doctrinaire Socialist in his early youth and that he and his brother Victor wrote some adolescent and rather idiotic nonsense about the alleged glories of the Soviet revolution.

To the best of our knowledge, Mr. de Toledano's summary of this unfortunate chapter in the Reuther story is more or less accurate. Whether or not he has served any useful purpose in writing about it at this late date is, of course, another matter. His motives are open to suspicion for the reason that he deliberately soft-pedals—almost completely ignores—the universally recognized fact that Reuther is now and has been for many years one of the most militant and effective anti-Communist in the United States.

Mr. de Toledano is honest enough to admit that Reuther was never a member of the Communist Party; also, more or less grudgingly, that "the Communist wanted Reuther out of the way because they could have regained control of the UAW." But instead of making this the central thesis of his vitriolic article, he lets it stand as an isolated and reluctant compliment in an otherwise unbroken series of direct accusations and awkward innuendos, some obviously petty, others perilously close to being libelous.

Among other heinous and horrendous crimes, Mr. Reuther is alleged to have his eye on the White House. I rather doubt that. But suppose he has? What's wrong with that in a republic in which every (non-Catholic, gentile) boy is encouraged to believe that he has a chance to be President of the United States? Are labor leaders ineligible for the Presidency?

Reuther and the late President Roosevelt, we are told rather cryptically, "had much in common." Reuther will undoubtedly be flattered by the compliment.

"As a demagogue," Mr. de Toledano continues, "Reuther bows to no man, with the possible exception of Harry S. Truman"—or, it might be added, of a certain contributor to the May issue of the *American Mercury* who is capable of stating rather casually but very demagogically that Reuther "as the leader of his chosen people . . . has been, in the words ascribed to Lenin, ready to 'use any ruse, cunning, unlawful method, evasion' to gain his ends."

These and similar descriptions (Arthur Schlesinger, Jr. of Harvard is characterized as "the Goebbels of Americans for Democratic Action") are merely the seasoning on the meat of the article. The meat of the article—the underlying thesis—is that Reuther is a dangerous radical who wants to go beyond the philosophy of the New Deal, a doctrinaire reformer who believes in economic planning through a system of Industry Councils.

"Reuther's dream" of an Industry Council Plan "was terrifying," says Mr. de Toledano, "but not original. An ex-Socialist named Benito Mussolini had thought of it first, as a means of ending Italys postwar chaos in the early 1920's. It had ended the chaos—and Italy with it."

Mr. de Toledano is no babe in the woods. He knows his way around the ideological world. He reads and writes for Catholic periodicals. Surely, therefore, he must be aware of the fact that Pope Pius XI advocated a system of Industry Councils as early as 1931, when Reuther was still enamored of Socialism. He must also be aware of the fact that Reuther is completely opposed, as was Pope Pius XI, to Mussolini's version of the so-called corporate state.

Reuther has come a long way since the publication of Pius XI's encyclical Quadragesimo Anno in 1931. He has his share of human weaknesses and faults—some of them catalogued sarcastically and with questionable propriety by Mr. de Toledano—but his economic philosophy, whatever its limitations, will stand up better in the light of Christian social teaching than Mr. de Toledano's. Reuther is no angel, but he would seem to be on the side of the angels in advocating a system of Industry Councils—a proposal which, far from being the exclusive property of the Catholic Church, is sympathetically treated, with qualifications, in a new book published under the auspices of the National Council of Churches of Christ in America.

Before he writes another article on the ICP, Mr. de Toledano would do well to read chapter 14 of this new Harber publication, *The Social Responsibilities of the Businessman* by Howard Bowen—the third in a series of six volumes sponsored by the National Council of Churches on "The Ethics and Economics of Society." Whether or not he agrees with Mr. Bowen's qualified endorsement of the Industry Council Plan, perhaps he will begin to recognize the fact that his own self-styled "minority report" on Walter Reuther is also a minority report on Christian social reconstruction.

This is not to say that Reuther's particular version of the Industry Council Plan is necessarily sound in every respect, or that it necessarily enjoys the unqualified endorsement of Christian social thinkers. It is merely to suggest that Mr. de Toledano, by reason of his own unqualified and highly emotional condemnation of the Industry Council Plan, has unwittingly told us more about himself than he has about Mr. Reuther. What he has told us about himself is unexpectedly damaging to his reputation as a social philosopher.

The Florida Catholic
May 1953

ANSWER TO FATHER HIGGINS

Father Higgins belabors me for having written an article critical of Walter Reuther in the May *American Mercury*. He impugns my motives in writing it, though he does not suggest what they may be. He unjustly represents the thesis and quotes from it with a rare selectivity.

I do not resent Father Higgins's attack. We live in a combative and hair-trigger era. Nor am I upset by the sideswipe at my motives. Those who know me are aware that I stand for, and fight for, the right of men under God to live in freedom and to choose between good and evil; that I stand against the economic Jansenism of our sorry intellectuals. I am deeply concerned, however, when a syndicated Catholic column misrepresents what I have written and then seeks to equate Walter Reuther's totalitarian position on industry councils with a misreading of two paragraphs in Quadragesimo Anno. (I will not mention Father Higgins's repeated use of "Pegleresque" as an epithet to discredit me, or his clear implication that my statements are false and "libelous.")

Father Higgins says that I "soft-pedal" the "universally recognized fact that Reuther is now and has been for many years one of the most militant and effective anti-Communists in the United States." Obviously, Father Higgins and I live in different universes. I readily concede that Reuther was an anti-Communist in his drive for power within the UAW. (As I pointed out in my article, he destroyed union democracy in the process of purging the Communists.)

But was Reuther an "effective" anti-Communist in 1950 when after the outbreak of the Korean war, he joined in the ADA's clamor for recognition of Communist China? Was he an "effective" anti-Communist when, in his first major move as president of the CIO, he readmitted District 65 (the Distributing, Processing, and Office Workers union)—expelled by Philip Murray and the CIO Executive Council as Communist controlled and still run by the same unregenerate leadership? Reuther's anti-Communism is strictly political—not moral or ideological. That may be enough for some, but it is not enough for me.

I am called a demagogue by Father Higgins because I say that Reuther "has been ready to 'use any ruse, cunning, unlawful method, evasion' to gain his ends." But Father Higgins's readers are not informed that in my *American Mercury* article, I carefully document that charge by describing Reuther's methods during the sitdown strikes in Detroit. I leave it to any reader who has read the article—or the documentation on which it is based—to decide whether Reuther did or did not employ ruses, cunning, unlawful methods, or evasions in gaining his ends.

But the meat of Father Higgins's argument is in his contention that "the meat of the (*American Mercury*) article—the underlying thesis—is that 'Reuther is a dangerous radical . . . a doctrinaire reformer who believes in economic planning through a system of Industry Councils." It is hard to see how the "meat" of my article could be the question of industry councils (I never mentioned economic planning) since I devote to it but two paragraphs in a piece running to over ten magazine pages.

Father Higgins does not specify what he himself means by industry councils—but Reuther is most explicit. He advocates a rigidly regimented system in which government-management-labor councils control every phase of the economy—from the allocation of materials to the movement of workers. This is a system which makes private property the adjunct of the State and destroys individual freedom—a system, moreover, which runs counter to Pope Leo XIII's Rerum Novarum and Pope Pius XI's Quadragesimo Anno. Father Higgins asserts that Pope Pius XI "advocated a system of Industry Councils as early as 1931," but a careful reading of the encyclical will show that this is not the case. A brief and cool description of the Italian corporate set-up, touching on the good and the bad, is hardly advocacy.

I do not believe that Reuther is a "dangerous radical"—a phrase which I nowhere use. Most "dangerous radicals," in point of fact, turn out to be much less dangerous than they seem. But I do believe that Reuther has a totalitarian direction of mind, that he is a socialist of the new type.

The Church stands firmly in opposition to Socialism—and I can refer Father Higgins to a number of encyclicals on this question, starting with *Quod Apostolici Muneris.*

Father Higgins may say that Reuther's economic philosophy "will stand up better in the light of Christian social teaching" than mine. But in view of Reuther's belief in the class struggle (a belief proscribed by the Church), his avowed disbelief in God, and his espousal of a social philosophy which in its pride substitutes the pragmatism of man for the revealed morality of God, I fail to see how Father Higgins arrived at his conclusion.

It saddens me to find myself in controversy with Father Higgins, the more so since, in announcing my fall, he describes my pedestal so generously. (I am not half the "social philosopher" he says I was.) I am certain that he attacked my article from the highest of motives. But I would have done an injustice both to him and to myself had I not answered forthrightly. In the last analysis, the decision is not in his polemic or in mine—it is in the article which he assailed. Perhaps Father Higgins will find time to read it again—and more dispassionately. He will see, I am sure, that my rancor is not against Reuther, but against Reuther's politico-economic a-morality. On this score, Father Higgins and I can hardly disagree.

The Florida Catholic
June 1953

Junior's Misses

As with Walter Reuther, it is expected by some that all criticisms of Arthur Schlesinger, Jr., by anyone right of the political center, would be based upon simple witchhunting or Red-baiting. Read then this thorough-going discussion. It attacks Dr. Schlesinger in his most vulnerable area, not his politics, but his thinking.

For a man so young, Arthur Schlesinger, Jr. has exerted a remarkable influence on the body politic. As ideologue-in-chief of the Stevenson presidential campaign, he was in large part responsible for its Fabian tone and its mocking treatment of the Communist issue. His column for the anti-anti-Communist New York *Post*, modestly headed "History of the Week," reaches hundreds of thousands of readers. As activist and phrasemaker for Americans for Democratic Action, the junior Schlesinger has done much to improve each shining prejudice of this curious and tiresome organization. His presence on forums and at other occasions where the elite meet to bleat is ubiquitous. (He also teaches at Harvard.)

At best and at worst, Schlesinger personifies the liberal conscience which, having descended to ideological adventurism, struggles periodically to justify its hog-wallow of sordid means and muddled ends. In polemic mood, he figuratively echoes the humorist Walt Kelly's ironic paraphrase, "I may not understand what you say, but I will fight to your death for my right to deny it." It is a sad commentary on the liberal disintegration that these misunderstandings are more frequently willful than not.

No one will fight to deny, however, that this professional young man has a very loud horn. If the notes are sometimes

cracked or shrill, if he garbles the score, at least he is on the
bandstand of history. (That he can also give a clear and sensitive
reading makes his other performances of startling significance.)
As a confessed "historian," Schlesinger has learned from Stalin,
Goebbels, and Charley Michelson that in the eternal counterpoint
of myth and fact, the booming drum carries farther than the
reedy oboe. And having pondered the philosophy of LS/MFT, he
knows that slogans, repeated frequently and firmly, have more
effect than volumes of reasoned argument.

Armed with these lessons, Schlesinger has become a shrewd
practitioner of what George Orwell called "doublethink"—an
advanced form of plural and convoluted logic which eventually
deceives the deceiver. In true liberal style, Schlesinger lards his
utterances with pious assurances of his scrupulous impartiality
and veracity. When he squirts bile at anti-Communists—
Schlesinger referred to Vice-President Nixon as a "junior
G-man"—it is always in the name of anti-Communism. When he
plumps for government regimentation, it is always in the name of
freedom. When he censures conservatives for the exercise of free
speech, it is always in advocacy of the First Amendment. When
he falsely accuses, it is always in the name of truth.

In a 1951 column, to cite an instance, Schlesinger took up a
favorite gambit of the non-Communist left—the smear of those
who testify against the Communist conspiracy. Louis Budenz, he
wrote, "obligingly put the finger on practically everyone in sight,
identifying as a Communist, for example, a man like John Carter
Vincent about whose political affiliations a year ago he had
professed ignorance." This charge of perjury had been manufactured out of the whole cloth by Joseph Alsop, a columnist of
musk and passion to whose writings Schlesinger is much devoted.

Forgetting his strictures against "character assassination,"
Schlesinger felt no qualms in repeating the libel. The record,
which was available to him, showed that Budenz, whose veracity
has been frequently upheld by Federal juries, never "professed
ignorance" of Vincent's political affiliations. On the contrary, he
had clearly stated, during the hearings in question, that he
"would prefer not to comment" on Vincent at the time for

reasons involving the FBI. Under oath before the Senate Internal Security subcommittee, Alsop was to withdraw the perjury accusation. But Schlesinger remained quiet.

This is not an isolated example of Schlesinger's historical method. Less than a month earlier, he had launched a somewhat broader smear, based on a cavalier revision of history, against former President Herbert Hoover. No honorable person had up to that time—or has since then—cast aspersions on Mr. Hoover's integrity. Nevertheless, in a letter to the New York *Times*, the junior Schlesinger charged Mr. Hoover with having condoned government corruption—the Teapot Dome Scandal specifically— during the early 1920's. Mr. Hoover was singled out at this late date because he had upbraided the Truman administration for having clung passionately to the demonstrable guilty or soiled in its higher echelons.

"Far from objecting to official corruption then," Schlesinger wrote, "Mr. Hoover sat in entire complacency as Secretary of Commerce, while his colleague, the Secretary of the Interior, sought to loot the Government . . . Not only did Mr. Hoover fail to make any public objection to Secretary of the Interior Fall, or to Attorney General Harry Daugherty . . . but . . . eight days after Fall's hasty resignation . . . Hoover wrote him" a warm letter of commendation. These, Schlesinger said calmly, were the "indisputable facts."

These "indisputable facts," as Admiral Lewis Strauss, now chairman of the Atomic Energy Commission, pointed out in an answering letter to the *Times*, were strictly of the junior historian's invention. Fall's "hasty" resignation had been publicly announced two months before it became effective. At the time, there was no suspicion that he was involved in any scandal. As a matter of fact, the New York *Times* editorially regretted Fall's departure from the Federal service. Not until months after Fall's resignation were the charges made and the investigation begun which led to the Teapot Dome fraud disclosures. It was, moreover, Mr. Hoover's Attorney General who sent Fall to prison—a fact which Schlesinger failed to pull out of his deep freezer.

Schlesinger's motivation in leaping to the defense of Professor Dirk Struik—and in the process suppressing the key facts—is somewhat more obscure. At the time that Struik was *indicted for sedition*, Schlesinger painted a picture of a persecuted teacher and added: "It is hard to see that *his opinions* constitute a danger to anybody. I have never heard of anyone *being influenced* by Struik; my nine-year-old boy could lick him in an argument." [Emphasis added.] Nowhere in his scoldings did Schlesinger point out that Struik was not only a professor of mathematics at M.I.T., but a member of a Communist underground cell of considerable influence in Massachusetts, and an instructor at the Samuel Adams School in Boston—a school which teaches the violent overthrow of the American Government and recruits students for the more advanced Communist academies of sub-version.

To what purpose this defense of a Communist by a man who is so careless of the reputations of anti-Communists? To what end this systematic falsification of history by one presumably dedicated to its disciplines? The answer does not lie in any stated or implied charge that the junior Schlesinger is a Communist, a fellow traveler, or a Russia Firster—for he is clearly none of these. When it has suited him, he has effectively opposed both domestic and international Communists. Nor does the answer lie in the implication that he is stupid or misinformed. He was educated at the best schools—Phillips Exeter, Harvard (from which he was graduated *summa cum laude*), and Cambridge. It would not be entirely fair to blame it on his associates in ADA, which today is being daintily cuddled by the Communist Party. It might be said that he would not love them half so much, loved he not Arthur more—but this kind of opportunism is only a surface phase of the junior Schlesinger's make-up.

Arthur Meier Schlesinger, Jr. is a product of his future. The shifts and turns, the given and withdrawn loyalties, the anti-Communism and the anti-anti-Communism, the strange alliances—all these make sense only when seen in this context. Along with the somewhat soiled figures of the Stevenson brain trust, he is riding a wave of the future which, until the Democratic defeat of 1952, was also a gravy train.

Only someone coasting on this greasy billow could have made such contradictory shifts in position as Schlesinger has fallen into: Truman was "hopeless" in 1946, but the saviour of America in 1949; Eisenhower was liberalism's last best hope before the 1948 convention, but the pawn of black reaction after the convention of 1952; there was "no reason why we can't coexist peacefully with Russia" in 1946, but he blandly favored a get-tough policy in 1948. In 1946, he made the flat statement that George Kennan's "containment" policy "is not a policy of threatening Soviet interests in what has become the settled sphere of Soviet power"; and in 1953, the equally flat statement that the same policy means "the liberation of the areas of Soviet conquest by peaceful methods."

There is only one constant, with its corollary, to be found in the writings and utterances of the junior Schlesinger: belief in, and support for, the "non-Communist left"—which means the socialist, forcible welfare-state left. He was lavish in his praise of Secretary of State James F. Byrnes (whom he detests today as Governor of South Carolina) for throwing U.S. support to the non-Communist left in Europe—a policy which is now costing us dear. And he was equally lavish to Secretary of State George C. Marshall for giving "new positions of authority" to such men as "Charles E. Bohlen [now our ambassador in Moscow] a brilliant student of Russia and *a persuasive champion of the non-Communist left thesis*, who had been discovered years before by Harry Hopkins." [Emphasis added.]

Although he denies it today (he admitted it when it was more fashionable), the junior Schlesinger is a non-doctrinaire socialist. Like other socialists, he believes in the equality of all men except those with an income larger than his own. He spouts hoary anti-capitalist bromides about the Eisenhower administration and the Republicans, referring to the "billion-dollar cabinet" and "plutocrats, profiteers, and pirates"—rather strange language from an "historian" who was hardly bothered by the tax looting of the

U.S. Treasury under Truman. Schlesinger obscures his socialism under a cloud of semantic irrelevancies and a style so fuzzy that it requires block and tackle to dredge up his thoughts. When his socialist espousals are quoted at him, Schlesinger has an answer: "I chose to write as if 'democratic socialism' and the 'mixed economy' were the same."

On the face of it, this is sheer intellectual dishonesty—and doubly so since "democratic socialism" and the "mixed economy" are one. For the "mixed economy" starts as a marriage of socialism and capitalism. But like the female praying mantis, socialism devours its mate, as the British and the French are learning. Schlesinger's disclaimer is therefore a flash of unconscious candor—the same kind of candor he demonstrated when, discussing the difficulties of writing current history, he remarked of his *Age of Jackson*, "All the witnesses are dead. There's no one to pop up and say, 'You were wrong—I was there.' " No one, for example, like Admiral Strauss.

The socialism of the junior Schlesinger is most apparent in his theory of the hobbled individual. Schlesinger writes: "The value of the individual . . . can become abstract and sterile; arrogant forms of individualism sometimes discredit the basic faith in the value of the individual. It is only so far as that insight [into the value of the individual] can achieve a full social dimension, so far as individualism derives freely from the community, that democracy will be immune to the virus of totalitarianism." Divorced from his obscurities of style Schlesinger is simply saying that the individual may be allowed freedom only so long as he does not exercise it significantly. For if individual freedom derives from the community, it exists as a form of charity which can be withdrawn by the community at will.

This is the crux of the socialist philosophy which showers love on the undifferentiated and collective mass, but which is jealously suspicious of individual free will—like Promethean fire, a gift of God and not the tentative grant of society. This is the anti-libertarian tie which binds Schlesinger to the New Dealers, the homeless Marxists, and those pathetic ex-Communists who can not accept the rigors of Soviet dialectics but who still cling to the deeper heresies of historical materialism. Like them, Schlesinger despises the Communists because they are traitors, trouble-makers, and competitors. But because he shares with the Com-munists their basic concepts of God and freedom, he ends up by tacitly defending what he hates. That the hatred is genuine merely serves to emphasize the ambivalence.

Writing for the socialist *New Leader* in 1952, Schlesinger declared that he "explicitly rejected the theory of socialism in the last pages of *The Age of Jackson* (1945)." Only by constricting socialism to the Maximalist doctrines of the early 1900's does this statement even approximate the facts. For in 1947, in an essay on "The Future of Socialism," written for the *Partisan Review*, he was supporting a theory of "democratic socialism" and proph-esying that "there seems no inherent obstacle to the gradual advance of socialism in the United States through a series of New Deals."

In 1949, socialism had lost some of its luster among the intellectuals. Schlesinger had not yet found a new name for the sweet-smelling rose, but he was still advocating the "liberal socialist" doctrine that the state "expend its main strength . . . in determining the broad levels and conditions of economic activity"—in short, a left-oriented corporativism. And having described the New Deal in 1947 as a "process of backing into socialism," he affirms in 1952 that he is, in fact, a New Dealer.

But it is not necessary to rely on sentences and paragraphs which, Schlesinger will plead, are taken out of context. There is the body of his work, starting with *The Age of Jackson*, the book which catapulted him into fame. Widely acclaimed as a great piece of historical writing—it had footnotes—chosen by the pro-Communist Book Find Club, and winning him a Pulitzer Prize, it was on a literate level the kind of historical manipulation which made a best seller of Howard Fast—and made Communist heroes of Thomas Jefferson and Abraham Lincoln. Though *The Age of Jackson* amazed the unlearned, such sober publications as New York University's *Journal of Economic History* found much of it "sheer romance" which failed "to make proper use of the work of scholars" and suppressed the established evidence when it ran counter to Schlesinger's thesis.

Jackson's battle with the Central Bank of the United States properly took up an important part of Schlesinger's book. But Schlesinger dealt with it in much the same manner as the *Posts*, both Washington and New York, deal with the McCarthy issue. "The landscapes at the Hermitage and Kinderhook smile in a fashion not noticeable where Whigs and Federalists live," the *Journal* remarked. "The Jacksonian leaders have a 'pervading insight,' their wrath is 'magnificent,' one or another of them is 'handsome,' 'grave,' 'masterly,' 'erudite,' 'thoughtful,' 'quiet,' 'intelligent,' 'brilliant,' etc., etc., and the old hero himself is touchingly fond of children. The opposition is a very sorry outfit. They are Bank 'lackeys,' they 'roar' and 'snarl,' they deal in 'hullabaloo,' they are 'phony,' they have 'fantasies,' they work 'backstairs,' their best minds are 'opaque,' and one gets the impression that Mr. Schlesinger never thinks of them as loving little children at all . . . He makes the Bank a dim sort of moneyed monstrosity" and misrepresents its function.

It is not very surprising that even after Schlesinger had begun to attack the Communists, the *New Masses* referred to *The Age of Jackson* as a book which "represents a statement of devotion to liberalism in politics," depicting "with the embroidery of formal scholarship a phase of the national struggle against the power of the bankers."

For all of its shortcomings—and its obeisance to liberal-leftist stereotypes—*The Age of Jackson* remains Schlesinger's most solid achievement. About a year later it was followed by his bill of divorcement from the "progressive" wing of the non-Communist left—an article on the Communist Party for *Life* magazine. It took some courage, in the Year of Our Lord 1946, for someone in Schlesinger's intellectual and academic milieu to anatomize the Communist Party. There was, moreover, the matter of his family background: the senior Schlesinger is and was a prodigious joiner of Communist fronts; his brother-in-law, Professor John K. Fairbank, was a member in top standing of the pro-Chinese Communist lobby and a close associate of Owen Lattimore.

Based in large part on the research of a New York *World-Telegram* reporter, the *Life* article was strong enough on such facts as it used. (By sheer coincidence, it failed to examine those Communist fronts which had won the senior Schlesinger's allegiance.) But in weighing the significance of these facts, Schlesinger slipped into a never-never land. He placed the Communist Party, which he had just described as an international conspiracy, in the same category as the Moral Rearmament movement and the Holy Rollers. He found "even freedom-loving Americans" looking "wistfully to Russia" because of the "faults and injustices" of the free enterprise system. And he cautioned against "witch hunts and Un-American Committees."

Though Communist espionage could not be "shrugged off," Schlesinger proceeded to brush it off by urging that it be left to the FBI to handle. By his own later admission, Schlesinger knew how the FBI was stymied in the Hiss case. It was no secret that in at least two important espionage cases (one involving the theft of atomic secrets), the FBI had been prevented by the State Department from making arrests. And as he later conceded, he knew at the time the *Life* article was written that Michael Greenberg, then working in the White House as an assistant to Presidential Aide Lauchlin Currie, was a Communist.

In *The Vital Center*, a book which quickly became the ADA's *Mein Kampf*, this sharp-sighted myopia continued. Schlesinger continued to berate the Communists for their betrayal of the great revolution, but he was willing to grant them, in 1949, the validity of the "class struggle," one of their basic tenets. "Class conflict is essential if freedom is to be preserved," he wrote. More important in a propaganda context were casual avowals that the Communist regime in Hungary "has done much for the common man" and "based itself on the trade union movement." That anything vaguely analogous to a trade union movement exists in the Communist world is, of course, nonsense. Or he can say, in the face of the Soviet Union's consistent record of genocide and anti-Semitism, that "the USSR stands plausibly . . . for racial equality. The shocking racial cruelties in the United States . . . compare unfavorably with the Soviet nationalities policy."

Latterly, Schlesinger has been devoting his efforts to his "History of the Week" column, his share of the loot when Mrs. Dorothy Schiff threw out her fellow-traveling editor-husband, T. O. Thackrey, and made James A. Wechsler his editorial successor on the New York *Post*. It is hard to tell who nourishes on whom, Wechsler or Schlesinger, but the relationship is clearly nutritional.

In his discussions of the foreign field, Schlesinger will sometimes fill his column with good sense. But for the most part, it is a dreary and all-too-often distorted series of lucubrations on current events—the allegations which are almost but not quite true, the amalgams which link conservatives with crackpots, the defense of the indefensible, the gratuitous smear, the running attack against the ex- and anti-Communist, and the constant deprecation of the Communist threat to the United States.

Examples come easily to hand:

ITEM. Owen Lattimore "was certainly for many years a notorious and unabashed fellow traveler," but "it hardly justifies perjury proceedings founded on trivial lapses of memory" even though under oath he proclaimed himself a constant anti-Communist. And Senator McCarran, whose subcommittee stated that Lattimore was "a conscious articulate instrument of the Communist conspiracy"—a more pointed way of saying what Schlesinger mumbled—is a dirty name for attacking the pro-Chinese Communist lobbyist.

ITEM. "[John Foster] Dulles, it is true, is sanctimonious, slippery, evasive, vain, and intellectually unscrupulous" because, among other reasons, he "called for the admission of Red China into the United Nations in 1950." There is no mention of the fact that Schlesinger and the ADA did precisely the same thing at precisely the same time.

ITEM. "The exposure of Communist infiltration into the United Nations staff continues. In a sense, *little could be more futile* than to insert agents into organizations which already have a full Soviet and satellite participation." There was "no excuse" for allowing "this drift of pro-Soviet American citizens" into the UN, Schlesinger adds—as though no excuse had been made by his heroes in the State Department for something which was not a

"drift" but a systematic penetration plotted with the aid of Alger
Hiss—but "after all [the little-bit-pregnant theory] *a very small
number of Americans working in the UN are implicated* in these
disclosures." The whole thing is merely one of "various unpleas-
antnesses of the past fortnight." [Emphasis added.]

ITEM. "Unless the President-elect [Eisenhower] . . . makes it
amply clear that he stands with Truman and Acheson [on Korean
policy] the process of unraveling will accelerate." In other words,
Schlesinger warns, the President must double-cross those who
voted for him in order to get rid of the Truman-Acheson policy
which placed Korea outside the defense perimeter of the U.S. and
invited the Communist attack.

Schlesinger blithely told his readers that the Yalta agreement
had no secret clauses, with the exception of Russia's pledge to
enter the Far Eastern conflict after the defeat of Germany. He
carried his myth-making penchant into the American scene on a
1951 Town Meeting of the Air when he asserted: "Mr. Truman,
it is sometimes forgotten, initiated the drive against the internal
Communist threat. The loyalty program was set up way back in
1947 and Hiss and Coplon were indicted by the Department of
Justice long before 1950. The loyalty program was set up, in
point of fact, after strong pressure from the 80th Congress which
Truman so passionately hated. And Truman fought the prosecution of Alger Hiss tooth and nail, calling the case a "red herring"
repeatedly.

On the same program, Schlesinger said, in defense of the Yalta
agreements, "Stalin must have had a hard time explaining to the
Colonel McCormicks of the Soviet Union when he got back what
had happened at Yalta." This assumption, couched in humorous
language, that an opposition in Russia could give the dictator "a
hard time," drew laughter. But a psychiatrist could have an interesting time with it.

This, then, is the picture of Arthur Schlesinger, Jr. This is the
"Pundit in Knee Pants," as a wit acidly remarked—the tabloid
Walter Lippmann, the crypto-socialist who steers the ADA tobog-
gon as it hurtles leftward.

"There he stands right in the middle, between Hank Wallace and Frank Biddle," wrote Morrie Ryskind. The placement is generous. For the vital center is anatomically no center at all, but lodged somewhere in the region of the kidneys. Politically and economically, it can be located between the clenched-fist collectivist state and the WPA of Harry Hopkins. Schlesinger himself placed it most accurately. "In a more fundamental sense," he asked rhetorically, "does not the center itself represent one extreme."

No one will argue this point. The extreme of the "vital center" has placed all the world—with the exception of the ADA, the ritualistic liberals, and the "progressives"—in a political and intellectual ghetto. Those who will not worship the vital center's extremities are thrust into the ghetto, wearing a yellow badge marked "forces of corruption"—Schlesinger's own phrase for those to the right of his center. It represents a new liberalism which brooks no opposition on pain of smear, calumny, and social ostracism.

And the result?

It has made of a potential first class citizen a force for political confusion. It has debased the intellectual currency and plunged the best minds of the country into a fruitless and undignified squabble. It has given aid and comfort to the Communists and their concealed allies.

The Soviet Union brandishes a hydrogen bomb; the Far East sinks into a Red tide; the Western world retreats steadily; victory turns into defeat. But Schlesinger and the "vital center," in a mass *trahison desclercs*, scream against those who fight the Communists with no reservations; they raise the false issue of "McCarthyism"; they see an anti-Communist under every bed; and they pontificate, as Schlesinger has, that "Communist ideas or influence present about the same danger as the snowball did to the fires of hell." Schlesinger strikes at the Communists with the flat of his sword; the cutting edge is reserved for the anti-Communists and for those who proclaim, without equivocation, a belief in the individual's sacred right to freedom.

"I did wish to see these people get what they deserved," Thomas Jefferson once wrote of some minor conspirators, "and under the maxim of the law itself . . . that in an encampment expecting daily attack from a powerful enemy self-preservation is paramount to law, I expected that instead of invoking the law to cover traitors, all good citizens would have concurred in securing them."

These words, ironically, were once cited by Schlesinger. The devil, it is true, can quote Scriptures—but we do not expect him to take them to heart.

Lodge: The Little Man Who Wasn't There

Though there are many others, this perceptive survey of 1964s political version of the 90-day wonder seems to me a particularly good and ample example of the journalistic fact that the author can give cards and spades to the gentlemen of the Left who are supposed to specialize in political insights but who, most often, specialize in nothing more or less than the indulgence of their own fancy fancies. To put it in another perspective, when such a reporter as Murray Kempton takes such a look as this at a member of his party, bells are rung and celebrations celebrated for the fearless objectivity of the man. When, as he does regularly, Toledano takes such looks at the members of his party, the gentlemen of the Left have been known to comment only that he is a conservative sourpuss.

Ambassador Henry Cabot Lodge, Republican ball-carrier for the Democratic Party, has been called the GOP's answer to Soapy Williams, the Grand Old Party-pooper, and the little man who wasn't there. He is all of these things—and much more. For it would be both unfair and unkind not to note that he is today the wonder-boy of American politics.

Both wonder and wonderment have begun to follow him. In Medford, Oregon, the editors of the *Mail Tribune* recently scratched their heads and asked plaintively: "Why should any Republican be attracted to a man who has lost elections, who is a lousy campaigner, who would be the oldest President to be inaugurated since James Buchanan, who is a member of the present Administration, whose views on the issues of the day are completely unknown, and who's 6,000 miles away doing a lousy job of running a nasty little war?"

Echo answers variously. The best guess yet is: "Republican masochism. It would be too much to believe that, in a state which once dumped Harold Stassen for Thomas E. Dewey after a debate in which Mr. Dewey took the soft side of the argument on outlawing the Communist Party, Ambassador Lodge is highly regarded because of his presumed toughness to the Soviets at the United Nations. But whatever the cause of the Lodge rash, even if it is only the latent Tom Sawyerism of the American voter, it is something which must be examined by the politicians as they move towards the important business of the San Francisco convention.

What manner of man is Mr. Lodge? Two stories are told about him. In one, a veteran Republican campaigner says in anguish: "Not only did he insist on a nap every afternoon when he was running for Vice President with Dick Nixon, but he had to climb into his pajamas to get it." In the second, an irate newspaperman sputters: "If he calls me 'my good man' once more, so help me, I'll stuff this notebook down his throat."

Both stories are true. They do not promise a happy campaign for the Republican Party if, by some zany quirk of fate, Mr. Lodge should be nominated. President Johnson will not be defeated by an opponent in Dr. Dentons who treats reporters as if they were flunkies. The press wouldn't like it—and James S. Reston would probably make it a constitutional issue. Though Presidential candidates are far too obsequious to the press, the pendulum can swing too far back.

If is, of course, a fact that the Washington correspondents who will cover Mr. Lodge when and if he returns to seek the nomination actively are predisposed in his favor. There is about the Saigon Sphinx a delicate scent of Liberalism. He was the man who joined in the posse which shot Senator Robert A. Taft in the back during the 1952 Convention. He was one of those who helped raise the cry of "Thou Shalt Not Steal" against a public figure whose integrity had never been challenged until then. The press looks back at this shocking performance with some degree of admiration. But by the dialectics of the political situation, Mr. Lodge will be treated with tenderness only while he stands in opposition to Senator Barry Goldwater. Once the main event has begun, most reporters will find that their affections have been fondly alienated by Lyndon B. Johnson.

The romance will begin to fade once a returning Ambassador Lodge realizes that like Garbo at the advent of talking pictures, he must someday open his mouth. "Lodge Speaks" will be a merited headline. But once the novelty of it has worn off, the bemused voter will begin to give heed to the words and their meanings. At this point, divinity will depart and the criteria of the political market place will once more obtain.

At this point, too, the pundits and press panjandrums will be forced to comment on Ambassador Lodge's past, present, and foreseeable future. They will begin to search his record and to call for declarative judgments from him on everything from Planned Parenthood to Planned Deficits. Biographers will comb newspaper files and the Reader's Guide to Periodical Literature for an index of his views and an insight into the life that has occupied him these 62 years. The search will be an arduous one and the results hardly worth the effort. Henry Cabot Lodge is like the rabbit Harvey. Even ectoplasm has more substance. In his political pronouncements, moreover, he has taken the politician's method of incoherence and carried it a step further to utter vacuity.

The proof of this spectral pudding is amply demonstrated by *Time* Magazine. In August of 1958 and September of 1960, the indefatigable researching teams of that newsmagazine could muster up only the thinnest of biographical fare. In two cover stories—the second largely repeating the first, there are many huzzahs for Mr. Lodge but very few facts about him. It is of interest that Mr. Lodge is descended from six United States senators and that the position of his grandfather on the League of Nations has been thoroughly distorted by the Liberal smearbund. Men with family traditions are personally enriched therefrom. The world of Boston aristocrats from whom Mr. Lodge is

descended contributed much to America. The sense of place has
unquestionably left its mark on him—even pejoratively as in this
tendency to condescend.

But these aspects of Mr. Lodge's family background tell us
little of how he stands today, how he acted in the Senate, or what
his responsibility may be for the murder of Vietnam's President
Diem. Like the lint in the umbilicus, they are useless in telling us
anything about the fabric of his coat.

But directly apposite to the present Lodge boom is one factlet
of his time as Richard Nixon's running mate. A Gallup poll in the
early weeks of the 1960 campaign showed Henry Cabot Lodge
running ahead of Mr. Nixon, John F. Kennedy, and Lyndon
Johnson. Today, the Gallup pollsters are again doing their bit for
Mr. Lodge—but who will prove that they are right today? Perhaps
he napped away his chances in 1960. In any case, a Gallup poll on
a man who—to quote *Time* in 1958—"looks about as much like a
grandfather as Marlene Dietrich looks like a grandmother" may
be amusing but hardly adds to the sum total of our political
knowledge. Neither does the fact that he is "cinematically
handsome." If this is the gauge of a President, Mr. Johnson
doesn't stand a chance against almost the entire field of Republican would-be candidates.

Looking back over the secret life of Henry Cabot Lodge, there
are some discernible milestones. He went to Harvard and was
graduated *cum laude*, a notable achievement when it is recalled
that he did the four years in three. The profession of law was not
for him. On leaving Harvard Square, he took himself to the
gentility of the *Boston Evening Transcript* where, uniquely for
the period, all reporters washed and minded their manners. A
stint with the *New York Herald Tribune* on the Washington staff
and some time as an editorial writer were enough to give him the
training in politics necessary to win election to the Massachusetts
legislature.

In 1936, a great political career seemed to be opening up for
him. Running for the Senate in the year of the great Roosevelt
landslide, Lodge bucked FDR's 174,000 lead in Massachusetts,
toppling James Michael Curley by a plurality of 135,000. As the

seventh senator of his line, he could almost claim membership in the small inner circle which runs the United States Senate and dominates its politics. The Presidential halo which had not settled on the head of a Bay Stater since the days of Calvin Coolidge seemed airborne for the young Mr. Lodge, and the kingmakers beamed on him.

But his record as a legislator, in terms of his impact on the Senate's workings and on measures bearing his name, was a meager one. His colleagues thought him aloof. He was never trusted by the leadership or liked by the Senate rank-and-file. No anecdotes gave color to his public personality—and it is doubtful whether he was ever seen at the New Carroll Arms, across the street from the Senate Office Building, indulging in the convivial drinking which acts as cover for much important legislative business. The Liberals thought him conservative and stuffy. The conservatives thought him Liberal and stuffy. He himself made no secret of his disdain for such roughhewn characters as Senator William Jenner of Indiana or Senator Joseph R. McCarthy of Wisconsin. In the Senate cloakroom, the word used to describe him was "evasive."

The evasiveness was most apparent when, as a Republican member of the Tydings subcommittee investigating Joe McCarthy's charges of Communist infiltration in the government, he was called upon to take a stand against the Democratic majority's steamroller tactics. Throughout those bitter and disillusioning days, the Republicans labored to blast open the inquiry and to get at the facts. But at no point could they count on Mr. Lodge's support. He acted always as if the entire matter were somehow unseemly—and it was only after the Democrats had nailed shut the barn door and thoroughly whitewashed it that Senator Lodge expressed himself and his umbrage. By that time it was too late—and there were some who, perhaps ungenerously, insisted that he planned it that way. The Tydings "investigation"—by the blatancy of its disregard for the stated aims of its mandate—cleared the way for the Senate Internal Security Subcommittee's monumental study into the ways and byways of the Institute of Pacific Relations. It also led to a brief period of

American awareness of the immediate dangers of Communist subversion. But Senator Lodge had little to do with this—and always he seemed to believe that looking into the depravities of the Kremlin's agents in this country was somehow a vulgar pastime for Midwestern louts.

At the outbreak of the Second World War, Senator Lodge resigned his office to enlist in the United States Army thus ringing down the curtain on this phase of the Ambassador's life. The next act is well-known and over-regurgitated. The Eastern Liberal kingmakers in the Republican Party needed a Presidential candidate to stop Senator Taft. From the Chase Bank and other environs of town-hall democracy came the call for Dwight David Eisenhower. The Tom Deweys, Harry Darbys and Jim Duffs labored long in the vineyard. The Paul Revere was Senator Lodge. It would be confounding history to say that he was *the* major Dwightist, but he worked so hard that many considered him the architect of the 1952 convention. His reward was a stunning defeat at the polls where a young congressman with good political connections took Lodge's seat in the United States Senate.

The man who helped elect a President found himself without a job. But this was only a passing misfortune. President Eisenhower appointed him Ambassador to the United Nations and a "personal member" of the Cabinet. As such he played a prominent part in welcoming Khrushchev on his 1959 visit to the U.S. To give Mr. Lodge his due, he did make some telling oratorical points against the Soviets. But oratory has never dented Communist armor. And even as he deplored the Soviet Union's blatant adventurism and disregard of UN rules, Ambassador Lodge could still refer to the Glass Menagerie on the East River as "the world's greatest adventure in building collective strength." The words are English, but the meaning is vague. Like many of Mr. Lodge's other utterances, it has a good ring. But what strength did it refer to—and who was collecting it? The "collective strength" did little to deter the rape of Hungary—a subject which occupied much of the Ambassador's rhetorical energies. Indeed he was so busy blasting away at the Soviets that he was of no help at all to Povl

Bang-Jensen when that UN official was fired for refusing to betray the confidence of Hungarian refugees.

Again ring down the curtain. Haul it up again when Henry Cabot Lodge, unemployed as a result of his failure with Richard Nixon to win the 1960 election and shummed by his party for an incredible boo-boo—the "promise" that a Nixon Cabinet would' include a Negro—appealed for work to President Kennedy. At that time, any hope of returning to electoral office was dim. The appeal to Negro prejudice had cost Mr. Nixon the South and perhaps the election, and the professional politicians wanted no shoot-from-the-hip hired guns on the Republican range. Mr. Kennedy was delighted to share his misfortune in Vietnam with a former Republican Vice Presidential candidate. Mr. Lodge was delighted to find himself once more in a post where he could my-good-man the local talent, whether journalistic or political.

He arrived in Saigon obsessed by the view that only simon-pure democrats should be allowed to battle Communism. Surrounded by the same kind of foreign service officers as those who had convinced Washington that we must jettison Chiang Kai-shek because there was "corruption" in the Kuomintang, Ambassador Lodge joined in gaily with the cabal which engineered the overthrow of the strongly anti-Communist Diem regime and put in a weak-handed group which allowed the Viet Cong Reds to score immediate gains. As a result of the coup, President Diem and his brother-in-law were murdered in cold blood. A second coup was necessary to bail out Ambassador Lodge and the United States. At present, the "nasty little war" continues, American lives are being lost, and Mr. Lodge wanders about the country like something out of a Hollywood movie.

The posture sought now by Lodge's artful dodgers of their candidate as Republicanism at Bay, or Virtue Triumphant, has a somewhat saggy-shouldered look as a result of the Ambassador's activities in Saigon. But what clutches a cold hand to professional political hearts in the Republican Party is Mr. Lodge's complete involvement in the Kennedy-Johnson Administration's second greatest foreign policy fiasco. Had Mr. Kennedy followed the advice given him on January 19, 1961, by the outgoing President, Laos would have been saved from the dangers and humiliations of a Communist-dominated "troika" and the anti-Communist position in Vietnam would not have been undermined. The coup d'état which weakened the resolve of the Vietnamese in their battle against the Viet Cong would never have taken place. By his presence in Saigon—and by his continual silence—Ambassador Lodge gives assent and blessing to policies which should become an important campaign issue for the Republican Party. His silence, moreover, gives rise to the question: Is Mr. Lodge a Republican? In this case, echo doesn't even bother to answer.

The irony of the Lodge candidacy, however, transcends such minor matters as wars for survival or party loyalty. He was projected into the campaign by General Eisenhower whose motives were, as always, pure. But the motives of those who gave Mr. Eisenhower *his* motives are subject to some scrutiny. And they are not as obscure as some would think. The Lodge candidacy was part of a strategy which can be outlined in a series of propositions:

1.   Barry Goldwater must be stopped if the conservative wing of the Republican Party is to be prevented from taking over.

2.   If Nelson Rockefeller can make it, then little goody two shoes.

3.   If Rockefeller cannot make it, then a situation must be created which will allow Nixon to accept the draft of a grateful party.

4.   The Rockefeller weaknesses are so great that someone else must be brought in. Who Else But Nelse must be replaced by Let's Dodge With Lodge.

5.   With substantial financial aid—and the fancy direct-mail campaigns in New Hampshire and Oregon really cost—Mr. Lodge can be the counterpoint to Senator Goldwater's point. But that is as far as it is to go. No convention in its right mind will nominate him.

As of this writing, this strategy is under scrutiny. The emergence of Ambassador Lodge as the pundits' choice has hurt Mr. Nixon badly. It has fragmented the "stop Goldwater" forces. And

it has given some of those who cynically came to the aid of the
Saigon Sphinx delusions of Presidential possibility. Meanwhile,
Senator Goldwater sews up delegates. The little man who wasn't
there, the Republican answer to Soapy Williams (or was it
"Honest Ave" Harriman?), and the Grand Old Party-pooper may
have, in the last analysis, done Barry Goldwater and American
conservatism a service. That, my good man, is funnier than any
dozen elephant jokes. Republican elephants, that is.

National Review
May 1964

The Book Reviewers
Sell Out China

To this day the interlocking directorship of the Asian specialists continues to operate, although with a few new names. And their fame continues to expand by the simple but terrifying device that was exposed in this significant story, i.e. each reviews the other, each extolls the other, each recommends the other and when the other receives new fame he returns the favor and so on and on and on while those lonely men who labor without the benefit of such a claque find it difficult even to get a publisher. In 1966, for instance, when hearings in depth on Asian policy were held in the Senate, the claque completely dominated the witness list while such men as Dixie Walker, George Taylor, and the veritable phalanx of scholars at the Hoover Institution either didn't get a look-in at all or just barely managed to squeeze a word in edgewise.

For the past dozen years, a group of free-wheeling writers and politicians has dominated America's China policy. That this group has labored to make China an arm of the Soviet power may be coincidence—or it may be part of a sharply conceived and shrewdly carried out plan. In either case, the result has been the same.

What is this group and how has it operated? The answer is so deceptively clear that most Americans have rejected it out of hand. Only a few political experts cried havoc, and they were branded a "China lobby" in the pay of fascists and disrupters.

Meanwhile, the real lobby—the four-plus propagandists of a pro-Communist line in Asia—prospered. Its stooges were able to seize such a stranglehold on the State Department's Far Eastern division that to this day, as we slug it out with the Chinese Reds, they are still unbudgeable. Working devotedly at their side has been a book-writing and book-reviewing cabal, busily plugging the old song that Asiatic Communists are all lover-boys who must be "understood" even when they shoot American prisoners in cold blood.

This real lobby is made up of all manner of folk: from Communist purveyors of classified documents (like Philip Jaffe) to eminently respectable diplomats who believe that it is better to bend than to break (like Prof. Philip Jessup); from the ambiguous Owen Lattimore (who advised that we let China and Korea fall to the Reds) to the late unambiguous Agnes Smedley (for years a Soviet spy in Japan). Some, like Jessup, can be accused only of having turned away their heads when the dirty work was being done. Others, like Jaffe, did the work.

It is not the scope of this article to probe the work of the pro-Communist lobby in the government or to page Alger Hiss. Overwhelmingly documented books like Freda Utley's *The China Story* can be consulted for this. The subject here is an analysis of how the pro-Communist cabal took over the book and book-reviewing field and, in matters Chinese, assumed a virtual monopoly.

The statistics alone are horrifying.

Of forty-two major books on China, written since Munich, thirty-one were pro-Chinese Communist, two straddled the issue, and nine were critical of Communism.

Who reviewed those forty-two books? Taking the three journals most important to the book trade—the *New York Times Book Review,* the *New York Herald Tribune Book Section,* and the *Saturday Review of Literature*—this is the breakdown:

Seventh-three reviewers were pro-Chinese Communist.

Twelve reviewers were fence-straddlers—the on-the-one-hand brigade.

Seven reviewers were known to have anti-Communist views.

This of course does not take in weekly magazines like the *Nation* and the *New Republic* which with almost unbroken consistency turned over all books remotely affecting Russia to a pro-Communist coterie—many of them party members or worse.

The pro-Chinese Communist cabal never stooped to hide this control of the leading book sections. The same names appeared over and over in the *Herald Tribune,* the *Times,* and the SRL: Agnes Smedley, Owen Lattimore (he scored a dozen times as reviewer or author), the late Richard Lauterbach, Edgar Snow, Nym Wales (Snow's wife), Richard Watts, Jr., Lattimore's friend Prof. John K. Fairbank (sometimes reviewing Lattimore), T. A. Bisson, Joseph Barnes, and Mark Gayn (arrested in the Amerasia stolen documents case and then released; he filed suit against the *New York World-Telegraph* for calling him a spy but dropped the case).

All of these people were good friends and associates, all propagandists for Mao Tse-tung's "agrarian reformers." A mutual admiration society of such magnitude should have been a public scandal, but no one raised a voice against its monopoly. So unabashed was the back-scratching process that Owen Lattimore placidly reviewed a book published by the Institute of Pacific Relations of which he was an important part for many years.

The prize topper came when Lattimore's tear-jerker, *Ordeal by Slander,* appeared. Though it lauded John Fairbank, the man who organized the Lattimore defense screech, the honorable professor shamelessly accepted an offer from the *Herald Tribune* to review the book. He did it fulsomely, too, in the exact meaning of that word. In scholarly circles, this is usually considered unethical, but none of Fairbank's Harvard colleagues drew back in disgust.

The other side of the coin is similarly etched, but hardly as prettily. For Lattimore and his bully boys did not merely praise their own works to the sky. With dagger and bludgeon, they assassinated any book with a contrary viewpoint. So completely were the book pages of the leading papers taken over by the pro-Chinese Communist cabal that one could predict in advance the fate of an anti-Communist book on China.

No matter how carefully documented, the book was certain to end up quickly in the publishers' overstock pile. The writer would be damned from hell to the Algonquin for "lack of objectivity," his political morals would be impugned, and he would be accused of selling his soul for Chiang Kai-shek's gold. Reviewers who might sympathize with an anti-Communist thesis were carefully screened out. Chinese experts as scholarly as Dr. Karl A. Wittfogel of Columbia University never stood a chance; they were banished to the small magazines—the *New Leader* gave many of them refuge—or lived in silent agony as they watched the betrayal.

The net effect, as Irene Kuhn demonstrated in *The American Legion Magazine* was to make publishers leery of books which parted with the Lattimorean line or assailed the State Department's suicidal Far East policy. What happened in the case of a book which violated the taboo can best be shown in the case of John B. Powell's *My Twenty-Five Years in China.*

Editor of the influential *China Weekly Review,* Powell had remained at his post when the Japanese captured Shanghai. Tossed into a prison camp for the duration, he was deathly ill—a skeleton of a man, both feet gone from Jap torture—when liberated. At the time his book appeared, late in 1945, Powell was dying in Harkness Pavilion. The pro-Chinese Communist cabal could not be moved to sympathy or respect. Three of its members seized Powell's book avidly.

Mark Gayn, just five months away from his *Amerasia* arrest, tore the book apart in the *Saturday Review,* berating the author for "strong prejudices [i.e., opposing Communism] which he never hesitated to air." Annalee Jacoby, a Time-Life Mao-worshipper, scolded Powell in *The Times* for not appreciating the Chinese Reds. Lattimore, pontifical and smug, informed *Herald Tribune* readers that this newspaperman who had spent twenty-five years in China had gotten all his information "second hand." With typical bad taste, he used the review as a medium for praising Edgar Snow's pro-Communist lucubrations.

And what kind of treatment did Lattimore himself get from the reviewers? The Panjandrum's word was never questioned. That his books are mutually contradictory was never noted by

the "experts." Nor did any one of the major reviewers point out
that the line of demarcation between his contradictions was the
Communist Party line, dictated by Moscow, which shifted in
1943 from praise to condemnation of Chiang Kai-shek and the
Nationalist government.

In 1942, the man who had seen in the monster Soviet purge
trials an evidence of "democracy" wrote that Chiang was "a real
genius," one of the great leaders of all time. And, Lattimore
added, China was "a democratic country in the sense that the
(Kuomintang) and the government represented what the vast
majority of the people want."

Some years later, writing about the same period in China's
history, Lattimore was shrilling in reverse that Chiang was
"fascist" and the Kuomintang "a party which owed nothing to
elections or to representative forms of government."

Since the pro-Chinese Communist cabal shifted along with
Lattimore, they found nothing cynical or dishonest about this
re-writing of history. Instead, the adulatory T. A. Bisson (his
political sympathies are the color of a fireman's underwear) said
in the *Saturday Review* of Lattimore's "Solution in Asia" that
"the breath of the future blows through this brief but stimulating
review of Far Eastern issues (which points to) a new and more
powerful role for the U.S.S.R. in postwar Asia."

And Edgar Snow, who but a week previously had told
Saturday Evening Post readers that the Chinese Reds had
renounced all intentions of "establishing Communism in China in
the near future," rhapsodized in *The Times* over Lattimore's
proof that the Russian Revolution was succeeding in Asia because
it "answers to real needs in the conditions of various countries."
Moreoever, he approvingly paraphrased Lattimore, conflict between the U.S.S.R. and the U.S., if it did come, would be our
fault and not Russia's.

When four years later, in 1949, Lattimore published *The
Situation in Asia*–still peddling the same old line–Snow made his
obeisances in the *Herald Tribune*. "A bucketful of sound sense,"
he wrote. Richard Lauterbach, a Time-Lifer closely guarding his
Communist philosophy, couldn't confine himself to buckets. It

was a "treasure house of wisdom," he said in the SRL. A sample:
"He . . . doubts the widely accepted notion that Chiang's defeat
means that the Kremlin can take over China."

In the same issue of the *Saturday Review* that ran Lauterbach's brilliant prophecy, the ubiquitous Snow was lambasting
George Creel, President Wilson's Public Information Officer
during World War I and an uncompromising enemy of Communism. In Creel's *Russia's Race for Asia,* Snow said with a
forthrightness that would lose him no lecture dates, "nearly every
page . . . is distinguished by errors of fact, judgment, and understanding."

Professor Nathaniel Peffer took up the crudgels for good
judgment in *The Times.* A non-Communist who spends so much
of his time battling for the Chinese Reds that it must leave him
little time to meet his classes at Columbia, Peffer found it "a
foolish book." Creel was not to be taken seriously because "he
fears Russia and does not like or trust the Chinese Communists."
In the *Herald Tribune,* another member of the cabal was also
horrified by the "startlingly biased judgments . . . a reductio ad
absurdum of Chiang propaganda."

When Lin Yutang exposed the brutality of the Chinese Reds in
Vigil of a Nation he suddenly saw his great popularity with the
American people vanish. Among the architects of this rejection
was Harrison Forman. Lin had pointed out that in stories from
Yenan, the Red capital, Forman had given to the Communists
whole areas liberated by Chiang's troops. Yet the openly pro-
Chinese Communist Forman felt no compunction about reviewing the book in the *Saturday Review.* And Forman made
good use of the opportunity, panning the book mercilessly. To
write of China and her politics, he stated, was beyond Lin
Yutang's "first hand knowledge."

Brooks Atkinson, on leave from Broadway and not yet
recovered from pro-Communist apologetics, was disturbed because "Dr. Lin denounces the Chinese Communists" and
"repeats the Kuomintang line of propaganda against the Communists." His evaluation for the readers of the Sunday
Times: Prejudice."

For riding Dr. Lin on a rail in the SRL, Forman was rewarded, also in the SRL. His *Report from Red China* was given to Richard Watts, a leading light of the Communist-front Committee for a Democratic Far Eastern Policy. Like Atkinson a play reviewer gone political, Watts was moved by Forman's "evidence" that the Chinese-Communists "form a free and independent body without subservience to Moscow and are not interested in . . . collectivizing China, but in bringing about a unified democratic nation." These gems appeared in the *Herald Tribune.* In the *Times,* Edgar Snow's word for the book was "historic."

The Challenge of Red China, by Gunther Stein (named a Soviet agent in a SCAP intelligence report) was folded to the bosom in *The Times* by Nathaniel Peffer and in the *Tribune* by Lattimore. Said Peffer: "The leaders of the Communists . . . are exceptionally straight-forward, simple, of unquestionable (sic) integrity. . . . (with a) paternal concern for the people over whom they rule." Said Lattimore: "The most up-to-date handbook, amazingly complete."

Six months after he was arrested for espionage, a charge later reduced to "conspiracy to . . . steal and purlion" top secret government documents, *Amerasia* editor Philip Jaffe published *New Frontiers in Asia.* The SRL and *The Times* judged the book for what it was, the *Saturday Review* pointing out its Communist bias. The *Herald Tribune* delivered it into the hand of Foster Rhea Dulles. The high praise he gave it may bear some relation to the fact that Dulles is a contributor to *Spotlight,* the journal of the aforementioned Communist-front Committee for a Democratic Far Eastern Policy. "The United States, (Jaffe) strongly feels, should encourage such progressive forces [as the Communists] ," Dulles reported.

Perhaps the most catalytic book on the Far East was *Thunder Out of China.* Written by two Time-Life correspondents, Theodore White and Annalee Jacoby, and chosen by the Book-of-the-Month Club, it seemed to have a double stamp of respectability. But to ensure its success, the top-flight reviewers of the pro-Chinese Communist cabal were on hand to give it a rousing send-off. Edgar Snow (SRL), Prof. John K. Fairbank (*Times*), and

Richard Watts Jr. (*Tribune*) gave it the highest praise. And their work was not in vain. Conservative businessmen, with little time to read, took its pro-Communist judgments as gospel truth and joined the ranks of the deceived.

In the cabal double embraces were not unusual. When Richard Lauterbach wrote *Danger from the East,* Mark Gayn (in the SRL) called it "one of the most brilliant reporting jobs done since the end of the war." When Gayn published *Japan Diary,* Lauterbach (in the *Tribune*) returned the favor with "in the richest tradition of American journalism." When Prof. Fairbank wrote *The United States and China,* Annalee Jacoby recalled Fairbank's kind words about *Thunder Out of China* and wrote (in *The Times*) that she couldn't "remember another volume which holds . . . as much scholarly information about a single subject."

The tally is almost endless. Bit by bit, and shamelessly, the pro-Chinese Communist cabal created the myth that Moscow's forces in Asia were merely "agrarian reformers," that they had fought the Japanese single-handed, "blockaded" by a vicious Chiang Kai-shek, that they were independent and could be won over to America. Steadily, they undercut the only armies in the field, Chaing's, which blocked the spread of Communism in Asia. Masterfully, they bolstered the tragic State Department policy which led inevitably to the Red invasion of Indo-China, the guerrilla fighting in Malaya, and the slaughter of American troops in Korea.

Perhaps, as he insists, Owen Lattimore was not the architect of this disaster. At the very least he was its chief propagandist. His views permeated the field; his writings blanketed the country. But let us be charitable. If the Soviet super-spy Richard Sorge smuggled a letter out of Japan to Lattimore (as the Willy Foerster affidavit attests), there was probably no skulduggery involved. It may be that Sorge was just forwarding a book review.

The American Mercury
July 1951

The Case of the Reluctant Prosecutor

To be perfectly frank, the conspiratorial theory of history never has appealed to me and the excesses to which it has been carried by some who have seen a Communist plotter under every rug has made it less and less palatable. This is a shame. Undoubtedly there is a substantial amount of conspiracy in our history. And, if there were more instances of careful coverage of it such as this we might, myself included, all be more sensibly aware of it.

Five men kept a studiously casual vigil on New York's lower Fifth Avenue. The streets had that cold, deserted look of Sunday night in any business section, anywhere in the world, The windows of shops and buildings were opaque and sightless.

Night after night, this group of men had rivetted their interest to a splash of light in one office of one building—No. 225 Fifth Avenue. Night after night they had strolled back and forth, hidden in the shadow of doorways, or stood on street corners as if waiting for the bus. Shivering a little in the blustery weather, they had taken their posts, waiting for the lights to go out in the office at No. 225.

On this Sunday night, they felt a small stir of excitement. No. 225 was dark. The men continued their vigil. When the night had moved well past the dinner hour, the office was still dark. One of the men stepped out of the shadows. The others gathered around him.

"This is it," he said. "Let's go." Within minutes, they had made their entry into the building. An assistant superintendent let them into the office which had occupied their attention for so many nights.

The first phase of the notorious Amerasia Case had ended.

It was a case which, for years, would hang like an albatross around the neck of the Administration which began it and then, inexplicably, dropped it. Two congressional committees, one in the House and the other in the Senate, would begin investigations which fumbled the truth and timidly dropped it in a flurry of contradictory statements. Periodically, there would be a clamor in magazines and newspapers for a merciless accounting of the facts. Ramifications of the case would reach into the touchy high echelons of the State and Justice Departments—of the White House itself. Men would rise and men would fall because of it. And the entire course of history in the Far East would be affected by it.

And always the question would arise: Why did the Prosecutor—not a single individual, but the collective forces of Federal law and order—tangle himself in so much reluctance when it came to bringing the Amerasia cabal to book? Why, moreover, did the theft of 1,700 classified documents in time of war fail to arouse the concern of the Attorney General and the White House palace guard which fixed the President's mind in policy matters? And why did politics-as-usual triumph over patriotism and justice? The answer to both the question and its corollaries lay in the events and circumstances of the Amerasia Case itself.

The Case of the Reluctant Prosecutor began in a nondescript building in Washington. From the outside, it looked like any of the old buildings which, in the Capital, are beggared by the imposing white columns of other government structures. Men and women, in mufti or in American and Allied uniforms, passed in and out of its doors. But the operations of the agency which carried on its business there was a military secret, for this was the headquarters of the Office of Strategic Services—the OSS, the nation's top wartime intelligence and espionage organization. It was the OSS which made the first dent in the front of a curious little magazine and its clandestine activities.

In February of 1945, an OSS Far East analyst was flipping through the current issue of Amerasia magazine when his eye fell on an article discussing British-American relations in Thailand. He began reading it, first out of a specialist's curiosity and then with a disturbed sense that he had read much of it before. Whole paragraphs seemed to repeat themselves in his mind. The analyst put the piece down, dug into his files, and came up with a secret report he had written on the same subject. Comparing the two, he found that whole sections of the Amerasia article had been lifted out of the secret document. Not only had the Amerasia writer read the document, it was clear; he must have had it before him as he wrote.

The Far East analyst immediately reported this leakage of classified information to the OSS security chief, Archbold Van Buren. Was it merely a case of indiscretion, Van Buren asked himself, or a clue to subversion and espionage in his own organization? He decided to find out. Hopping a plane for New York, he appeared at the inconspicuous hotel on Eleventh Street where Frank Brooks Bielaski had set up an investigations unit for OSS, which he headed.

Tackling the problem at the government end was impossible. It was determined that the secret document in question had had a distribution of over 50. Counting in the secretaries who also handled it, this made well over 100 people who might have given the report to the Amerasia writer. There was really no way to check quickly and efficiently on the security of so many people. Bielaski decided to work from the other end. He put several investigators on the job of learning all they could about Amerasia, its editors, its policies.

Though Amerasia was widely read among State Department personnel, the investigators learned, it was a small frog even in the small puddle of Far Eastern research. Its readers numbered considerably less than two thousand. An OSS researcher, sent to the Public Library, reported that for some seven years the chairman of the editorial board had been Frederick Vanderbilt Field, the millionaire Communist. Board members and contributors were, with a few exceptions, either demonstrably pro-Communist or generally sympathetic to the Communist position in the Far East.

A further check disclosed that Amerasia was an unofficial off-shoot of the "respectable" Institute of Pacific Relations, of which the Senate Internal Security subcommittee was to conclude in 1952 that it "disseminated and sought to popularize false information . . . originating from Communist and Soviet sources." There was a clear "interlocking of personnel" in the Amerasia and IPR organizations. But what gave OSS investigators their first real jolt was the material they dug up on the editor and owner, Philip Jaffe.

From government security files, they learned that Jaffe was a Communist, though his actual membership could not be determined. Under the name of J. W. Phillips, he had edited an outright Communist magazine, China Today. He had contributed large sums of money to the Communist Party, was an intimate of the then Communist chieftain Earl Browder, and frequented the Soviet consulate in New York and the Soviet Embassy in Washington. It was Jaffe's money—he was the owner of a profitable nonunion printing plant and a wealthy man—which kept the magazine going despite its sizable deficit. His co-editor, Kate Mitchell, had a record of Communist-front affiliations.

All of this was interesting, but it did not solve Bielaski's problem. He decided to search the Amerasia offices at night for the stolen document—a procedure sanctioned by precedent and probably by law. If the document were found, he reasoned, the OSS could begin to move against Amerasia's editors and to plug a leak in wartime security. On this long chance, the decision was made. A night surveillance was set up and the long wait began.

On the night of March 11, when for the first time activity ceased in the Amerasia offices, Bielaski gave the order to enter. With him were Brendon P. Battle and William J. Losti, both ex-FBI agents; Olaf Oleson, a onetime investigator for R. H. Macy & Co.; and an expert on locks from the Office of Naval

Intelligence. Bielaski was prepared for a long and difficult search in the Amerasia suite. He scattered his men throughout the rooms, taking the front room for himself. He had just begun going through a pile of copy and dummy sheets, when one of his men interrupted, excitement in his voice.

"We think you better come back here," he said. "We found some stuff you ought to see. Something is going on back there."

Bielaski followed the investigator down the corridor. On the right was a photographic darkroom containing elaborate photocopying equipment. It was hardly the set-up, Bielaski noted, for a magazine which published no photographs and ostensibly devoted itself to scholarly matters. He gave the room a fast scrutiny and continued down the corridor. At the rear, there were two offices—Kate Mitchell's and Philip Jaffe's. On Jaffe's desk were some twenty photocopies of documents, not quite dry. Bielaski was interrupted again, this time by Oleson.

"I think you had better come in the library," Oleson said. "I have something to show you."

The library table was covered with documents and photocopies of documents. Oleson pointed to a large manila envelope.

"You haven't seen anything yet," he said. "Let me show you what's in the envelop. Bielaski noticed that across its face, written cater-corner, was "John Hersey," the name of a famous author and newspaperman. Inside the envelope, each with the newspaperman's name on it, were at least a dozen secret documents. Before Bielaski could read them, Oleson said:

"Wait a minute. You are looking at the wrong place. Look in between them."

On newspaper copy paper were typed six documents, all marked "Top Secret." One of the documents, according to Bielaski's report of April 12, 1945, when the search was still vivid to him, "dealt with the disposition of the Japanese Fleet subsequent to October 1944, giving the location and class of each ship. The second document dealt with the schedule and targets for bombing in Japan." There was one document which meant nothing to him at the time, but which he recalled after the Hiroshima and Nagasaki raids. It was marked "A" bomb.

The search continued. Behind a door, the OSS men found a bellows-type suitcase stamped "P.J.J." and two briefacses, all locked. The Naval Intelligence expert opened the locks. All three were packed with original secret documents. Bielaski spread them out on a table. In the pile, there were documents from Naval Intelligence, Army Intelligence, British Intelligance, the State Department, OSS, the Office of Censorship, the Office of War Information. Some of the documents were up to 150 pages long. All of them bore an official stamp warning that unauthorized possession was a violation of the Espionage Act.

And there, with these papers, was the OSS document they had been searching for.

By 2:30 a.m., the OSS team had tidied up the Amerasia offices, relocked the suitcase and the briefcases, and departed—leaving everything as they had found it—or almost. Of the estimated 400 documents they had found in the office, Bielaski took those which had originated in OSS and several others from the State Department.

"No one can possibly miss these," he said to himself. "If I go back to Washington without proof of what I've seen, they'll say, 'The man's crazy.'" For the systematic and wholesale pillage of America's military and diplomatic secrecy was enough to throw off balance even an experienced counterespionage agent. Frank Bielaski was taking proof with him both to convince his superiors and to reassure himself.

A plane rushed him back to Washington. From the airport, he went straight to OSS headquarters. One by one, for dramatic effect, Bielaski laid the recovered documents on the desk of Security Chief Van Buren. The climax to the performance came when Bielaski handed his superior a paper which revealed the nation's most closely guarded military secret: MAGIC, the code name for a magnificent Navy operation which had broken the Japanese code just before World War II. Through MAGIC, the U.S. had been privy to Japan's diplomatic secrets before Pearl Harbor. It had allowed Washington to intercept the signal, ignored or misunderstood, that the sneak attack was about to be launched. And in every important naval engagement of the Pacific fighting, it had allowed the Navy to have advance knowledge of Japanese strategy. The details of MAGIC were found in the Amerasia office.

That evening, Van Buren got through to Brigadier General William Donovan, head of OSS. Since the documents recovered from Amerasia bore the receipt stamp of the State Department, Donovan decided that Secretary of State Edward Stettinius should be the first to be told. Less than 24 hours after Bielaski had entered the Amerasia offices, Van Buren, Donovan, and Assistant Secretary of State Julius Holmes met in the Stettinius suit at the Wardman Park Hotel in Washington.

"Good evening, Ed," Donovan said to Stettinius. "I've got something here that will be of great interest to you." He handed the documents to the Secretary of State who looked at the headings and glanced over them as Donovan told him of Bielaski's search of the Amerasia offices. When Donovan had finished speaking, Stettinius turned to Holmes and made a cryptic remark.

"Good God, Julius," he said. "If we can get to the bottom of this we will stop a lot of things that have been plaguing us."

His sense of urgency was translated into official cognizance. At his insistence, James V. Forrestal, the Secretary of the Navy, and other cabinet-rank figures in the Administration conferred. It was agreed that only the FBI could cope with a case of this magnitude and seriousness. Within four days, the case was turned over to Director J. Edgar Hoover. The FBI was already overtaxed by its wartime duties of counterespionage and anti-sabotage work. The security of nuclear experiments by the Manhattan Project—and the first hints that this security had been breached by "idealistic" scientists—was one of the bureau's greater concerns. But Hoover yanked 75 special agents from other assignments and appointed one of his assistants, Myron Gurnea to direct the investigation.

Philip Jaffe, the Amerasia editor, was put under 24-hour surveillance—and the Case of the Relectant Prosecutor went into its third phase.

There are no cloaks and daggers in the FBI. Each man knows that it is neither heroics nor extraordinary cunning which succeed, but the patient and intelligent teamwork of trained men—the long hours of surveillance, the minute search into a suspect's past and present, the careful evaluation of the pertinent and the irrelevant, the piecing together of evidence until an airtight case is built up and handed to the Attorney General for prosecution. Several times during the war—notably in the cases of Arthur Alexandrovitch Adams and the jet-propulsion spy Schevchenko—the FBI had gone through this painstaking process. Then the State Department had stepped in, barring arrests because prosecution might annoy the Soviet Union and allowing the guilty to escape.

In the Amerasia affair, however, the State Department had seemingly put aside its usual coy worry over Soviet sensibilities. Whatever his other shortcoming, Secretary Stettinius was a patriotic American; he had approved FBI action. Under Secretary of State Joseph C. Grew, who for much of this period was Acting Secretary, was so scrupulous that he asked not to be given the names of suspects until arrests were made. State Department personnel were involved, he realized, and he wanted to make sure that possible feelings of friendship did not interfere with the investigation.

Thus reassured, the Bureau moved in. It started out with one tremendous advantage: knowledge that the stolen government documents were being funneled through the Amerasia offices for photocopying before transmission. It therefore knew that one or more couriers were running a shuttle service between New York and Washington. No. 225 Fifth Avenue was the center of the apparatus; the State Department was the source of information. The procedure to be followed was a classical one.

Men were posted outside the Amerasia office. Every person who entered the premises became a subject of inquiry, to be discarded if investigation showed him to be a legitimate and demonstrably innocent visitor. In this manner, the FBI began building up its list of suspects, and with it the evidence that could convict in a court of law. Philip Jaffe's peregrinations were the most fruitful. Unconsciously, he led the FBI to some fifteen people whose background and activities warranted individual surveillance. They were, for the most part, State Department employees. All of them had records of close association with the Institute of Pacific Relations.

The records of the Amerasia case occupy thirteen fat volumes in FBI files. Like all such records, they are a meticulous account of the normal activities of a group of people under round-the-clock scrutiny—when out of the house, what restaurants eaten at, what movies or plays seen and with whom, what friends encountered, what love affairs indulged in—coupled to those actions which, seemingly humdrum, are the warp and woof of the conspiratorial pattern. Of the suspects, five led all the rest as the case developed.

Two of them were Amerasia's co-editors, Philip Jaffe and Kate Mitchell, in whose offices the OSS had found the first batch of incriminating documents. Jaffe, the FBI discovered, had been in close association with Agnes Smedley at the time when she was most actively working with Richard Sorge's Soviet spy ring in China and Japan. He had, at least once, penetrated with Owen Lattimore into Yenan, the inaccessible capital of the Chinese Communists. In Yenan, he had been on terms of gentle camaraderie with Mao Tse-tung and Chu Teh, the leaders of the Red camarilla. Jaffe led the FBI to the other three.

Just five days after the FBI entered the case, Jaffe made one of his frequent trips to Washington. He was met in the lobby of the Statler Hotel by Lieut. Andrew Roth, USNR, and Emmanuel Sigurd Larsen of the State Department. Jaffe and Larsen were carrying briefcases, Roth a large manila envelope. The three drove away in Jaffe's car. Larsen was dropped at his office. Jaffe and Roth drove by what the FBI described as a "circuitous route" to the Library of Congress. They remained parked on the east side of the Library, then drove to Roth's apartment where they left the car. That evening, Mark Gayn entered the picture.

Who were these people?

Roth had been a contributor to Amerasia and a researcher for the IPR in his civilian days. He frequented the Communist-front Washington Book Shop. As a student of the College of the City of New York, he had been known as a fellow traveler. Despite a "totally adverse" report, prepared by the Office of Naval Intelligence, he had been commissioned in the Navy and assigned to the sensitive job of serving as liaison between the State Department and the Office of Naval Intelligence. How Roth was able to get a Naval Intelligence assignment after Naval Intelligence had tried to keep him out of the Navy became one of the mysteries of the Amerasia case.

Attempts to discover the source and nature of the influence exerted on the Navy were met with the kind of distressed silence which is more tell-tale than a noncommital answer. Privately, it was conceded that the pressure had come from the White House which, in the person of Lauchlin Currie—a Presidential assistant with Far East connections and IPR attachments—was later to intercede for the Soviet agent Nathan Gregory Silvermaster. The FBI knew one thing: Jaffe had openly boasted that Roth's commissioning was his doing.

Larsen was an Old China Hand. He had worked in and around the Chinese government, scavenging in that tragic country's vast bureaucracy. Larsen's admitted record was dubious—police spy, strong-arm boy, violator of extraterritorial treaties. The FBI discovered that he had been forced to resign from the Chinese Postal Service, that he had misbehaved as an employee of the British-American Tobacco Company, and that he had deserted his first wife and child. With this to recommend him, he had become a protege of Mortimer Graves, head of the American Council of Learned Societies. Through Graves, he had gotten a Rockefeller Foundation Scholarship and a job in Naval Intelligence handling classified materials. In 1944, he had transferred to the State Department.

Gayn was a Manchurian-born Russian, educated in Soviet schools in Vladivostock, who had been associated with Chinese revolutionary student groups in Harbin. In the United States, he had worked for the newspaper PM, his articles and stories always streaked with a tender regard for the Soviet Union. Gayn was free-lancing at the time of the Amerasia investigation. An article, accepted by *Collier*'s at the time he was under surveillance, was published with an editor's note that the material came from "confidential reports from various diplomatic and military sources." Significantly, it dealt with a subject covered by one of the documents which had been seen in the Amerasia offices by Bielaski: the bombing of Japan. The FBI also learned that Gayn was in and out of the OWI offices in New York. He had access to classified materials there.

Surveillance reports show that during April, May, and June, there were an unusual number of meetings among the members of the suspected group. At most of these encounters, manila envelopes were passed to Jaffe or returned by him to the suspects. Sometimes there were several such transfers of material in one day. On April 12, 1945, Mrs. Andrew Roth visited the Amerasia office. She was carrying a large manila envelope when she entered but was empty-handed when she left. She later denied having visited the magazine.

An FBI agent trailed Mark Gayn when he left the Amerasia office. The two men boarded a bus together, the FBI man seating himself behind Gayn. With hardly any concern, Gayn reached into his briefcase and pulled out several typed sheets. They were stamped "secret" and later identified by the FBI man, who had peered over Gayn's shoulder, as government property. On the face of the document, the agent was able to spot the standard stamped warning that illegal or improper possession was a violation of the Espionage Act.

The FBI was not guessing in its reports that the flow of documents to the Amerasia office was continuing. Shortly after moving into the case, it had made a quick search of the Amerasia premise. The 400 documents examined by Bielaski's men were no longer there. At first, the Bureau believed that the apparatus had been warned or had noticed some suspicious disarray after the OSS search. But a later entry by the FBI found the office again crammed with classified documents.

On April 18, the FBI advised Assistant Secretary of State Holmes and Mathias Correa that it was ready to present a case for prosecution. Correa, an assistant to Navy Secretary James Forrestal, and Holmes requested that the investigation be continued for another sixty days so that both Navy and State could be certain that other employees of those departments were not involved. The FBI agreed. Within 24 hours, the case had developed a new lead. The Amerasia Five had grown to the Amerasia Six.

In the lobby of the Hotel Statler in Washington, Philip Jaffe met John Stewart Service of the State Department. Service was a Foreign Service Officer who had served in China in various consulates, had risen to the rank of secretary of the United States Embassy, and had built up a considerable reputation among left-oriented officials of the State Department. As political officer to General Joseph Stilwell, he had exerted considerable influence on American correspondents in China and on the American military. Along with Stilwell, he was responsible for the "hate Chiang Kai-shek" attitude of many who traveled out to Chungking. Service's reports to the department during the war years had brutally undercut the Chinese Nationalists, praised the "democracy" of the Chinese Communists, and described their program as one of "agrarian reform" and "civil rights."

The meeting between Service and Jaffe had much of the strange about it. Service had never met the Amerasia editor before. From the start, he felt an irking antipathy to Jaffe. Yet at this first encounter, he brought with him copies of classified reports which he had written—reports which he had refused to show newspapermen like Brooks Atkinson of the *New York Times* but which he allowed Jaffe to read and eventually to carry off to New York. The next day, Service spent the morning in Jaffe's room at the Statler. Subsequently, when he traveled to New York, he stayed over at the home of Mark Gayn—a man he had met but once and casually through Jaffe.

The meeting with Jaffe assumed considerable and shocking importance for the FBI. Agents had planted a microphone in Jaffe's room and recordings were made of what was said there. In the course of a discussion of political, military, and policy matters, Service was heard to warn: "Well, what I said about the military plans is, of course, very secret." On another occasion, Jaffe pressed Service for a bit of strategic military information on a topic then under wide public discussion: Did the United States intend to invade the Chinese mainland?

"I don't think it has been decided," Service answered. "I can tell you in a couple of weeks when Stilwell gets back." The FBI was counting on an indictment of conspiracy to commit espionage. Service, it believed, met the requirements.

FBI "routine" picked up a valuable witness—Annette Blumenthal, an IPR typist. At Jaffe's orders, she had innocently typed copies of a number of classified documents. Miss Blumenthal talked freely to the FBI agents who interviewed her, identified several secret documents as among the papers Jaffe had given her to copy, and agreed to testify.

By May 29, 1945, the FBI had completed its case against the Amerasia Six—Jaffe, Kate Mitchell, Gayn, Roth, Larsen, and Service. The top people in the Bureau felt that they had gathered enough evidence to link the six in a "conspiracy to commit espionage" indictment. With such an indictment, each individual case gathered strength from the overall evidence. On that day, the complete Amerasia file was turned over to the then Assistant Attorney General in charge of the Criminal Division, Tom Clark, who assigned James McInerney, a special assistant to the Attorney General, to handle the case.

McInerney was fully briefed by FBI representatives. They reviewed for him the nature of the evidence and told him precisely how it was gathered and what investigative procedures were employed. With this knowledge, he authorized the next step—arrest and prosecution of the six. Years later, he was to plead with two congressional committees that the evidence was weak and that it could not be used in a court of law—but on May 29, he voiced no objections.

Two days after the Justice Department took over the case, it had squeaked to a halt. McInerney informed the Bureau that it was to hold the arrests in abeyance, pending the termination of the UNO conference in San Francisco. Secretary Forrestal, whose job was not diplomacy, had warned Tom Clark that the arrests of six Americans might anger the Russians and hurt the negotiations for a United Nations charter. Who put this idea in Forrestal's head is another one of the minor Amerasia mysteries. His objections came to nothing. Assistant Secretary of State Julius Holmes informed President Truman that the Justice Department had been called off, the President called the FBI to order in energetic terms all necessary action. He was concerned over the Amerasia leaks and over the problem of Communist subversion—a concern he learned to temper as he gained White House experience.

The FBI waited now for an opportunity to make simultaneous arrests of the suspects when they were at home or—in the case of Jaffe and Miss Mitchell—in their offices so that a lawful search, incident to the arrests, could be made of premises. FBI agents had previously entered Larsen's apartment to check his typewriter—an entry which was subsequently to offer a feeble but sufficient excuse for the Justice Department to fumble the case.

On the night of June 6, the Justice Department rounded up the six suspects. Roth had been summarily suspended by the Navy that same day. When he was arrested, a Navy officer accompanied the FBI special agent in order to ritualize the act by ripping the gold buttons from Roth's uniform. Why Roth was allowed to beat a Navy court-martial which would have made him subject to the death penalty has remained a more guarded secret than the details of the atomic bomb.

The FBI agents who went to Larsen's apartment asked him if he had any classified documents there. He admitted that he had and turned some over to the men taking him in custody. In his presence, they made a further search and found other documents in a dresser drawer. Larsen then claimed that he had no idea how they had gotten there. In all, the FBI found 270 documents in his apartment.

In the Amerasia offices, they found 467 more—in Jaffe's desk and in Miss Mitchell's filing cabinet. When arresting officers called on Gayn, they found him "apparently preparing to flee the country." The Larsen and Amerasia documents were of varying degrees of military and diplomatic importance. For example: "Very Secret—One Reason Why Wedemeyer Returned To

Washington" including a memorandum to the Joint Chiefs of Staff (in Larsen's apartment); "Secret—Chaing Kai-shek's Treatment of the Kwangsi Clique" signed by John Stewart Service (in the Amerasia office); "Secret—Yen Hsi-Shan's Dealings With the. Japanese" signed by John Stewart Service (in the Amerasia office); a Military Intelligence Division report entitled "Air-Field, Seaplan Anchorages" pertaining to Japan, Korea, and Formosa (in the Amerasia office).

The following morning, *The New York Times* gave page one prominence to the arrests:

FBI SEIZES 6
AS SPIES, TWO
IN STATE DEPARTMENT

The FBI laboratory had been busy all that night processing the documents and other papers seized in the arrests. A report made by D. Milton Ladd, assistant to J. Edgar Hoover, detailed this work:

Laboratory examination of material disclosed latent fingerprints of Kate Mitchell, Mark Gayn, and Emmanuel Larsen [on the documents recovered]. One document contained six latent fingerprints of Mark Gayn, one latent fingerprint of Jaffe, and one latent fingerprint of Emmanuel Larsen, indicating that all three individuals had handled that particular one. Typewriting examinations disclosed that a number of those documents in Jaffe's possession were typed by Annette Blumenthal and several were typed on a machine belonging to Mark Gayn. Through typewriting comparisons it was further determined that two items recovered in the offices of Amerasia were carbon copies of items recovered in the possession of Emmanual Larsen.

A handwriting examination disclosed three items in the known handwriting of Andrew Roth and a large number of documents which bore the handwriting of Emmanuel Larsen. Most of the documents recovered were definitely determined to be of Government origin. . . . They originated primarily with the State Department, Navy Department, Office of Strategic Services, Office of War Information, Military Intelligence, and Foreign Economic Administration. The subject matter of these documents included military as well as political information.

Admissions, both oral and written, made by the subjects reflected
they were fully aware of the fact that they possessed confidential
government documents ... containing wartime secrets. ... We knew
then of the Communist connections of Jaffe and had every right to
assume that the information would have been used against the best
interests of the United States.

The arrest of six American on an espionage charge exploded
over the nation, eerie and startling as a Verey light. The contours
of a political no-man's-land were suddenly illuminated. The
Communist threat seemed hardly as funny as the sophisticated
wisecracks about seeing a Communist under every bed. People
who had taken as truth the government's reassurances that Russia
and the Communists were allies and friends faced a new
verity: treason. The proportions of the conspiracy gave it
another dimension which the average citizen could not quite
grasp.

But behind the steel doors of the Communist Party's inner
sanctum, on the notorious Ninth Floor of 135 East 12th Street in
New York, the American Politburo knew that disaster had joined
the circle. The first reaction of the Communist leaders was one of
panic. They thought immediately of denouncing Jaffe as a
Japanese spy, thereby ridding themselves of his taint. This was a
little too extravagent, even for the Red Machiavellis. The next
plan was to instruct Andrew Roth to make contact with Alger
Hiss—occupied then with starting off the United Nations on the
wrong foot—and to have him intercede with the Secretary of
State on behalf of the arrested six. After some discussion, this too
was rejected. Hiss was too important an apparatus man to risk on
such a venture. There is sworn testimony in the files of congressional committees which indicates that the final decision was to
hand the assignment to Owen Lattimore. As a semi-private
citizen, it was felt, he could drop a word here, pull a string there,
for the Amerasians.

Simultaneously, a double strategy was mapped out: Party
members and their dupes on newspapers and radio were instructed to play up the Amerasia arrests as (1) an attack on
"freedom of the press" and (2) as a spite plot cooked up by

Acting Secretary Grew to discredit critics of his policies. Grew was to be further smeared as a dark reactionary who wished to maintain the Japanese militarists in power after the defeat of Japan. The Amerasia case was to be described as the first engagement in a battle to drive the "liberals" out of the State Department. The "liberals" had long since laid the groundwork for this propaganda line; throughout the prepwar and war days, they had denounced the State Department as a center of "black reaction" sabotaging the efforts of a well-meaning President Roosevelt.

Heretofore, Grew and his right-hand man Eugene Dooman—two able, experienced, and honorable career diplomats and, incidentally, staunch opponents of Soviet and Japanese expansionism in Asia—had been the targets of polemicists in the Communists press. Suddenly, the same sort of attack began to spot the columns of the legitimate press. Carefully planted and disguised Communists, aided by the indiscriminate liberals, were as always able to pump up a spurious hysteria in the media of mass communication—and as always their colleagues accepted the illusory as the real. Grew, who had conscientiously refused to know the names of the suspects before the arrests, was accused in legitimate newspapers of having plotted the case in order to suppress a forthcoming book by Roth which "exposed" him. The New York Herald-Tribune, a Republican newspaper then under the Svengali-like influence of Joseph Barnes, in a muddled editorial ascribed the arrests to "Red-baiting" and charged that anyone in the government "to the political left of the State Department." must "maintain a mouse-like quiet." The New York Post published a series of articles by Andrew Roth, both self- and Amerasia-serving.

Four days after the Amerasia arrests, Owen Lattimore wrote to President Truman asking for an appointment. On July 3, he was closeted with the President. The only account of what went on in the executive office that day comes from Lattimore himself. Among other things, he has conceded, he urged the President to get rid of State Department officials who had backgrounds of service in Japan (Grew had been Ambassador to

Tokyo, Dooman had been his counselor in the Embassy) and to replace them with career men from the State Department's Chinese section—the section, it might be added, which delivered China to the Communists. Lattimore kept this visit a closely guarded secret until, in 1952, he was forced under oath to divulge the fact that it had occurred, as well as a grudging and partial account of what had been said.

Roth's articles in the *New York Post*, accusing Grew of "sowing the seeds for a third world war"—the standard charge— gave the public a first class red herring to sniff after. The real work was done in Washington. So powerful were the forces working against prosecution that a State Department public relations man, Tom Blake, let it be known to newspaper friends that the "fix" was in. James M. Mitchell, co-editor Kate Mitchell's uncle, had powerful political connections. He put his Buffalo law firm on the case and dispatched a member to Washington to confer with Justice Department lawyers. Subsequently, one of the government attorneys on the case was hired by the Mitchell law firm.

Representative Emanuel Celler, elected to Congress on the Democratic and pro-Communist American Labor Party tickets, called on Attorney General Tom Clark. Cellar's law partner, Arthur Sheinberg, acted as Philip Jaffe's attorney. Mortimer Graves, who had gotten Larsen into the Office of Naval Intelligence, gave him a $75-a-week job to tide him over until the case blew over. He also helped create a fund, to which State Department people contributed, for Service's defense. Service himself went to see Lauchlin Currie for help and advice. Currie was a Presidential assistant who had successfully blocked an attempt to get N. Gregory Silvermaster, a Soviet spy, out of government service and who had entrusted Owen Lattimore with handling his personal mail at a time when Currie was out of Washington. And Currie sent Service to see Thomas Corcoran—"Tommy the Cork"—a tremendously powerful figure in New Deal Washington.

Two things happened at this point: Attorney General Tom Clark took all the Amerasia files out of the office of his appointee, Assistant Attorney General in charge of the Criminal

Division Theron Lamar Caudle, a man loyal to Clark but unpredictable in matters which might be morally or politically dangerous. And, for reasons which have never been explained, the charge was reduced from conspiracy to commit espionage, which neatly tied all six suspects together, to illegal possession of government property. This latter step automatically destroyed the case against John Stewart Service. Though his activities fitted into the scope of conspiracy, subject to adjudication, he had taken no illegal possession of government property.

After some delay, the Amerasia case was presented to a Federal grand jury in Washington. Until the minutes of that grand jury are opened, only the Justice Department and the members of the panel will know precisely what went on during its secret deliberations. This much has been divulged, however:

The jury was led to believe, by government attorneys Robert Hitchcock and James McInerney, that the stolen documents "could be seen in almost every magazine and newspaper office in New York." The grand jury was never told of Jaffe's Communist affiliations. Service was not, it has since been admitted, given a penetrating examination. Mark Gayn told the jury that he was merely a working newspaperman, going about his normal business. He said that he had gotten material from Jaffe, but merely unclassified typewritten memoranda. And he swore that he had never seen any government documents. That an FBI man had seen him holding one such document, with a top secret stamp, and that his fingerprints had been found on others taken from the Amerasia office at the time of Jaffe's arrest was seemingly of such little relevance that the grand jury was not informed. Brushing aside the matter of fingerprints again, the Justice Department decided that Kate Mitchell's only culpability lay in her editorial relationship with Philip Jaffe.

Despite the lackadaisical charity of the Justice Department, the grand jury brought in indictments against Larsen, Jaffe, and Roth. Service, Miss Mitchell, and Gayn were no-billed and released. It was no understatement when J. Raymond Walsh, then a fellow-traveling radio commentator, broadcast that Service's arrest had "brought some exceedingly powerful people within the government to his defense." Walsh never elaborated on this statement—nor did anyone ever press him. Like so many other aspects of the Amerasia case, it was another arrow pointing down a road which no one dared to take.

The Reluctant Prosecutor—in the persons of Hitchcock and McInerney and Tom Clark—now had three indictments to take into court. Under every law and every legal precedent set by the Supreme Court, the cases against Jaffe, Larsen, and Roth were ironclad. The documents and papers seized in the Amerasia offices were evidence enough to bring the three men to trial and—granting a normal reaction by the trial jury—to get a conviction. There was a possibility that the courts might rule that the FBI's entry into the Amerasia offices and the Larsen apartment, prior to the arrests, was illegal. But this would do no damage to the government's case. Federal doctrine, as outlined in the classic text Wigmore on Evidence, is very clear on this point.

Evidence gathered through illegal entry, in normal cases, would usually be considered "tainted" and inadmissible in court. But in the Amerasia case, the entry had been made to recover stolen government property involving the national interest and held illegally by the defendants. Therefore, whether the illegal entry rule applied was a highly debatable matter. The issue, moreover, was irrelevent since illegal entry could only "taint" the evidence taken from the personal premises of the defendant against whom it would be used. Even if the courts were to rule that the entry into Larsen's apartment had been improper, "tainting" the evidence found there, the documents recovered from the Amerasia offices were, under the rule, admissible in any litigation against Roth or Larsen. This same evidence, since it came not from Jaffe's home but from a corporate entity— Amerasia—could also be used against Jaffe. The question of "taint" was, therefore, not one which a lawyer would take seriously.

This was the status of the Amerasia case on the eve of the trial. But the Reluctant Prosecutor would not have it so.

On September 28, 1945, Larsen's lawyer went into court with a motion to suppress all the evidence against his client and to quash the indictment. He was armed with affidavits to prove that the FBI had entered Larsen's home prior to the arrest. That Larsen's lawyer should have so moved was natural. No good lawyer fails to use any tactic in the defense of a client, even if it is a long shot, and his was a textbook maneuver which might serve some purpose in an appeal. The routine procedure at this point would have been a thorough study of legal precedent by the Justice Department and a brief to present to the court, countering the Larsen motion. As a matter of fact, FBI and Justice Department attorneys were assigned to prepare such a brief. But before it had been completed—in fact almost before they had gotten down to work—McInerney and Hitchcock demonstrated that their reluctance cut only one way. They called in Jaffe's trial lawyer, Albert Arent, and offered him what he had been seeking for some time: a deal. In return for a guilty plea, the government agreed not to press for a jail sentence but simply to ask for a $5,000 fine.

On September 29, 1945—the day after the Larsen motion—the government and the defense went into court. It was a Saturday and no reporters were present to publicize the proceedings. After the usual preliminaries, the case was laid before Judge Proctor. Arent delivered a short but heart-warming talk in which he painted his client Jaffe as a scholar and a patriot.

"If Mr. Jaffe has transgressed the law," he said, "it seems he has done so from an excess of journalistic zeal." There was, he added, "no intent to jeopardize the welfare of his country."

Then Hitchcock rose to tell the court that he agreed "in substance" with Arent's evaluation of Jaffe. He asked for "less than five minutes" to present the government's case. In those minutes, he assured Judge Proctor that Jaffe had taken the documents merely to increase Amerasia's circulation. Not only was there "no evidence" that Jaffe had meant "injury or embarrassment" to the government, he added, but there was positive evidence to show that Jaffe's intent was, "quite to the contrary," innocent. (Five years later, Hitchcock was to state under oath that he had not mentioned Jaffe's Communist affiliations because he had been certain that Judge Proctor had read about them in the newspapers!) And he never described to the court the importance or the secrecy of the stolen documents.

Proctor took both Arent and Hitchcock at their word that there had been no thought or act which "had a tendency to injure the government." He made it very clear that he was relying on Hitchcock's evaluation of Jaffe's loyalty when he added: "It would make quite a difference to me if I did not have that assurance." The Arent-Hitchcock deal for a $5,000 fine was also forgotten by the Reluctant Prosecutor of the pleasant and unique litigation. Jaffe was fined $2,500. Thirty-four days later, the case of Larsen came up. It was equally brief and amicable. Hitchcock again assured the court that "there was no element of disloyalty involved" in the Amerasia case. The same Jaffe he had exculpated in the earlier proceedings was now described as the "corrupter" of Larsen who pleaded *nolo contendere*. He was fined $500, the money coming out of Jaffe's pocket.

This left the case of Lieut. Roth. The evidence against him was in no wise "tainted." The Justice Department had his fingerprints on stolen documents and memos in his handwriting. But the file on Roth remained cozily locked up in Attorney General Tom Clark's office. The heat was off and the Justice Department, presumably, lost interest. It dropped the case completely, and the indictment was dismissed. Five years later, Justice Department lawyers "explained" that they had decided not to prosecute after Philip Jaffe gave his co-conspirator Roth a clean bill of health. There were other scandals to occupy the public—and those men in the State Department who might have pressed for prosecution were safely out of the government.

So ended the legal phase of the Amerasia case. Throughout this phase, Assistant Secretary of State Dean Acheson looked on with disapproval, much to the satisfaction of the *Daily Worker* which hailed him as "one of the more forward-looking men in the State Department." While the Amerasia case had languished in the courts, the political issues had been drawn—a clearcut struggle between the pro- and anti-Communist forces in the department. Roosevelt had maintained a politician's balance between the two forces. A bewildered Harry S. Truman did not even know that they existed. The battle for control of the State Department was beyond his comprehension and he had already begun to fall under the influence of the Acheson clique. Only the Communists were fully aware of what they were doing—and what they wanted. Behind the Aesopian language of their press, they reported the struggle.

The day after the Amerasia arrests, the *Daily Worker* had begun calling for the removal of James Clement Dunn, a career diplomat of high standing whose crime was that he was "one of the most ardent anti-Sovieteers in the Department." Nelson Rockefeller, another assistant secretary, who had promoted the "good neighbor policy," was also on the ax-list. Averell Harriman and Admiral Leahy, the President's personal chief of staff, also came into the line of fire—Harriman because he was suspicious of Soviet intentions, Leahy for his experienced anti-Communism and his influence on the President. Behind the Amerasia smoke-screen, Rockefeller was forced out of office and Dunn was shuffled off to a UN conference in London. With Rockefeller went the "good neighbor policy" and there began the aggravation of American difficulties below the Rio Grande.

Tired and in ill-health, Grew resigned from his key office of Under Secretary. Whether or not he was pushed out is still a matter of controversy. A diplomat always, he still insists that he was not forced out. Significantly, Eguene Dooman was nudged out at the same time. And Dean Acheson stepped in as Under Secretary. With the old and experienced diplomats out of the way, Acheson immediately began promoting the left-wing career men—John Carter Vincent was one of them—and embarked on a policy of baiting General Douglas MacArthur. From the Acheson-Vincent team came a set of directives which would have utterly destroyed the Japanese economy and left the country a prey to the Communists. When MacArthur balked, Acheson took the unheard of step of rebuking him publicly. It was not until Secretary Forrestal stepped in that the directives were rescinded.

The collapse of the Amerasia case was merely the final icing on Acheson's cake. A new Secretary of State, James F. Byrnes—unaware of the incriminating evidence collected against Service—

reinstated him and signed a note congratulating him on "this happy termination of your ordeal." The group which had been threatened at the time of the Amerasia arrests was now fully in control. The consequences in Europe were felt immediately. A State Department directive of October 17, 1945, to General Eisenhower, incorporated all the main points of the Morgenthau Plan for the total destruction of the German economy—a plan, incidentally, which had been drafted by Harry Dexter White and Gregory Silvermaster, both Soviet agents. Men like Harlow Shapley and Archibald MacLeish, Communist-front joiners *par excellence,* received State Department appointments as American representatives to international conferences.

In the Far East, the consequences were catastrophic. Owen Lattimore became the ideologue of our policy; the Acheson-Vincent-Service team became the implementers of the Lattimore line. The virtually avowed aim of the State Department became the destruction of the Chinese Nationalists. General George C. Marshall, who had earned his retirement, was sent to a mission to China to force Chiang Kai-shek to accept the Communists in his government. Marshall had no understanding of the problems involved, but he was well briefed by Acheson and Vincent. When Chiang refused to commit suicide—prefering murder at the hands of his American allies—Marshall cut off all military aid, boasting that "with the stroke of a pen" he had "disarmed the Nationalists." When the Marshall arms embargo was lifted, after eighteen critical months in which the Communists gained the ascendancy, the State Department saw to it that large Congressional appropriations never reached anti-Communist China.

When public indignation began to mount—and when members of the Senate began to protest—Acheson, now the Secretary of State, made diplomatic history by issuing a mendacious White Paper which torpedoed a friendly government and laid the groundwork for the Communist invasion of South Korea.

And during this time, what had happened to the Amerasia suspects. Those who had not been arrested continued to prosper. (One of them is still with the International Monetary Fund.) Service went back to his job at the State Department where a grateful government assigned him the task of passing on the promotions of his fellow diplomats. The President's Loyalty Order did not touch him. Gayn went abroad for the newspaper *PM*. When it folded, he moved behind the Iron Curtain, a free-lance writer who increased his income by black market deals.

Kate Mitchell dropped out of sight except as an occasional sponsor of a Communist front. She seemed on the verge of coming into notorious prominence when the Senate Internal Security subcommittee found personally, though not politically, incriminating correspondence addressed to her in the 150,000 letters and papers it subpoenaed from IPR files.

Philip Jaffe prospered until he came a cropper with the Communist Party for being too friendly with the ousted chief Earl Browder. Then he drifted into the amorphous ranks of the Titoists. Called as a witness by congressional investigators, he refused to divulge any details of past or present activities, standing on the Fifth Amendment. But to close friends, he indicated that he would gladly speak up were he granted some kind of immunity.

Andrew Roth was given asylum by the pro-Communist weekly, *The Nation*. As its foreign correspondent, he traveled through the troubled areas of the Far East, always filing stories which gave maximum aid and comfort to the Communists and none at all to the United States.

And Larsen went up hill and down dale, first denouncing his former colleagues in anti-Communist magazines, then defending them at Loyalty Board hearings and from congressional witness stands.

As for Amerasia, it limped along for awhile—then ceased publication. Its unexpired subscriptions were taken over by the IPR magazine, Far Eastern Survey. There is no record that any of Amerasia's readers complained.

In 1950, the Amerasia case—which had been liberally coated with whitewash in 1946 by a House committee—was once more put on display by a Senate Foreign Relations subcommittee—the so-called Tydings Committee. Although enough of the facts were read into the record to warrant a public castigation of the

Reluctant Prosecutor, the Tydings Committee gave the Justice Department its public benediction and found nothing ill-advised in the way the case had been handled. Instead, it gave further currency to the canard that the Amerasia documents were "teacup gossip."

But the second coat of whitewash somehow didn't take when applied to John Stewart Service. The Tydings Committee ignored Service's "military plans" conversation with Jaffe at the Hotel Statler, but it was forced to publish the transcript of the hearings it had held, most of them in executive session. Under pressure from the Republican minority in the Senate—and in the context of Senator Joseph McCarthy's charges of security laxness in the State Department—Secretary Acheson's elaborate defense began to crumble. The President's Loyalty Review Board, which had been hampered in its work by faulty directives, imposed a change in regulations and began to reconsider the cases of Service and others in the light of information presented to the country by anti-Communist senators.

On February 14, 1951, at a secret meeting of the Loyalty Review Board, the Service case came up for reconsideration. In the discussion, one member of the board said:

> "On this loyalty business—now, take the Service case, where the record shows that the man was living over there with a Chinese woman who we know and the record shows was under the pay of the Russian government, and he's in love with that woman, and you say that he can be loyal, perfectly loyal to this government. . . ."
>
> "In this particular case," another member said, "[Service] came over to this country [in 1945, when he returned from China to become involved in the Amerasia case] with the intention of divorcing his wife . . . so that he could marry the Chinese girl . . . "
>
> A third member said: "About the Service case—that was passed on three times by the State Department's Loyalty and Security Board, and now it's before us for post-audit; so all the information we have has been know to them . . . "

Late in 1951, the Loyalty Review Board ruled on the last of the Amerasia suspects. Reviewing material long held by the State Department, it found that there was a "reasonable doubt" as to

Service's loyalty. To find otherwise, the board said with polite irony in outlining Service's Amerasia role, "would, we are forced to think, stretch the mantle of charity too far."

More than six years after Frank Bielaski had entered the Amerasia offices, Service was fired from the State Department. Neither law nor justice—nor the ordinary instincts of patriotism and self-preservation—had accomplished the job. The government's hand had been forced by the aggressions of the Soviet Union and by a public opinion whose sense of law and justice were acuter than that of the Reluctant Prosecutor.

In the six-year time lag, the Reluctant Prosecutor had prevailed. By the time the facts were known, American boys were fighting and dying in Korea and the world stood again on the verge of calamity. As in the Hiss case, public awareness and public indignation had come too late. Had the Amerasia prosecution been carried out energetically, a different set of public characters would have held the stage of history. Other eyes would have penetrated the dust which blinded the Achesons, the Services, and the Vincents. For small though the Amerasia episode may have been in the great drama of empire, it set the mood for the play. The Case of the Reluctant Prosecutor was a curtain raiser. But who today can ring down that curtain? And will it ring down on Man?

1953

A Spy for Stalin

It has often occured to me that studies of intra-Party intrigue such as this are quite possibly what has led many readers to the conclusion that Toledano must have been a member of the Communist Party at one time or another. He was not. He was and is, however, one of a literal handful of reporters in this country who determined early-on that Communism was a major story of the times and that just as one might reasonably decide to specialize in medical reporting that one could reasonably decide to specialize in reporting the pathology of Communism. For their pains all, and notably Toledano, have been called not Red-reporters, for instance, but Red-baiters. By exactly the same logic, such a notable science writer (and, indeed, scientist) as Joshua Lederberg would, I assume, be called a science-baiter.

Mark Zborowski stands indicted of one count of perjury. The law, in its picayune majesty, accuses him of lying when he denied some fifty meetings with Jack Soble, convicted member of an atomic spy ring, and of association with Vassili Zaroubin, Soviet master of espionage in the United States. But whether or not the courts decide that the grand jury spoke true in its charge, they will not consider Zborowski's admitted apprenticeship as Stalin's spy in the 1930's among those prisoners of frustration, the Trotskyists. Nor will any human judge pass sentence for Zborowski's betrayal of his closest friends—or for the brutal deaths which resulted from that betrayal.

221

He was a struggling student at Grenoble when the NKVD approached him with an offer of money and future academic kudos in the Soviet Union, from which his parents had fled. The year was 1933, the cellars of the Lubianka had begun to fill with those who would figure in the Great Purge trials, and Stalin dreamed that every footfall on the Kremlin's pavement white was a Trotskyist with serpentine and syenite. He wanted his personal agents to penetrate the Trotskyist movement, to report the names of those still in Russia who maintained a relationship with Communism's Fallen Angel.

Others would be assigned to smash a pickaxe into Trotsky's restless brain. It was Zborowski's job to make himself an intimate of Leon Sedov, Trotsky's ill-fated son and a leader of the Fourth International's European operations. Eventually, Zborowski was told, he would be expected to lure Sedov to a place where he might be kidnapped for transshipment (dead or alive) to the Soviet Union. The NKVD manufactured a "revolutionary" past for Zborowski and gave him a monthly salary of 4,000 francs. This was a munificent sum (at the prewar rate of exchange) and Zborowski explained his affluence to the poverty-ridden Trotskyists as an "inheritance" from a capitalist aunt in Poland.

In the fervid world of Trotskyist intrigue, Mark Zborowski posed as a willing worker against Stalinism. A great show of security was made in the Fourth International, but Zborowski's account of his political antecedent was accepted without any check. He became one of Sedov's trusted lieutenants—and of sufficient importance to the NKVD to be given their secret phone number at the Soviet Embassy in Paris. Alexander Orlov, a high-ranking NKVD official who subsequently defected to the West, read Zborowski's reports to Stalin. And so we know that the Trotsky-Sedov correspondence—"correspondence," says Orlov, that "embraced everything of importance to their movement including secret information from and about Russia"—was regularly digested by Zborowski. The names of secret sympathizers in Russia therefore became the property of the NKVD— and of Stalin, who had ordered that all Zborowski's reports be sent to him. The rubber-tired Soviet equivalent of the tumbril rolled in Russia.

By 1936, the Fourth International was at its busiest and most influential. The rising terror within Russia, the stirrings in Asia, the growing influence of the trade union movement, and the Spanish Civil War found the Trotskyists deeply involved. British Intelligence and the *Deuxième Bureau* had little time for an examination of these activities, but the NKVD was immensely interested. In July of that year, the Fourth International called a secret conclave in Paris. Elaborate plans to keep the Soviets from spying on the meeting were made. The delegates, as they arrived in Paris, were to make rendezvous with a trusted courier, at various Metro stations. The courier would conduct them singly to the meeting place. Sedov looked about him for a man untainted by suspicion to serve as the courier. He chose Zborowski.

Their reports from Russia indicated that there was a serious leak in Trotskyism's leadership. To protect the Trotsky archives, invaluable in rebutting the charges of the Moscow trials, they were packed into fifteen large bundles and moved secretly from a private home to the International Institute of Social History, a center of Marxist studies run by Boris Nicolaevsky. Four people knew of this—Sedov, Nicolaevsky, Mrs. David Dallin, and Zborowski. On the night of November 6, 1936—days after the transfer—the Institute was burglarized. Money and other documents were untouched—but the Trotsky archives were stolen. Zborowski protested the raid to his NKVD superiors. "This will throw suspicion on me," he said. He was told coldly to mind his own business. "Those papers are a present to Stalin on the anniversary of the Revolution," was the explanation.

But Zborowski fingered more than papers. In 1937, Ignace Reiss broke with the Soviet apparatus in Western Europe—and there was consternation in the ranks. Reiss was a veteran of the underground wars, a hero of the German struggles. He knew Richard Sorge, another spy then posing as a Nazi as he built up a fantastically successful espionage ring in China and Japan. Reiss' high rank, moreover, gave him first-hand knowledge of the structure and scope of Soviet operations in the West. It was mandatory that he be murdered before he could talk. Hunted by the NKVD and suspicious of the capitalist police, Reiss turned to Sedov. Three people knew that Reiss had agreed to leave

Lausanne for a meeting with Sedov in Rheims—and one of them was Zborowski. When Reiss' bullet-torn body was found in the woods near the French border, a ticket to Rheims was in his pocket.

Trotskyist leaders, en route to Spain, stopped off in Paris to see Sedov—and the NKVD phone at the Soviet Embassy rang loudly. A report that Alexander Barmine, youngest Soviet general and key diplomat, was in flight from Stalin reached the NKVD—via Zborowski. When General Walter G. Krivitsky, chief of Red Army Intelligence in Western Europe and a friend of Reiss, broke with his past in those nights of the long knives, Sedov gave him a bodyguard—Zborowski—and the NKVD moved in. One unsuccessful attempt was made on Krivitsky's life in Paris, and the French police assigned men to keep an eye on him. Orlov reports that the NKVD decided to bide its time. (Suicide was committed on Krivitsky in a Washington hotel room early in 1941.)

By 1938, Zborowski had promoted himself to a Damon and Pythias relationship with Sedov. When Sedov was suddenly stricken, Zborowski rushed to a phone to summon an ambulance—and alert the NKVD. Friends of the healthy young man felt that he would recover quickly—but they tried to keep his illness and the name of his hospital secret. Yet Sedov died, under circumstances which are considered mysterious. To students of Stalin's secret service, however, they were no more mysterious than the sudden death in Cuba of Tina Modotti, an NKVD *apparatchik*, whose health deteriorated dramatically after she had broken with the Red underground.

When Alexander Orlov could no longer stomach his work in the NKVD, he too broke. Unlike many who had departed before him, he kept his own counsel. Knowing about Zborowski, he stayed away from the Trotskyists. But he wrote a detailed anonymous letter to Trotsky, warning him of the Soviet agent in the Fourth International. Mrs. Dallin was in Mexico at the time, and Trotsky showed her the letter. Anonymous letters were not new to him. The NKVD used them to denounce his most trusted followers, hoping to plant a seed of suspicion, to cause dissension

in the Trotskyist movement. He showed Mrs. Dallin another
letter, accusing her of being a Stalinist agent. When she returned
to Paris, she told Zborowski about it. "Smears," he said. And he
laughed.

The collapse of Europe brought Zborowski to the United
States in 1941. At first, he earned his living as the foreman for a
metal products company in Brooklyn. One summer day in 1943,
as he strolled along the Coney Island beach—or so he says—
Zborowski was approached by a stranger. "Finally we have found
you again," the stranger said. Zborowski swears that he refused to
accept an order to return to work for the NKVD. But within days
he had quit his job, moved to Manhattan—and to the same house
where some of his former Paris associates lived. In 1945 he turned
up at Columbia University, doing anthropological research and
being cultivated by such people as Gene Weltfish—later to charge
that the U.S. was using germ warfare in Korea. A grant from the
United States Mental Health Institute brought Zborowski
$24,000 for research.

He seemed free of all suspicion. Then, in 1954, Alexander
Orlov came out of hiding. His articles on the NKVD had caused a
sensation when they appeared in *Life* magazine. He began to
mingle with New York's Russian colony. One day, David Dallin,
then gathering material for his book on Soviet espionage, asked
Orlov how thoroughly the NKVD had penetrated the Trotskyist
movement. "The closest friend of Trotsky's son was an agent,"
Orlov replied. And then he asked, "Is it true that Sedov cried like
a child in 1936 when he read that Zinoviev and Kamenev were
executed?" It was a question laying bare that curious senti-
mèntality of the *apparatchik*—an intimate and damning detail
from one of Zborowski's reports.

The Dallins confronted Zborowski. He calmly admitted that
he had spied for the NKVD. Yes, he had reported on his friend
Sedov, he had informed the NKVD that Krivitsky was in Paris.
All this was true. But he had always reported "late"—after his
information had lost its value—never when it could do harm. And
he had been very angry when the NKVD had stolen the Trotsky
archives. He had not known they would do such a thing. He was

sorry, so sorry that he wrote a "confession" for the Dallins. Two years later, he repeated the same story to the Senate Internal Security Subcommittee. Everything that he admitted had occurred in Paris, beyond the reach of American law. He returned to his anthropological research on the cultural components in responses to pain.

But the wheel was spinning. The Soble-Abel-Albam atomic spy ring was broken up by the FBI. Jack Soble turned State's Evidence. Among those he named was Mark Zborowski. Fifty meetings, said the government. None, said Zborowski. The indictment was handed up. The rest of the story remained untold. But guilty or innocent, the story already on the record could never be expunged.

National Review
May 1958

Gouzenko:
An Exclusive Interview

As in the preceding story, this one is the result of professional and able specialization in a very special field of journalism. Interestingly, the sheer journalistic expertise of the story seems to have overwhelmed our old colleagues at Newsweek. It was rare, indeed, in the years that followed, at any rate, that Newsweek would accord such prominence to a story treating so coldly of Communist felony as opposed to Communist mellowing.

The phone rang and a cheerful Canadian voice said it was calling for "our friend." "He'll call himself 'Mr. Brown,' which I think is overdoing it a bit. We'll get in touch with you again presently." The meeting with Canada's most private citizen—arranged by letter drop to the Royal Canadian Mounted Police, and by wire and phone with a "contact"—still seemed distant and unreal. An hour later, I was in a car, being driven to a house whose owner and location I will never know. There, I was ushered in to meet Mr. and Mrs. Igor Gouzenko.

Until then, he had been only a name and a history. In September 1945, he had walked out of the Soviet Embassy in Ottawa, carrying with him 109 documents (taken from the military attaché's files) which exploded an atomic espionage ring operating in the U.S. and Canada. His escape and his vain attempts to tell his story in newspaper and government offices had the terrifying frustration which makes the suspense in a

Hitchcock movie. But to the world, he was a faceless man, an object moving in the vacuum of official secrecy.

The former cipher clerk is, however, no mere cipher of history. A slim, dark-haired man, he is of forceful personality, direct, full of energy. His mind is acute and it is easy to understand why as a student in Russia he won top honors. Clearly, he understands the world of conflict in which he lives. Svetlana Gouzenko is blond, vivacious, pretty, with a Scandinavian cast of features. Her face mirrors her moods, sweeping quickly from laughter to indignation.

Today, Igor Gouzenko has emerged from eight years of self-imposed obscurity. He has thereby confronted the Canadian Government with the one fact it would like to forget: his existence. Though he is still wrapped in a cloak of security, there is little doubt that his partial emergence has made the Canadian Government acutely uncomfortable. Many say that too many skeletons rattle in too many closets when he walks by.

Gouzenko is not working on any great listing of spies. He had told all he knows, although only part of it was recorded in the report of the Royal Commission. But he has a mission, quietly pursued during his years of obscurity and as quietly ignored by the authorities. Now he is anxious to pursue it as publicly as is consistent with his safety. "There is no reason why my case should be an exception," he says. "Among the many secret agents, we have secret friends."

The problem, as he sees it, is to make these secret friends come forward as he did with fresh documentary proof that will expose whole espionage apparatuses—not merely turn up a spy here or a cold trail there.

"Not fear of death, but fear of ingratitude and fear of uncertainty" keep the secret friends within the enemy camp, Gouzenko says. Once the escapee has turned over his documentary evidence, will he be left to shift for himself? Will he be protected from Soviet pressure and revenge?

Gouzenko's mission is to induce Congress and the Canadian Parliament to pass legislation which will assure a future to potential escapees. He is certain that they will come over to the side of the free world if laws are passed granting immediate citizenship to "every escapee who brings documentary evidence leading to the uncovering of Communist spy activity." In addition, escapees should be given lifelong protection, if they want it—and guarantees of economic security to go with it.

"If such a law is passed," Gouzenko says, "no Communist spy master will ever again be sure of his men." Gouzenko has worked out the ways and means to exploit the law he envisages—and it's for this reason that he indicated willingness to see the Jenner committee.

Gouzenko pleads earnestly that time is short. He does not see war tomorrow, but he feels that within five years the Soviet Union will be ready for armed conflict. Meanwhile, the West permits the future enemy to infiltrate its home bastions. He is certain that some nine Soviet rings are operating in the U.S. and Canada.

Gouzenko's conversation was frequently interrupted by his wife—because, she said to him: "My English is better than yours." Passionately and volubly, she seconded the points he made, adding details of her own. The talk shifted to that terrible day in 1945 when neither she nor Igor knew which would arrive first, aid from the Canadian Government which stubbornly refused to believe their story or a knock on the door from the NKVD. "There were men outside the house," she said. "Some were NKVD and some were Mounties. We did not know what would happen. Do you know what I did? I hung out the diapers."

Since that hairbreadth escape, the Gouzenkos have changed homes six times and name twice. The Canadian Government has fabricated complete pasts and identities for them. Neither of the two children—a boy of 10 and a girl of 8—know who their parents really are. The family moves about with a certain measure of freedom, but the Gouzenkos must always be watchful and wary.

They live quietly in a country community. Their mode of existence is, of necessity, modest. "People say we have an annuity from the Canadian Government," Mrs. Gouzenko says, "but it's not true. We live on $300 a month."

Despite the pressures of enforced anonymity, Mrs. Gouzenko is very active in community affairs, she keeps up her home, she gardens, and she paints. But about her other hobbies she is reticent. "If I tell you what they are, our many friends will be able to identify me."

Gouzenko has been busy, too. For the past four years, he has been working on a novel. It is a massive work, running to some 300,000 words, and it will be published in England this spring. The publisher is planning on an advance printing of 100,000 copies. "They say it is like Dostoevsky," Gouzenko says. The book is important to Gouzenko. "If it is a success," he says, "then I will be somebody."

Newsweek
December 1953

The War's Retrospect

A WARTIME TESTAMENT

Of this moving piece, I will only say that it reveals another Toledano significance, if not secret. He is a Christian scribe, as I have said. He also is a poet. And with that latter judgement, who can disagree?

In the early spring of 1944, cold winds still whipped across Pine Camp. The winter snows of upstate New York had barely disappeared from the bleak parade ground and from company streets pitted by tank treads. In our section of the half-deserted post, barracks which had echoed to the boisterous American shouts of the 45th Infantry, or of the 2nd and 3rd Armored, now restrained the quieter excitement of Italians—men captured in Africa and Sicily who were being trained by us as auxiliary QM troops to relieve GIs for service in Europe and the CBI.

In that chill spring, I did my day's work in the Intelligence Office. I wrote the daily news bulletin and turned it over for translation to an Italian lieutenant whose family had published the music of Giuseppe Verdi; I wrote and edited the bilingual post weekly; I poked into the lives of former prisoners whose rejection of fascism was still in doubt.

After Retreat and chow, I joined the other men who piled into rattling taxis and sped to Watertown—to drink, to see old movies, and to watch the V-girls go by. And like these men, I waited for the day to come when my name, rank and serial number would turn up on a shipping list. It was not combat we feared, but the process of being tossed into a manpower pool in a repple-depple—and from there to company, platoon, squad, where all personal loyalties had already been assigned and where we would face war uncoached and unbefriended.

The anxiety in me was deepened. At home, my wife was having a child, and I knew that I might be shipped out before the child was born—before I could see its face and hear its cry. That I might fight and that I might die had been a fact of daily existence from the moment I put on the uniform; that I might die before I had seen the proof of my immortality—this was another matter.

For nine or ten nights of that Pine Camp spring, I sought to circumvent this possibility. I might have prayed, but instead I wrote letters. Sitting on the edge of my bunk, a writing pad on my knees, I beat a path of communication to a child unborn, of sex undetermined. As in all such undertakings, of course, the path was not to my child but to my own soul. They were not good letters; they were full of tag ends and sudden silences; but they have spoken to me ever since.

"There are many things I should like you to know," the cramped handwriting of the first letter says, "things which I may not be able to tell you till you have moved out of childhood—or perhaps never. You are one of a cheated, precious generation, born of people whose love has been tempered by war and hovering death. For your father is a soldier. . . .

"There is a dirty, bitter job to be done by men not trained to war or military discipline. It is a job worth doing only because it must be done. That is why I am away from you . . . why you may not have me about as reassurance against the dark, uncertain world which closes in on the young and sensitive.

"So I must give you more than a fleeting picture of me. . . . I must let you know what I feel and believe. All I can give you is words. . . . But my life has been bound up in words, and beyond those abiding loves which are my private endowment, words and their bright, poignant significance have been a passion to me."

So I wrote, and in the following evenings, when the loud bustle had turned to an easier drone, I filled the pages.

"What I would most like to pass on to you now is a deep sense of obligation as a way of life. *Noblesse oblige*—nobility compels—they say. But it is the sense of obligation, not to a vague humanity but to the individuals who make up our lives, which is paramount. The will to do right can be broken; the obligation can not. If the good is a matter of choice, it loses its authority. It must be an obligation which can not be ignored. We are *obliged* to the people we love, to the ideas we cherish, to the God we worship. We are *obliged* to ourselves, and to the honor within us."

With a kind of penitence, I wrote: "They told us that it was foolhardy to have a child in wartime. They told us that it was a demonstration of faith in victory and security. Never believe these things. You were conceived because two people can wait only so long before having children if love exists between them—and because there was a war and I was a solider who might never return. For myself, too, it was pride in what I come from that made me want to perpetuate this heritage in you, richened by what your mother brings. And I wanted you because no man dies alone whose blood still breathes the living air. And though I am not afraid of death, I do not want to die alone."

Floundering in mortality, I wrote:

"Wind and rain pass over earth, washing away its substance. But the core or man's conscience is hard and stubborn; sometimes it survives." And again:

"I think I started to grow up when I ceased to be afraid of saying things that had to be said merely because they sounded like platitudes. When I was in school, it was considered shameful to speak of honor and dignity, of love of man and love of God. We were all historical materialists and anti-idealists. Man was selfish and economic; when the proper strings were manipulated, the puppet danced.

"We posed as cynics till we became cynics, and the boredom was profound. For historical materialism did not give us what God had given our elders. It left us without motivation and without grace. It is only now that I am learning that without God, man has no dignity; and without dignity he is an animal. I am learning that without God, man has no purpose; and without purpose, he is a useless mechanism.

"Perhaps negation will again be fashionable when you are in school. Perhaps the small craft scooped out from the tree of our new hopes will not weather the tempest of this war. Perhaps decency will not survive and a new set of half-truths and ex-pediencies will arise to confuse you and me. Then we will live again in evil.

"But I think that something will remain, at least some remnant for us to use in reconstructing the whole. At great price, the war has forced some of us to revaluate our ideas, to reforge our ideals, to purify our faith. It has pressed upon me a shining under-standing of the dignity of life in freedom, the impossibility of life without dignity. And from this has grown a morality of spirit too intransigent to perish easily. Even before you are born, you are pledged to it. And you will come to the struggle with clean hands."

I knew then, as I know now, that we were the expendables. "This war of vengeance and reprisal for a world self-betrayed will not dirty you as it will dirty me. Wars may be necessary, but they are never justified. We will pay for it with more than our lives, our fortunes, our suffering, our loss of self-respect. Whether we go through mud and death, or pass the war behind desks, we are all marked men. We shall never be the same.

"The tragedy of war is not that men die in great numbers, but that men must kill; not that men must obey commands like automatons, but they they must give them without conscience— and with this the living tissue of human dignity atrophies. It is not a shame to obey, except when obedience is the product of fear and compulsion. To die is common; to kill is horrible. And the men who have lived with that horror, no matter how remotely, can never order their lives in balance and tranquility. . . .

"As a student, I was a pacifist. War was something unreal and impersonal at which we scolded. But Spain came, like a hand at the throat, and in those years of bitterness and anger, we all knew that before the decade had ended heaven and earth would shake.

So pacifism was sand in our mouths and we had nothing. Political faith, moral faith—both of these were gone, and in their place was a gnawing blankness worse than fear."

In the innocence and exaltation of the times, I could write: "Only one horror is greater than the horror of war: slavery of the soul. Freedom is not a luxury, not a right but an obligation. It is not something that decent men can take or leave alone. Freedom can live only when it is an imperative which moves men to action and high anger at its violation. It is the keystone in the arch of our world. It must live deeply in the heart and in the mind, jealously guarded from any encroachment. There can be no compromise with freedom, as there can be no compromise with breathing.

"If our lives are consecrated, it is to that principle. That is why I am glad you are an American—not because Americans are superior to other people, but because the history and tradition of America is one of continual and troublesome preoccupation with freedom, of a sense of obligation to freedom."

My last letter, written in early April, reflected a doubt that I had floundered. "I have tried to be rational and detached in telling you that by holding to a tradition of obligation, by believing that one's acts are not random but build or destroy on a continuous pattern, we move toward a seasoned and better world. The course of history shifts and God takes notice.

"I have tried to say that only in the emotion of knowing what we believe, in the comradeship of purpose, can we begin to find the basis of personal peace and personal justice. But in writing of these things, I have been moved too often by the thought of you and the thought of myself; the thought of the man and woman who bore me and raised me; the woman who will bear you; the thought that perhaps she will raise you alone.

"I have tried to tell you things that are just beginning to grow in my mind, and in this groping I have left out much that is important, too. I have not written to you of music and my love of cities, of the feeling for form which disciplines our love of beauty and liberates it. I have not written to you of the small tenderness for little things. I have not written of laughter and of silence, of friendship and courage.

"I have not written to you of evil or the bitter frustration at witnessing its triumph, of light in the morning and darkness at night. I have not written to you of the sweetness of woman—you will be a son, I am sure of it—of the goodness of swimming and running.

"These are things you will find out for yourself, and in finding them you will grow and learn, you will reach and pass me. I have written more than less at random, but close to the core of my beliefs. My thinking has not been clear or direct. I have written merely to give you a taste of me as I am today—and for myself, to feel with a surging mixture of joy and melancholy that I am near you, within sight and sound of you, my son. Whether I have written stupidly or profoundly does not really matter before this fact.

"This is a time of anguish and turmoil for the world and for us. God speed us through it till we have found quiet and a warm sun together."

I did not die. I did not go into combat. I saw my son shortly after he was born—and before my name, rank and serial number had turned up on a shipping list. And we have never found quiet and a warm sun together. There is war again—or its Korean dress rehearsal. And the world is in exile from itself once more. It weeps by Babylonian waters.

I have two sons now who will grow up and wear uniforms; and perhaps they will fight, where I did not. I may show them the letters, as a token of my lost innocence. Perhaps they will know then that, by the grace of God, evil is eternal even as good is eternal, that it is man's fate to choose eternally between them.

The hope of that cold spring has vanished. The victory of American arms which we could see on the horizon has been destroyed by a conspiracy of weak men and evil purpose. The future is in sordid hands. My sons will inherit it. All I can tell them is that man lives and man dies—but the fight for freedom goes on forever.

The Freeman
December 1952

MISLAID GENERATION

Interestingly enough, at least for me (and you must thus be patient with the thought) this essay and the one that follows indicates an area in which mystic Toledano and rationalist Hess fully can agree but with which Communists surely could not. To the 'mystics of muscle' it seems that mere life is itself the irreducible value of man. To the rest of us, in the other two categories mentioned, there must be added the condition of life. Life lived as less than human is life not worth living. To give one's life in the attempt to live as a man is not a sacrifice. It is an honest trade. The sort a man must make.

The "lost generation" which had its laureate in Hemingway has become a literary cliché, a joke and an excuse. Living in a post-war world of disillusion, of bitterness at a sweet dream gone, it could look about and say: These are our complaints, that we lost our bearings, our ideals, our sense of order in the shuffle of battle; that the outlines of our world were revealed as tinsel in the piercing glare of the war.

The sham, the deception, the vicious materialism of the new century were discovered to the men of that generation. The point of rest on which to base moral Value had been shattered. They could be cynical or "brave." They were lost.

The years after the war brought depression, inflation, boom, depression again—and then that mass of heterogeneous impulses which we call the New Deal. The lost generation was absorbed into the stream of living; it had become domesticated in offices and kitchens, belatedly birthing new freedoms (which were not the New Freedom of another idealism) sired by cynicism and jemenfoutism. Irreligious, it took to heart the simple words of Ecclesiastes: There is no new thing under the sun.

Then another generation came, and another. Each labeled itself New. Each one orated: We are the Youth. One was cautious.

It tried to examine without judging. For the most part, it built up
and tore down theories. It argued—good God, how it argued! And
its heritage to the following generation was the destruction even
of cynicism.

The young men of today have seen the studpidity, the futility
of cynicism. (They are wonderfully good at seeing futilities.)
Their carryover from the "lost" is an abiding suspicion of
idealism. They are like a collar-button which has rolled into a
corner of the drawer. They are not lost: they are mislaid.

So that is what we are: The Mislaid Generation. There is a
certain positiveness about being lost. We are nowhere. We even
lack a laureate. We have only a saying, a password: Where do we
go from here, boys!

Where do we go from here?

For the most part we are fed. We are badly educated, all of us,
in schools which taught: A is equal to B, but only today and here.
Tomorrow it may be equal to C or D—or A may not be here at
all. It really adds up to a good Groucho Marx theorem. We have
been taught names, dates, places, trends, and then told that our
fine materialistic monument is built on quicksands. At best, we
rub noses with phenomena.

But the eternal verities, what of them? Without the courage of
our cynicism, we coyly mention that Utopia means Nowhere,
that no man has drawn a blue-print of a concept. So we are
skeptical. We do not even bother to argue any more, except as a
kind of intellectual setting-up exercise not taken too seriously.
And we are "practical." You can see us by the millions being
practical, all shined up, like collar-buttons based on sound physical principles to keep collars in place. But we remain in the
corner of the dresser drawer.

And there is only one verity which we ever accepted: that we
would grow older and marry, have children and die. There was no
stardust in this truth we clasped to our meager bosoms. But in the
winter nights of our adolescence it was something to warm us
against the winds of despair.

Oh yes, it *was*. But it is no longer. We know as of today that,
before God, many of our polished brass-plated collar-button souls

will be shuffled out of the drawer and acquire an unwanted significance. We know as of today that millions of us will stop bullets and fall in our tracks dead. They are not even giving us music and drums this time to drown out the quiet sound of this fact.

Not that we do not want to fight this war. It is our war and it must be fought. We are no less brave, no less determined to fight, no less afraid to die than our to-be-lost cousins of another day. But we want to know what it means. We are asking, Where do we go from here, boys? And no one has an answer—no, not President Roosevelt. We know what we are fighting about. But for the first time in the world's recorded history, we find a mislaid, misfit, and mishandled generation which is skeptical of what it will get.

Each generation finds its God in the patterns of its examined behavior. Other, older men believed in ends, in the burnished goal. But ends are never upon us.: we wallow in the means. So ideologically, we live from hand to mouth, trusting in the immutability of the human spirit, the transiency of evil. But these are not slogans to take into battle. Nor are they the drum, the fife, and the beating heart which carried the day for us once before.

In this hard Spring of 1942, I offer you these facts and moods. They have disturbed me; I doubt that they will offer you any consolation. Expanded into a book, with appropriate footnotes and references, they would make interesting reading to a historian of this epoch in a glorious century. I propose them as a challenge to the dark, ill-kept drawer which is our world; as an answer to the morale builders who do not find us lynching Germans and skinning parboiled Japanese. Timidly, I offer them to the men who hold guns in hand and get no joy of it, to those of my years who lost the questions, suspect the answers and have no hope of hell.

New Leader
April 1942

NOTES FOR A FAREWELL

No man wants to die. Yet no man can stay behind in this time
of great decision, remaining glued to the seat of his own selfish
interest. We struggle against the final moment when we must give
up the sights and sounds we love. But when the call comes, as
men we are glad, and as participants in freedom's enterprise we
are glad. The Army, even America's civilian army, is unknown
and fearsome territory. Before it, I am reluctant. And military
discipline will at best be a burden. But looking ahead to it, there
is a surge of feeling, call it patriotism if you will—or the
recognition that at last I am taking my place in the ranks of
vengeance.

It feels strange to be writing this—and stranger still to be
feeling it deeply. Mine was the generation which lived through the
false dawn of "world peace." We talked of Einstein's two percent
plan, of the Oxford pledge, with a dishonesty born of the
realization, not quite subconscious, that shielding us from the
horrible facts of war were the French poilu and the British tar.
Unfortunately for us, the strength of ten was not in the pure in
heart. Or perhaps the hearts were not so pure.

At any rate, when the Teutonic tribes let loose their dogs upon
us, the only answer we had was a panicky: "Down, Fido!" But
Fido would not be downed, so men were beaten in Berlin and
shot in Vienna. Courage was born in Spain, but the "No
pasaran!" was never heard in London or Paris or Washington. Nor
did you and I hear it, for all our big talk. When Spain fell, we
were weeping, not fighting.

It has taken the Selective Service Act to make men of us.

For some time now, men of my age lived in the approaching
presence of swift and violent death, either as soldiers or as
soldiers to be. Whether in fear, or bravely, or with the resignation
that is any man's mite, I know that before this war is over certain
sharp, pressing facts of blood and endurance and pain must be
faced. It is important for me to ask now: "Where shall I seek the

struts to brace my inner self, the nerve or the guts, the stiff upper
lip? What sources of strength shall I draw on to survive this flood
of calamity, to ride out this hurricane of evil?

I know this: that wars are won by men who are willing to
catch a bullet or spill their guts in battle—for bread or hate or the
fear of God or the safety of a particular fireside. Men fight for
simple things, and in naive ways they die. In the gloss of history,
the crude stuff of human emotion is forgotten and only the
beautiful, unheard words of the leaders remain. Yet, here and
now, it can be emphasized that no man has died in this war with
choice selections from the Encyclopedia of Social Sciences on his
lips.

I mention this because the propaganda of scholars has convinced us that there is no salvation save by the grace of
specialized vocabularies and academic occultism. Organized intellect, which like everything else has become a vested interest, can
be of small comfort to my contemporaries as we are being
measured for uniforms. Even in ordinary life, it failed signally in
moving us to an understanding of anything but physics and
chemistry. But beyond the realm of matter, it has destroyed faith
without giving us certainty.

For myself, writing on the eve of a new phase in my life (and
can anyone say if it will lead me to the second front or to a safe
desk in some obscure Army post?) I find that I can leave the isms
and the ologies to those busy thinkers who are all head and
bottom. They have weighted down with distinctions the truths
that I seek and tied them to earth with a Lilliputian weave of split
hairs. They have used Promethean fire to heat their tea. They
have befuddled us with dialectics and saddled us with the base
fiction that men's acts are solely of economic motivation.

I prefer to turn to such outmoded words and concepts,
founded on the spiritual needs of people, as honor, dignity, hope,
love, courage, common reason, brotherhood, decency, the
holiness of man. These words have been met by snickers in a time
of glib complexities. They are starting to have a new significance
for me. I believe, profoundly, that each man is a holy vessel, too

often corrupted by his own weakness and bearing the seeds of his
own destruction, but holy nevertheless since the good of society
is held within him. In each man's salvation lies the world's
salvation.

The pie-in-the-sky of theology is not what I mean at all, but
salvation in terms of the democratic ideals which we all share.
And it is precisely here that I launch my faith in the common
reason of the men of good will and decency, those heirs to the
Judaeo-Roman tradition of the Western world and its inspired
belief in law and morality, its reliance on the accretion of small
rights and duties as a means to the high justice which lives after
the slick blueprints have been trodden underfoot.

For what we call democracy is an expression and an extension
of the individual good consciously developed. The working classes
have no monopoly on it, nor does it shun the wearers of
particular ties. I am sick at heart watching men labelled and
therefore damned without conscience. It is a disease we have
caught from the totalitarians, a means of evading careful judgement of an adversary. I too caught the infection for a while and
can testify to its virulence. It provokes anarchy and produces
hate.

The last war destroyed men's faith in their ability to conquer
the evil within and about them. It crushed the individual's faith in
himself and in his power to meet the world head-on. As much as
your economic ·motives, this is what gave ideological fascism its
hold and its impetus. This was the real failure, a failure of *faith* if
you will. Yet in the countries with the strongest individualist
tradition, fascism had no chance. That is why Britain was able to
stand alone; that is why America was able to rouse itself, despite
the confusion and fascist-making antagonisms in our society; that
is why even the tortured French had to be destroyed from
without before a totalitarian system could be imposed upon
them.

The struts to brace my inner self, I am afraid, are but in the
making. I am still groping for meanings and explanations, for
seaworthy truths to weather the gale. But for the first time, I feel

that I am on solid ground. I feel safe in America, in the contradictions of America, in the blatant individualism of America. There is trouble ahead be sure of it. We have always had the mechanism to meet it; I believe we are creating the state of mind to fight it, the goodwill and the confidence.

These are notes for a farewell. The real farewell cannot be written until I come back. Standing before a morning when death stampedes the sun, it might have been easier to say, "God love us all . . ."

New Leader
April 1943

NOTES FROM
A FURLOUGH DIARY

Mostly it is a strange feeling to be home on furlough, to see the life that is no longer mine continuing without me, to find that though I have changed, the sounds and smells and sights of New York are still the same. It is a little frightening to think of being a civilian again. The Army has become, in a short a time, more than a routine and a formula. It is, perhaps, a sanctuary or an escape. Probably this sounds fantastic: an escape into a machine geared for death and destruction. If I could explain it, a service would be done to so many who have sons and brothers, lovers and husbands, in the armed forces.

If I could explain it. . . .

Remember the returning soldiers in the Dos Passos and Hemingway novels. They could never talk about the war or the Army to the folks back home. They were inarticulate before the overwhelming gap which exists between the soldier and the civilian—even between the trainee and the civilian. It seemed to us when we read those books that Dos Passos and Hemingway were merely creating a literary convention in order to avoid a little work. And we thought that they were being that much phony by adding to the silent hero tradition a jigger of 1920's *Weltschmerz*.

Both Hemingway and Dos Passos were reporting with absolute fidelity. For some time I have known this, but it has been brought home to me with pressing clarity, these days of my furlough. Scores of well-meaning or merely curious people have asked me, "Well, how does it feel like to be in the Army?" And I have said, "It feels fine." But of course that was no answer at all. For to crawl on your belly for 100 yeards is not fine at all. Nor does fine describe the surge of joy which hits you for no reason at all in the midst of an ordinary day's routine.

I have come back and seen you sitting at your desks, felt the gladness of your handshake. I have walked along those city streets which meant so much to me, mingled with the crowds which are the bloodstream of New York. But where I had felt a kinship with all this, an emotional response, my reactions now are purely intellectual.

As I walk along, I think: These people may work hard; they may work much harder than I do. But at night they go home to their own beds, their own chairs, their own walls. They are attached to some sort of permanence and privacy. The clothes they wear are of their own choosing; they can select their own friends. And then, I look down at my uniform. It is the good uniform of a good Army. I am proud of the uniform and happy that I am wearing it today. But wearing it, I am no longer the same person. The clothes, you see, really can make the man.

And this is only a very small part of it.

I have learned a lot of things, some commonplace, others poetic, but if you ask me what they are I will stutter a weak answer, an answer that makes you suspect my sincerity. But the proof of this particular pudding is that any soldier will tell you how impossible it is to talk to civilians. Soldiers wives belong to our club and speak our language; we can be frank and at ease with them. There is a good article in this subject for someone who has the time and the energy to write it.

It is a shock the first time you are given the command, "Fix bayonets." Suddenly, death by steel becomes a very pertinent fact. You can understand why brave soldiers have turned and run in the face of a bayonet charge. When you fire a rifle or a machine gun, you are merely acting as the intelligence for a mechanical contrivance to end life. But with a bayonet, you are actually pushing the steel. In training, you actually feel it bursting through the burlap and cane dummy. Imagination can carry you the rest of the way.

Well done, the bayonet drill has all the precision and grace of a modern ballet. Its movements are calculated to give you the utmost power in thrusting, slashing, parrying, striking with the butt—all these while the body remains in perfect balance and in fluid motion. This same juxtaposition of beauty and terror you will find in the wonderfully tooled parts of machine guns and light artillery pieces. Handling them, you are struck by the pleasure you feel at their mechanical integration, by the boding sense that this cam will move in that camway to broadcast immediate death.

The pacifist strain that once was in me still has enough life to stir in wonder at this.

It is with a feeling of return that I have picked up the old habit of reading a morning newspaper. The reward is not very great in terms of what I get out of the papers themselves. In Walter Lippmann's phrase, they are full of "gossip journalism, pipe-line journalism, intrigue journalism. . . ." But newspaper reading is a sign of our civilization and I enjoy the feeling of community which reading the paper gives me. To be fair, there is more than this involved. I was moved this morning, again by Lippmann, who writes. "In the supreme moments of history terms like duty, truth, justice, and mercy—which in our torpid hours are tired words—become the measure of decision."

It takes courage to say those words today. Before you know it, you are being branded a mystic and a reactionary. I still remember the smug smiles which succeeded the frowns when, about to enter the armed forces, I wrote in The New Leader:

"I prefer to turn to such outmoded words and concepts, founded on the spiritual needs of people, as honor, dignity, hope, love, courage, common reason, brotherhood, decency, the holiness of man. These words have been met by snickers in a time of glib complexity. They are starting to have a new significance for me. . . ."

I have been exposed lately to direct and simple people whose emotions have been direct and open, untouched by the ingrown ideological suspicions current here. In many ways I have come to share this simplicity. Thinking of them and of myself, I know I do better in standing by my old sentiments than in joining the throng of "realists" turning cartwheels in the square of history.

New Leader
August 1943

Unconventional Ambassador

Of such reports as this it can be said that were it not for the hardy handful of which Toledano is a member, stories of persistently anti-Communist members of the Federal establishment would be classifiable somewhere on the order of hens teeth.

E verybody likes Jack Peurifoy. Everybody, that is, but the Communists. They can never forget how thoroughly he did them in the eye when he was Ambassador to Greece. They are not likely to forgive the "coincidence" that Peurifoy was on hand when they got the boot in Guatemala.

The gallery of Peurifoy's admirers runs a gamut from former Secretary of State Dean Acheson to Senator Joe McCarthy. Acheson likes him because whatever passes for blood in his icy veins responds to a good administrator. McCarthy likes him because he shares the view of most legislators on Capitol Hill. This view was summed up by Representative John Taber, the witty and splenetic chairman of the House Appropriations Committee. "I don't like any of those bastards from the State Department," Taber once said. "They lie and they hedge and they don't know what they're talking about. All of them, that is, except Jack Peurifoy."

John Emil Peurifoy does know what he's talking about—even when his official position causes him to express himself strangely. He was born to an arguing Southern family—in Walterboro, South Carolina—and weaned on the *Congressional Record*. In a legal household, he learned the value of quick thinking and clarity of

247

mind. As a State Department official, a Foreign Service officer, and the American representative to Communist-troubled nations, he has utilized both. His own experience has taught him that the direct approach is often much better than the circumlocutions of traditional diplomatic discourse.

To arrive at this experience, Jack Peurifoy traveled no royal road. Outrageous fortune kept him on a seesaw for many years. He was just about halfway through West Point when his father died, and young Jack had to quit and go to work. There were no plushy jobs open to him—he had to take what he could get. He put into cold storage his ambition to become President of the United States and started out on a clerk's tour of the nation. Tutor and bank clerk in Kansas City, insurance salesman and night cashier in New York—these were the kinds of jobs he held.

But New Deal Washington was the lure in those depression days. It became the only boom town in the U.S. Franklin D. Roosevelt, however, wasn't waiting at Union Station to offer Jack Peurifoy the keys of the city. He settled for a $90-a-month job running an elevator in the Senate Office Building. This was his introduction to Federal service.

But he wasn't discouraged. Within months, he had gotten himself a post with the Treasury Department. It paid only $1,620, but in the early years of prosperity, that was not so bad. The job wasn't much either, but it had to do until the real thing came along. On the strength of this advancement, he married Betty Cox, an Oklahoma girl who also worked in the Treasury. They set up modest housekeeping and waited for the big break to move them into a big Georgetown house. Instead of the big break, however, Jack got a pink slip from the government, just before the Christmas of 1937.

It wasn't that Jack Peurifoy had fallen down on the job, merely that the government—violating all rules—had abolished his department entirely. Jack worked the Christmas rush in a Washington department store as a floorwalker, perhaps the only job he ever held which was cut to the traditional pattern of diplomacy, and then grabbed the first thing that came along. In the Capital's Botanical Garden, he did manual labor—shoveling snow, washing out flower pots, shoveling snow, and mixing manure. This lasted for only a brief period until the Treasury Department eventually welcomed him back, and by late 1938, he stepped into the State Department. Today, Peurifoy says that he moved into the Department because something about diplomacy had always attracted him. The chances are, however, that if you had asked him then why he was changing, he would have said, "It's a better job."

It was a lucky decision. The systematic infiltration of the Treasury by the Communists—an infiltration which by far exceeded the State Department's—was well on its way. In that atmosphere, dominated by Harry Dexter White and his tightly-knit policy espionage cell, Peurifoy would have been elbowed off the road to advancement. The State Department had its hazards, but the elbowing was more subtle and the Communists there, from Alger Hiss down, were less dominant—personnel-wise.

Advancement in the State Department is slow and arduous, even when such hazards are eliminated. But Jack Peurifoy took it like the 100-yard dash. In seven years, he covered a lifetime's ground and rose to the top of the Civil Service pile and the highest pay classification: $10,300 a year. He cut no corners in running this course; he just moved fast. But he made no effort to advance by getting shoe polish on his tongue. He ignored the usual rules, appeared at the office out of uniform (slacks, lumberjacket, and old shoes were good enough when he put in a weekend of work in the gingerbread edifice which then housed State), was frank and direct, and never affected the prim manner which sooner or later takes hold of the State Department official. If there was ever a choice between a cocktail party and a baseball game, Peurifoy ended up in the bleachers eating a hot dog.

In 1945, when the State Department began preparing for the United Nations Conference in San Francisco, Alger Hiss was made secretary-general—and Jack Peurifoy got the short end of the bargain—housekeeper of the meeting. On his shoulders fell the task of finding 5,600 hotel rooms for delegates and staffs in a war-crammed city. He also had to set up worldwide communications for diplomats and the press and create a translation service.

If a delegate was unhappy, it was up to Peurifoy to find him joy;
if the Russians were irritated, Peurifoy mollified them. He did
this hydra-headed job so well that he came to the attention of
Dean Acheson, then Under Secretary of State. The two men
became friends—and Peurifoy has never turned his back on
Acheson. Neither has he let that friendship interfere with his
sense of duty.

In 1947, John Emil Peurifoy was appointed Assistant Secretary for Administration by Secretary George Catlett Marshall. (He
was later promoted to Under Secretary for Administration—the
same job with a fancier title and higher pay.) Handling personnel
and security, he was hardly in a spot to be loved by the assorted
crew which had been jammed into the State Department when it
absorbed O.S.S. and O.W.I. And the Foreign Service boys weren't
happy either. They looked down their noses at a man who had
once run an elevator and shoveled manure. They also violently
resented Peurifoy's efforts to "desnob" the department. He did
his job, attempting to bring order out of the chaos of State
Department organization, coping with the feeble security regulations behind which men of doubtful loyalty hid, and—most
important from the bureaucratic standpoint—winning friends and
influencing Congressmen. That he was genuinely liked and ad-
mired on Capitol Hill is a matter of record; how he achieved this
bit of black magic has never been adequately explained.

"It's just that he's a nice guy," says one Senator. "He doesn't
put on any side," a Congressman declares. "He didn't mind
putting down a few; he liked a bull session as well as the next
man; he never acted as if Congressmen were created by God after
he ran out of human flesh," says another.

Then, in the summer of 1948, the Hiss case broke with a loud
bang. The worst suspicions of Communist infiltration into the
State Department were dwarfed by the facts as they were
unveiled in that historic proceeding. When the House Un-
American Activities Committee processed the rolls of microfilm
which Whittaker Chambers had saved over the years, Jack
Peurifoy was called in to evaluate the importance of the classified
documents they represented. Until then, Assistant Secretary

Peurifoy was hardly a public figure. His testimony projected him into the headlines for the first time.

Unlike some of his colleagues, who pretended that the documents had been taken in good clean fun and represented no more threat to American security than a batch of Grandma's recipes, Peurifoy laid it on the line. The colloquy went like this:

Q. In your opinion, would you say that the very existence of these rolls of microfilm is evidence of an espionage plot against our government?

A. I would.

Q. Do you believe that they could have been taken only by a person . . . desiring to harm our government?

A. I believe this. Under our security regulations no official of the Department could ever remove such documents—not even to take them home at night to work with them.

And then Peurifoy added: "I would like to say this—and this is purely gratuitous comment on my part—but what I regard as most serious about this whole thing . . . is that the documents were taken out of the State Department . . . and to me that means that our codes were being read by foreign nations during that whole period."

This straight-from-the-shoulder testimony destroyed the prepared ground to which many Hissite partisans retired when it could no longer be denied that Hiss had passed the documents.

During the Senate investigation of Senator McCarthy's charges of Communism in the State Department, Jack Peurifoy was chosen to run interference for Secretary of State Acheson. Despite this onerous task, Peurifoy did not lose the friendship or respect of most anti-Communists. The Tydings hearings ended in a whitewash for the State Department—a victory for the Administration Peurifoy served—and shortly thereafter, he took himself out of Civil Service and joined the Foreign Service—at the top.

Ambassador to Greece was his first assignment—and he stepped into a ticklish situation which might have been disastrous to that nation and this. The Communist invasion had been defeated, but it was touch and go for the legitimate government.

But Peurifoy acquitted himself excellently, breaking down the barriers of protocol and establishing himself on a firm footing with both the Greek government and the Greek people. Presenting his credentials to Prime Minister Sophocles Venizelos, he said:

"I think we will get along better if we talk man-to-man. If I have anything to say to you, I will tell you myself. If any third party says I have told him something I have not told you about the position of my government, you can ignore it. By the way, my name is Jack." By the time he left Greece, half of Athens was calling him Jack. This was in July, 1953, after he had helped the Greeks stabilize their government and had done a notable job in administering ECA funds.

His next assignment was Guatemala, already thoroughly dominated by the Communists. And Peurifoy's ambassadorship was no cinch. The Red-controlled press openly insulted him, one newspaper threatened his life, and President Jacobo Arbenz blatantly shunned him. After his first meeting with Arbenz, Peurifoy remarked to an intimate: "If he isn't a Communist, he'll do until a better one comes along." As the situation in that small Central American country worsened, Peurifoy sat tight and cultivated those who might be of service in the future.

When the revolt of Colonel Castillo Armas broke out, Peurifoy strapped a shoulder holster under his arm and made himself available to anti-Arbenz elements in Guatemala. When the military leaders of the country came to see him, he had good advice for them. An anti-Communist government was set up, as the Ambassador looked on approvingly.

But though Peurifoy's quiet activities paid off, destroying the major Soviet beachhead in the western hemisphere, the career boys in the State Department were upset. They didn't think that the shoulder holster he wore during the days of fighting was quite seemly. John Emil Peurifoy had gone sleepless for days, in the critical period of the revolution, but he didn't allow the criticism of the "cookie pushers" to annoy him. He had gotten results, and in his book, that's what counts.

The American Mercury
October 1954

Whose Civil Liberties?

The date of this is important. The ACLU has come quite a way since then, although Toledano probably disagrees. He, incidentally, was the reporter most closely to cover the efforts of at least one branch of the ACLU to buck the entrenched racism of some major labor unions.

On the night of November 24,1953, Edward R. Murrow's telecast "See It Now" presented to the country what purported to be an objective account of a controversy between the American Civil Liberties Union and the Indiana Department of The American Legion, headed by Roy T. Amos of Indianapolis. The locale of the show was Indianapolis, where a group of people who wished to start an ACLU chapter were refused the use of the Indiana World War Memorial. Murrow, in his trademarked voice of doom, set the stage and then turned the presentation over to two CBS reporters and two photographers.

Whether by malice or misfortune, the Murrow telecast gave the impression of a studiously contrived piece of special pleading designed to show that the Indiana Legionnaires were a collection of fascist-like crackpots and the ACLU a bearer of the Jefferson-Lincoln tradition. The strongest statement of the Legion's position, by Cale J. Holder, was not heard. Instead, the Legion's case was presented on the Murrow show by utilizing camera techniques to create pro-ACLU sentiments. Shots of the Legion's trooping of the colors were so edited that they looked like a Nazi display of military ritual.

On behalf of the ACLU, the most glaring sin was the careful deletion from a speech by Arthur Garfield Hays of everything but the most pious sentiments on civil liberties and the right of dissent. His statements defending the rights of communists to teach in the public schools and blasting all investigation of communism were not heard by the nation's televiewers. Nor, for that matter, did Hays' cockeyed and self-contradictory assertion that no one in the U.S. could speak up in defense of civil liberties "because the danger is too great," seem of interest to Murrow's editors.

The total effect was unconsciously summed up by John Crosby, the snydicated radio-TV columnist, who wrote: "Mr. Murrow showed the two meetings—the Legion's and the Civil Liberties Union—jumping back and forth from the regimented atmosphere of the Legion's to the democratic reasonableness of the Union's . . . Murrow simply presented the facts (and the faces) and let them speak for themselves." How could Crosby know that the facts (and the faces) were carefully chosen to have precisely that effect on him? Curiously, Murrow did not catch the Legion on the point where it was demonstrably off-base—the false accusation by Indianapolis Legionnaires that ACLU had defended the atomic spies, Ethel and Julius Rosenberg. Perhaps he didn't know.

In itself, the Indianapolis incident is of small consequence. The attempt to build it up into a national issue died. The anti-Legion case was so palpably feeble that it aroused only the professional breast-beaters. The ACLU was aware of this, for it kept its anti-communist staff members in complete ignorance of Murrow's intervention until the last minute. But the Murrow broadcast did serve an important purpose. However imperfect and grudging, it brought to the fore questions which have bothered many people.

Is the American Civil Liberties Union a communist front? Is the net effect of its work subversive? Does it fight honestly and with clean hands for civil liberties? The American Legion has repeatedly asked for a congressional investigation of these questions. But the ACLU is too much of a Sacred Cow to be so subjected. The questions should be answered. After a careful study of the ACLU's literature, of its leadership, and of its activities, I have come to the following conclusions:

1. In the established sense of the word, the American Civil Liberties Union is not a communist front—even though Earl Browder, in sworn testimony at the time he was the red boss in America, characterized it as a "transmission belt" for communist ideas.

2. It is nevertheless of tremendous value to the communist movement. In the guise of serving civil liberties, it disseminates to all corners of the country the kind of propaganda which best serves communist purposes by spreading dissension, confusion, and misinformation.

3. Despite claims of impartiality, it has set up a double standard in evaluating civil liberties issues—one standard for the left, the other for the right.

4. The ACLU has, on several occasions, perpetrated conscious fraud on the American people. Its literature, moreover, is packed with gross and glaring contradictions of fact and doctrine.

5. For the most part, its general statements of purpose are noble, but in specifics the ACLU has been both equivocal and selective. Its protestations that it abhors communism must be judged in this context.

6. The ACLU has shown considerable impartiality in its litigations and legal briefs, but it has issued press releases and reports which have been crudely partisan.

It is not to be gainsaid that the ACLU has done tremendously important and socially useful work in fighting against discrimination and segregation of Negroes, for the extension of the franchise in areas where some have been denied the vote, against pre-censorship of books and films, etc. It has also entered the courts in behalf of rabble-rousing crackpots like Father Terminiello, defending a free speech principle. The ACLU's perfidy, if I may so call it, has been in the area of the communist conspiracy, of cold war tensions, and of the germinal disagreements between liberals and conservatives.

Three case studies will demonstrate the nature of my criticisms:

The Merle Miller Case. In 1950, the ACLU commissioned
Merle Miller,[1] a professional liberal of anti-anti-communist persuasion, to make a "searching inquiry" of the blacklisting of
communists and sympathizers in the Radio-TV industry, and the
boycott of programs featuring them. With an appearance of
impartiality, the ACLU also asked Miller to look into charges that
anti-communists had been similarly excluded. The Union's concern was sparked by the publication of *Red Channels*, a small
volume listing the communist-front affiliations of some 150
radio-TV artists. (It may be noted that the ACLU gave its
blessings to a boycott of the sponsors of the TV "Amos 'n'
Andy" show because the show allegedly was offensive to
Negroes.)

The ACLU's position on this controversy had already been
made abundantly clear. Conveniently forgetting its reiterated
concern over freedom of the press, it had joined the Liberal-
communist onslaught against *Red Channels*, and its sponsor, the
newsletter *Counterattack*. The Union's counsel, Arthur Garfield
Hays, who was coincidentally earning private fees as attorney to
some of the people listed in the book, was leading the vigilantes.

Aided by Alan Reitman, the ACLU's publicity man, Miller
wrote *The Judges and The Judged,* which was published by
Doubleday, in a flurry of publicity, with the Union's impri-
matur.[2] The book was such a fraud it produced a split within the
ACLU. It falsely contended that those listed in *Red Channels*
were unable to find work, that in "not a single instance" had an
anti-communist been blacklisted. To prove his point, Miller
"quoted" a number of anonymous and mythical producers. He
invented stories out of whole cloth to smear anti-communists; he
falsified statistics.

Reviewers on major newspapers who hailed the book didn't
bother to check the facts. That task was left to Merlyn S. Pitzele,

---

[1] Miller's orientation can best be shown by his statement that the "real
threat to . . . the United States, to the world, is not from the Left but from
the Right."

[2] The ACLU spent $2,980.53 of its funds for research and advertising of
the book.

a member of the ACLU Board and one of the country's outstanding labor experts, who published two devastatingly careful analyses of *The Judges and The Judged*. He demonstrated that the book was full of "half-truths, distortions, and lies," and he furnished evidence which showed that Miller and Reitman had deliberately turned down proof that *over the years anti-communists in radio-TV had been blacklisted*. Finally, Miller grudgingly admitted many of the errors, but explained that if his "math" was wrong it was because he relied on a "researcher."

The Pitzele rebuttal widely discredited Miller, but the Authors League elected him as its president. The ACLU hastily set up a committee to study Miller's book. But when the committee sustained Pitzele, the ACLU suppressed its report. Publicly, the Union admitted some "important errors," but managed to slap Pitzele. *To date, the ACLU has not repudiated the book*. It has, in fact, *announced its "continued sponsorship."*

The Teachers Union Case. In July 1952, the New York Civil Liberties Union held a meeting protesting a ban on the use of public school auditoriums by the communist-controlled Teachers Union. At this meeting, ACLU counsel Hays acclaimed the Teachers Union as "our kind of people," and read a long statement prepared for him by Rose Russell, the TU's political commissar. When Daniel James, then managing editor of the socialist *New Leader*, rose to offer a viewpoint slightly at variance with that of the ACLU, he was drowned out by the organized boos of the communists in the audience.

"What astounded me," James has written of the incident, "was that the communists should be aided and abetted by such stalwarts of fair play and freedom of speech as Arthur Garfield Hays and Osmond K. Fraenkel (ACLU Board member), who acted as chairman ... I was rarely able to utter three or four consecutive words without being heckled, hissed, abused, and threatened by the communists, and being restrained—sometimes physically—by the chairman ... Seizing my arm, he directed me at the height of the communist attack to cut short my speech ... Mr. Hays did not utter a single protest." *To date, the ACLU has not rebuked Hays or Fraenkel* for their betrayal of the principles of free speech. Is the ACLU an impartial champion of free speech?

The Peekskill Case. In August 1949, a group of veterans paraded in protest against a concert and rally scheduled ih Peekskill, N.Y., by Paul Robeson, communist singer, and the Civil Rights Congress, a communist front. As a result of the parade, a riot resulted, a veteran was stabbed by one of the Robeson ushers, and several others were injured. Robeson never sang. A week later, a second attempt was made by the communists to hold their "concert." This time they brought with them some 2,500 guards, armed with bats and bottles and organized in paramilitary fashion, many of them members of goon squads from the communist fur workers union. In the interim, certain anti-Semitic and anti-Negro elements in the community sought to make capital of the incident, unleashing some ugly passions. A second riot broke out, following the concert. A grand jury was impaneled which found that the communists had staged a planned provocation. It also exonerated the police of communist charges that they had deliberately encouraged the riot.

But before the grand jury had made its findings, the ACLU rushed into print with a report. According to James Rorty and Winifred Raushenbush, who did an extensive study of the riot for the Jewish magazine *Commentary*, the ACLU report was cited as "an impassioned indictment of the Peekskill community, its press, the veterans, and the police. In contrast, the communists are flatly acquitted by ACLU of any responsibility for either riot." The writers discovered in the ACLU report "a rather cavalier, and partial, handling of the facts. The grand jury presentment justly said: 'Much of its text and some of its conclusions are so far from the truth as to be scandalous.' " Rorty and Raushenbush itemize some of these scandalous mis-representations. The American Jewish Committee dissociated itself from the ACLU report and excoriated it in a pamphlet of its own.

These are not isolated instances. The history of the ACLU is full of cases in which a double standard was applied. In the case of Edward Rumely, an extreme right-winger who pleaded the

First Amendment before the Buchanan Committee and was indicted for contempt of Congress, the Union remained strangely silent, though the facts blatantly demonstrated a violation of constitutional guarantees. When the Supreme Court ruled in Rumely's favor—and when he was no longer in peril—the ACLU belatedly indorsed his position, giving the impression that it had supported him all along. Yet when the pro-communists Corliss Lamont and Julius Emspak speciously pleaded the First Amendment before the congressional committees, the ACLU rushed into print with defense of their "rights."

The indictment under the Smith Act of a group of "alleged pro-fascists" in 1943 stirred up lukewarm indignation in ACLU hearts—and the Union reserved judgment on the case until the government had presented its evidence in court. Not so when the eleven top communists were indicted in 1948. The ACLU had no need to hear the government's evidence. It was immediately clear to ACLU leaders that the Constitution was in jeopardy, and the ACLU's director freely predicted from the start that the Supreme Court would reverse a finding of guilty by the lower courts. (The Supreme Court sustained the judgment on the "clear and present danger" principle—long a darling of the left—which immediately became suspect to the ACLU.)

When in *U.S. vs. Shapiro*, the courts suspended the protection of the Fifth Amendment in OPA cases, the ACLU looked briefly and turned its head away, finding no violation of the Constitution. When the West Coast racketeer Mickey Cohen was driven from city after city, without due process, the ACLU was elsewhere detained. During the Kefauver Committee investigation, the senators and staff hauled up witnesses with no notice of charges, abused them and held them up to shame and ridicule before TV cameras, inserted loaded summaries in the record, refused those accused of confrontation and cross-examination. The ACLU remained silent, though it has screamed loudly at anti-commuunist Congressional committees for allegedly similar practices.

The LaFollette Committee's questions (and enforced answers) on the political associations and activities of employers elicited no complaints from the ACLU—nor did its bulletin decry then the employment of "guilt by association." The principles the ACLU espouses for communists did not apply to employers.

The ACLU has failed to supply The American Legion with a statistical breakdown of its "right-wing" cases. Since 1951, the Legion has been requesting it, but despite repeated assurances that a list was being compiled, it has never been forthcoming. Without such a list, no guess is valid as to what part of the Union's efforts has been devoted to the communists. Estimates run to as high as 90 percent.

It certainly is not hard to understand why the ACLU's activities in behalf of the extreme right have been grudging and strictly legalistic, whereas its entry into judicial and public arenas in behalf of communists and left-wingers has been fervid, crusading, and fraught with publicity releases and cries of anguish at capitalist malevolence. The reason for this imbalance has been given by Roger Baldwin, until recently Mr. ACLU, in an article he wrote for the propaganda organ, *Soviet Russia Today*.

"Those of us who champion civil liberties in the United States and who at the same time support the proletarian dictatorship of the Soviet Union are charged with inconsistency and insincerity . . . If I aid the reactionaries to get free speech now and then, if I go outside the class struggle to fight censorship, it is only because those liberties help to create a more hospitable atmosphere for working class liberties. *The class struggle is the central conflict of the world; all others are incidental. When that power of the working class is once achieved, as it has been only in the Soviet Union, I am for maintaining it by any means whatsoever.*" (Italics Baldwin's.)

This statement, written in the middle Thirties, is a dead giveaway of a position still held by dominant forces in the ACLU. Eliminate the straight communist orientation, which Baldwin now coyly disavows, and it still applies. For the net effect of ACLU activities has been to inflame rather than minimize the class struggle, to stir up hatred against "big business" and those whom the Union raucously labels the "professional patriots," to weaken America's will to resist acts and ideas which historically have been repugnant to the republic.

Though it still pleads for civil liberties, the constitutional safeguards, and judicial due process, the ACLU has systematically betrayed these principles by subscribing to the bureaucratic abuses of big government, whenever they help leftist ends.

The ACLU's blithe unconcern over encroachments of administrative law—in which the judicial process was assumed increasingly by the President, in which the income tax statute reversed Anglo-Saxon tradition by laying the burden of proof on the accused in both administrative and judicial action, in which the executive subpoena suspended the Fifth Amendment—vanishes promptly when the Attorney General lists a few communist fronts.

The genesis of the ACLU is an interesting one. Its progenitor was the American League to Limit Armaments which itself was conceived in December 1914 at the Railroad Club in New York. In time, the group changed its name to the American Union Against Militarism. The change of name did not mark a change of purpose: To agitate and organize against American entry into World War I. When President Wilson's ill-conceived diplomacy was soured by British vinegar into outright military intervention, the organization changed its name, becoming the National Civil Liberties Bureau. Its mission was to encourage conscientious objection to military service, to defend conscientious objectors, and, following the call of Roger Baldwin's heart, to come to the aid of those rough and tumble revolutionaries, the Wobblies. In 1920, the NCLB became the American Civil Liberties Union.

To avoid misunderstanding: I do not question the right of Baldwin and his assorted organizations to defend whomsoever they would, or to use the Constitution and the courts as their weapons. I do resist their right to do so as embattled Americans fighting in the name of Washington, Jefferson, and the Bill of Rights. When the ACLU came to the vocal defense of the Wobblies who broke up a peaceful Legion parade in Centralia and murdered four Legionnaires, it had about as much interest in the

Constitution as a group of street fighters, barricaded in a church, have in the Sermon on the Mount.

The dedication to honest principle of the ACLU has had no better description than the words of Roger Baldwin, written in NCLB days, to a fellow worker: "We want also to look like patriots in everything we do. We want to get a good lot of flags, talk a good deal about the Constitution and what our forefathers wanted to make of this country." It took the Stalinists until 1936 to arrive at this tactic, at which time the ACLU gratefully reported that its "defense work was greatly strengthened by the new policy of the Communist Party, which has encouraged the formation of united-front committees to bring together diverse agencies in common and harmonious action."

It is of some significance that the forces of labor were once considerably more suspicious of the ACLU than they are today. President William Green of the AFL denounced it in 1934 as an organization whose "practice is almost exclusively the defense of communists." John L. Lewis, then an AFL stalwart, wrote in 1924 that the ACLU "has not, in a single instance, come to the assistance of a man or woman who did not profess radical sentiments, or who was not allied with the communists, the anarchists, the revolutionary, or the radical movements of America. Fifty-two persons, holding a total of 325 directorates in 45 organizations (of which the ACLU was one) are in control of the radical and revolutionary campaigns now being waged in this country."

In 1935, the ACLU published a pamphlet, *Who's Un-American? An Answer to the "Patriots"*, which lumped William Green and the AFL with crackpots like Elizabeth Dilling, and protested against *"patriotic" agencies* for wanting to "make it a crime to incite soldiers and sailors to disobey orders." It accused the Hearst press of such high crimes as "loyalty to private initiative, capitalist enterprise, and the right to get rich."

The ACLU listed among "un-American" organizations the Elks and the D.A.R. Applying the doctrine of "guilt by association," it sought to discredit its pet enemies as "associates of Russian Czarist aristocrats," a phrase taken from the red lexicon of smear.

Though the ACLU loudly proclaimed the right of "advocacy of force and violence"[3] against the state, it objected to certain groups and individuals because they advocated rearmament, free enterprise, and what it characterized as "distrust of democracy." The Elks and others, said the Union, had "much in common" with fascism.

In 1942, the ACLU, having the nazis in mind, demonstrated its vaunted impartiality by announcing that the First Amendment (free press and speech) did not apply to those believed to have contact with the enemy. "Today a man must be judged in part by his motives," said Roger Baldwin. "We didn't defend the *right* of Father Coughlin to *publish* the magazine *Social Justice*. We would never defend a paper like *Social Justice*, which, *it is reasonable to assume*, was voicing enemy propaganda." He suggested the use of common sense in judging a pro-nazi. "Has he associated with known enemy agents?" Baldwin asked. To date, neither he nor the ACLU has applied the same set of criteria or the same assumptions to those who associate with communist agents.

In the year 1937, when the St. Marys, Pa., *Press* published an editorial critical of the CIO and the National Labor Relations Board, NLRB officials called on the editor, and, according to *Editor & Publisher*, "cross-examined him upon matters not at all relevant to the industrial hearing and compelled him to reveal, against a well-accepted journalistic principle, the name of the writer of the editorial . . . What was crystal clear was the effort of the examiner and the board's attorneys to discredit the paper . . . to intimidate its editor and other editors who might [wish to criticize] the board and its administration."

The ACLU found no issue of press freedom then; it found none when a Senate committee ransacked the private files of William Randolph Hearst. This led Walter Lippmann to write that "the directors of the Union have missed one opportunity after another to prove that they really stand for the thing they profess to stand for, that they care for civil liberty as such . . . and not

---

[3] And advocacy of murder.

merely because it is a convenience for communists." Again, when the Government sought to classify the Associated Press as a "common carrier," subject to regulation, the ACLU found no civil liberties issue.

When James A. Wechsler, editor of the anti-anti-communist New York *Post* and kissing kin to ACLU board member Osmond Fraenkel, was questioned by Senator McCarthy on the policies of his newspaper, the Union jumped in with publicity release and loudspeaker, sounding the alarm against this "threat to the freedom of the press." Wechsler was admittedly a member of the Young Communist League in the Thirties.

The flexibility of the ACLU's views on civil liberties was further demonstrated during WW II. The Union did not protest the activities of the Friends of Democracy and other "anti-fascist" groups which systematically prepared blacklists of all those who had expressed pro-Axis opinions, who had joined America First, or who had opposed U.S. entry into WW II. A book by John Roy Carlson, financed by the Friends of Democracy, which had a wide sale was never challenged by the ACLU as blacklist, nor did the Union hire a war-time Merele Miller to write a counterblast.

As a matter of fact, the ACLU's 1944 report, *In Defense of Our Liberties*, began with the glowing assertion that "the third year of the war has maintained the unexpected record of the first two years in freedom of debate and dissent on all public issues and in the *comparatively slight resort to war-time measures of control or repression of opinion* . . . Marked advances have been made under the impact of the professed aims of the war, *particularly in meeting the claims of racial minorities.*" (Italics added.)

It is only after one has read through these sonorous sentences that their true meaning becomes apparent. For as the report states calmly later on, the period it covered was distinguished by such "marked advances" as the arrest of 30 Americans for violation of the Smith Act (a case in which the ACLU refused to intervene, in glaring contrast to its passionate opposition to the prosecution of communists under the same act), the conviction of

29 members of the German-American Bund charged with ob-
structing the Selective Service Act, legislation against persons of
Japanese ancestry in Arizona, Colorado, and Utah, the suspension
of habeas corpus in Hawaii, the discrimination against German
refugees, etc., etc.

What the ACLU presumably meant by "marked advances," of
course, was that in this time of gory friendship with our gallant
Russian allies, few communists found themselves in the pokey or
under attack.

As communist perfidy and communist infiltration became
more apparent to the American people, and as the piled-up
evidence became incontrovertible, the ACLU's reports to its
members and the public became more hysterical, more illogical,
and more politically partisan. In *Times of Challenge*, issued in
August 1947, was a carefully snide attack on the Republican
Party, the American businessman, and all conservative values. It
bemoaned the expression of the popular will which resulted in
the election of a Republican Congress in 1946 as an indication of
the lamentable desire "to repudiate experimentation in government and to return to the presumably sound leadership of private
business." Characterizing the Taft-Hartley Act as a "legal strait-
jacket," and labeling as "unreasonable" the President's belated
loyalty program to rid the Federal service of "any employees
suspected of communist sympathies"[4] the Union admitted that it
could only point to vague "tendencies," of lost civil liberties
(based perhaps on a reading of the civil liberties Ouija board
which it operates in its Fifth Avenue offices), and conceded that
the year was "marked by a large number of minor gains."

The 1947 report was remarkable also for the following:

1.   Citing no facts, it blasted the House Un-American Activities Committee as being "almost exclusively occupied with
ferreting out communist influences by the same irresponsible
methods of innuendo, scare-head publicity and unfair treatment
of witnesses."

---

[4]No one is ever proved a communist to the Union's satisfaction, and
everyone is persecuted for sympathies.

2.   It pooh-poohed the communist menace by stating that
the "President's [loyalty order] and the general excitement
aroused by it reflects the *widespread belief, unsupported by
substantial evidence*, that communists with a 'primary loyalty to
Russia' have infiltrated into many Federal departments." (Italics
added.)

3.   "In Congress the Republican leadership *apparently* considered a move against the poll tax good *political strategy* and
therefore ordered hearings on the bill to abolish [it] ." (Italics
added.)

4.   On the exclusion of the American Youth for Democracy,
which it conceded was the "successor to the Young Communist
League": "It is conceivable that though the national organization
may be communist-controlled, this may not be true of its locals."
The ACLU might have added, with equal intellectual honesty, that
though the Communist Party might conceivably be under communist control, this would not necessarily be true of the Kings
County branch of the party.

5.   "Though the Philippines became independent on July 4,
1946, *its conservative pro-American government managed to win
a popular vote* for measures tying the islands' economy closely to
American capital . . . The Union had objected to the
measures . . . as unduly restricting Philippine freedom." (Italics
added.)

The 1949 report, *In the Shadow of Fear*, started out with the
usual reverse homily: "The imagined insecurity of the strongest
democracy in the world in the face of the cold war with
communism has created an atmosphere in which fear makes the
maintenance of civil liberties precarious." This was sheer poppy-
cock, as the author of the report must have known had he read
the later print of his own product, which demonstrated an
increase in civil liberties throughout the two-year period.

Let it be remembered that this covered the period of the early
Hiss case, and of the encyclopedic and documented evidence of
widespread Soviet espionage. The 1949 report, however, deliberately ignored these vital facts, but summed up the work of the
House Un-American Activities Committee as "inflammatory and

irresponsible exposures." And it went on, the "excessive and jittery concentration on the communist danger, *so little justified by any activities at home* . . . has inevitably resulted in strengthening the conservative anti-communist forces . . . the FBI's functions have been expanded under laws now penalizing opinions and associations, [what laws?] risking for the first time in our history the creation of a secret police system." This, as ACLU General Counsel Morris Ernst has demonstrated, is a rank libel.

Of some interest, since the ACLU is constantly referring to its defense of the civil rights of Ku Klux Klanners, is an item in the 1949 report which noted with approval that Alabama had suppressed the organization. "The Union's Southern representatives," the report says blandly, "were active in assisting the authorities" in this suppression.

The black silence of hypocrisy reigned over the 1949 report, for it said not a word, nor wept yet a tear, over the blacklisting by Hollywood of such men as Morrie Ryskind, the late James Kevin McGuinness, and others who had appeared before the House Un-American Activities Committee as friendly witnesses. Following their testimony, these Hollywood writers and directors, who had committed the unpardonable sin of exposing communist shenanigans, found themselves unable to work. The infamous Hollywood Ten, communists all who improperly pleaded the First Amendment and consequently went to jail for contempt of Congress, had the support of the ACLU, which attempted to file an *amicus curiae* brief on their behalf with the Supreme Court.

In 1951, the ACLU's report *Security and Freedom: the Great Challenge*, demonstrated a shift in emphasis. Roger Baldwin, who had written the earlier reports, was no longer executive director, and the report reflected the absence both in the loss of his flamboyant anti-anti-communist bias and his crisp polemic style. The new executive director, Patrick Murphy Malin, combined a new turgidity with an occasional realization that perhaps, after all, and maybe, the anti-communists were not Constitution-chomping monsters or the communists suburban reformers. With

Malin, however, something new was added—the misuse of the term
"due process." From that point on, anything at all, including a
speech or an article whose opinions Malin found unpleasant,
might find itself characterized as "violative of the spirit of due
process"—whatever that means.

Due process, however, did not enter into the ACLU's evaluation of the stormy Tydings Committee hearings. The scandalous
treatment of pro-McCarthy witnesses, the vicious injection of the
religious issue, the exclusion of minority counsel from the
hearings, the smear against people who were refused permission
to testify, the political chicanery and outright fraud of the
majority behavior—fraud later admitted under oath by Senator
Tydings—did not faze the ACLU. It rejoiced instead over the
"fairness of ex-Senator Tydings" subcommittee in investigating
[Senator McCarthy's] charges."

The ACLU protested that "small risks" must be run in order
to maintain our liberties—a view which must amuse the Russians,
who have seen such "small risks" walk off with our most precious
military, diplomatic, and atomic secrets. But the ACLU argued
further that the judicial process must also be subverted by the use
of communists on juries. "Discrimination on political grounds
(sic) . . ." said the 1951 report, "established a bad precedent . . . Furthermore, indictments handed down by a grand jury
from which communists have been excluded, might be invalidated; they would certainly be invalidated if handed down against
communists." This novel concept, which would make it mandatory to include in juries persons with a direct interest in the
litigation, was not invoked by the ACLU when Robert Best and
Tokyo Rose were tried—even though no nazis or fascist sat in the
grand jury room or the jury box to insure justice.

By far the longest report in the ACLU's history, *Freedom,
Justice, Equality* runs to 160 pages of small print. It covers the
period between the 1951 report and June 1953, and it might have
done an important job of clarifying issues which the ritualistic
liberals had deliberately muddied. The 1953 report acknowledged
that its litigative function had declined, owing to a sharp increase
of interest by the legal profession in civil liberties cases. The ideal

function of the ACLU was therefore one of education. But the Malin-Reitman booklet strays far from this objective. Page after page of my copy is bright with underscoring of discredited bromides, half-truths, distortions, and false conclusions—too numerous to itemize here.

It is difficult to assess blame for this. In Malin's case, it seems clear to me, the fault lies in his inability to clamber out of the box of paradoxes which the ACLU has constructed over the years. With Arthur Garfield Hays one enters a never-never land of frustrations and contradictions. On the one hand, he has lent his name and been party to some outrageous campaigns of smear against ex- and anti-communists. But he has also come to the aid of controversial anti-communists like Jan Valtin, supported the Soviet escapee Leon Volkov, and served honorably with the Fair Trial for Mikhailovitch Committee at a time when it was considerably more unpopular to do so than it might be today. There are reasons for Hays' split personality, none of which are the concern of this article, but they go much deeper than any presumed crypto-loyalty to communist purposes.[5]

The case of Alan Reitman is something else again. As publicity director, his influence is covert but great. The stream of publicity releases which emanates from his office is largely responsible for the charge in certain circles that the Union is primarily interested in yanking communist chestnuts out of the fire. But Reitman's motives are as obscure as his political past, which includes a period of work for the CIO-Political Action Committee.

The confusions of Malin, the predilections of Hays, and the shadowy operations of Reitman have been bolstered by a hard ideological core made up of Walter Gellhorn and Osmond K.

---

[5] Hays has been listed as a member of nine organizations cited by the U.S. Attorney General as communist fronts; was affiliated with or participated in activities of eleven organizations cited by the House Committee on Un-American Activities as being connected with the Communist Party; and was affiliated with or participated in activities of five organizations cited by the California Committee on Un-American Activities as being connected with the Communist Party.

Fraenkel (stalwarts in the National Lawyers Guild which has been repeatedly cited as a communist front), and Corliss Lamont, whose denials of communist membership must be believed simply because he is of more value to the party out than in. Until 1940, communists like Elizabeth Gurley Flynn and crypto-communists like Dr. Harry F. Ward sat in joyous comfort on the ACLU's Board of Directors and left only as a gesture of protest against a dead-letter by-law which had been passed, barring from the Union's governing body those who gave support to communist causes.

Against these anti-libertarian influences, a small group fought a valiant but all-too-often losing battle. Among them were Clifford Forster, the Union's special counsel[6]; Irving Ferman, its Washington representative; and Merlyn S. Pitzele, who was recently forced out after eight years of *sturm and drang*. With others of like mind, they have battled for a reasonable appraisal of the complex issues arising out of the cold war, for a clear-cut statement on the nature and activities of the communist conspiracy, and for impartial action and propaganda on all civil liberties cases—both right and left. But they have been thwarted by the ideological recalcitrance of the majority, and by the systematic communist infiltration of key ACLU local chapters which backstop the "dirty hands" civil libertarians at all points of conflict.

The effects of this conflict can be discovered in the 1953 report, in its sins of omission, and its sins of commission. When considered in the light of the ACLU's formal statements on labor

---

[6]Forster has since resigned because the ACLU's Board of Directors refused to take a positive stand against communism. Shortly after Forster resigned, the ACLU did an about-face and adopted an anti-communist resolution recognizing that communism is a world-wide conspiracy and not a political theory, but making no reference to the espionage aspect for which Forster had been fighting. However, even the watered-down version failed to get the votes of Osmond Fraenkel, Dorothy Dunbar Bromley, Dorothy Kenyon, Gen. Telford Taylor and Walter Gellhorn. In view of the internal opposition, it will be interesting to see how the organization will implement the resolution in its work.

and on subversion, the form of the onslaught on the public consciousness becomes clear.

After eight years of cold war, the ACLU refuses to accept the vast body of testimony and documentation which lies behind Supreme Court Justice Jackson's dicta in *American Communications Association vs. Douds*. Two points therein are pertinent:

1. "The Communist Party alone among American parties past or present is dominated and controlled by a foreign government."

2. "Every member of the Communist Party is an agent to execute the communist program." Membership in the C.P. is thereby removed from the constitutional areas of free speech and association; it is an overt act against the duly constituted authority of the Congress.

Yet in its discussions of the loyalty program and the academic freedom question, the ACLU persists in dealing with communist membership as if it were an expression of dissenting beliefs, analogous to membership in any of the dissident or revolutionary parties which have periodically sprung up in American political life. It concedes that no teacher should "advocate any opinions or convictions derived from a source other than his own free and unbiased pursuit of truth," yet concludes by objecting to any action, whether by investigating committees or school authorities, which removes disciplined communists from their posts. Only a blatant act of academic sabotage will satisfy the ACLU, and since communists are clever enough not to commit such acts, this is a quietus on all reprisal.

But the ACLU, which would grant full license to communists, shies away from granting full citizenship rights to Senator McCarthy. It took no notice of *Time* magazine's abuse of press freedom in an attack on McCarthy—an attack, incidentally, in which certain allegations made against the Senator ran directly counter to every scrap of research in *Time's* files—but the Union objected vocally when, failing to receive a retraction from *Time*, McCarthy exercised his right as a citizen by calling the libels to the attention of advertisers. This, said the ACLU with perplexing logic, made him "prosecutor, judge, and jury."

Similarly, the ACLU completely misrepresented the so-called "book-burning" episode, which developed around McCarthy's legitimate attempt to show the American public that U.S.-operated propaganda libraries in Europe and Asia were carrying communist books and periodicals, and his justifiable attempt to get them off the shelves. This, in the ACLU's fervid opinion, was "censorship." (Ironically, the ACLU did not raise a peep when hundreds of thousands of books and school texts were turned into pulp in Germany, by order of General Clay, because they were written by people suspected of nazi sympathies. Among the books destroyed: Noncontroversial texts and Holy Bibles.)

The ACLU banned communists and sympathizers from its board of directors in 1940, but it refuses the U.S. Government the right to ban communists from government employ, on the theory that "a free society takes its major risks on the side of liberty." But it is the ACLU's considered opinion that labor unions, which are a kind of enforced public utility in many cases, need not take these risks. "Any demands for union democracy must be tempered with a clear recognition of the serious obstacles which face unions in maintaining democratic standards. Historically, many unions have had to struggle for survival against deadly attacks by employers who did not hesitate to use spies, bribery, intimidation, or even physical violence." The parallel is clear, though the ACLU's standards aren't.

In advocating greater union democracy—within the delimitations of union "risks," however—the ACLU has nevertheless plumped for the nineteen Taft-Hartley Act revisions which former Labor Secretary Martin Durkin proposed. One of these points would have immeasurably strengthened the control of union leaders, permitting them to force an employer to fire a member for "disclosure by the member of confidential information of the union." The ACLU has made it clear, in *Democracy in Labor Unions*, that union leadership has often used every means to stifle opposition. By the Durkin clause, any union member bringing his opposition to the leadership to the floor of an open meeting could forfeit his job, with no recourse to the "due process" which the ACLU so frequently invokes in communist cases.

The sad fact remains that "due process" is a convenient argument, as conveniently forgotten when it suits the ACLU's philosophy. It was not invoked when the National Labor Relations Board acted as "prosecutor, judge, and jury" in the early Wagner Act days. It was not invoked when, under the New Deal, administrative edicts supplanted the acts of Congress. It was not invoked when the State Department censored Trotzky's biography of Stalin. It becomes sacred when communist and left-wing toes are trod upon.

Is the ACLU a front or a fraud? Or is it a legitimate grouping of sincere but sometimes misguided civil libertarians? When the ACLU insists that loss of "civil liberties" to communists is the first step to loss of civil liberties for all, does it really mean it? I have neither a yes nor a no answer. But on this, I can be categorical:

Until the ACLU cleans its house of special pleaders and its mind of false concepts it will and should be suspect in the public mind. No amount of hand-wringing and protestation will change this. What the ACLU needs is a couple of overt acts—on the side of freedom.

American Legion Monthly
1956

How Communism
Demoralizes Youth

*When this was written, obviously, the author felt there
was no need to discriminate carefully between those
who, as in the case of Ayn Rand, to cite the most
cogent example, can maintain moral values on a completely rational basis and those who, as he says, "make
all standards of justice and decency merely 'relative.'"
That there is a wholly rational alternative both to
so-called conventional Christian morality and Communist immorality is a significant fact which, I trust,
Toledano would no longer ignore, as he seems to in the
following discussion.*

There are over eight thousand members of American Youth
for Democracy in our schools and colleges. They are the storm
troops of a new totalitarianism which is attempting to put a
halter on America's youth, to blindfold it so that it can be led
down the Communist road to its own destruction. If eight
thousand seems a small number to accomplish this task, let it be
remembered that for each of these AYD zealots there are
thousands of other young people who are taken in by the
propaganda, who mouth the same slogans, who follow the same
cynical leadership, and who believe that any attempt to expose
Stalinoid fascism is "red-baiting."

I have talked to these earnest, aggressive, misled young people.
Most of them are not vicious but have merely succumbed to the
same disease which afflicts too many of our men in high place.

The story of their error is a complex one. How did they get that way? And is there anything we can do about it?

It might be well to begin this account with the young Italian prisoners I talked to, or with the tough-bodied and sullen Afrika Korps boys who swung pick and shovel near our barracks. This was youth too, given to a like heresy, and as Eugene Lyons once put it, "deliberately mobilized to beat civilization into a pulp."

These were the heirs to that backwash of history which to the strains of *Giovinezza*, of *Horst Wessel*, unleashed terror, rapine, and desolation over three continents. Now they were bewildered and unhappy as they went about their tasks, guarded by an American kid from Kentucky or Brooklyn whose loaded shotgun was merely the outward manifestation of his strength. They had been blindfolded and the sudden sight of the sun, coming with defeat, had made sick people of them.

Or perhaps the starting point should be the student who had subscribed to another "wave of the future"—the second in one generation—who had sold his birthright for a mess of verbiage, and then seeing it plain in a flash of intuition had come to me with tears in his voice as he murmured: "But I don't understand, I just don't understand . . ."

This young man had been lured into the Communist youth movement, not pressured into it. Like most of the students who joined the Communist-controlled AYD, he came from middle class background and went to a fairly expensive college. Contrary to current belief, idealism had only played a minor part in his conversion. He had gone into it because of an emptiness in himself primarily. Gregariousness, an inverted rah-rah spirit, and a hankering for ritual and totemism, all these were involved in his choice. And once in, there was social pressure, a sense of being in the know, a big shot, and a pumped-up feeling that he was showing the adult world a thing or two by this courageous stand in favor of bloody revolution and the holiness of Joseph Stalin. But in the main, it was merely that in succumbing to Marxist immoralism, he was taking the final step in a walk which began early in his education.

For the blindfold began to be applied when the whole moral structure of our society was questioned by what has been called *scientism*. Democracy is based on moral premises, self-evident principles. Totalitarianism begins with a total denial of any moral code and sets up in its place power and material advantage, no matter how achieved. It is one of the deep ironies of our misfit society that the scientific spirit, which developed in the expanding and unrestricted world of a free enterprise democracy, is today the root of the evil which threatens it. For scientism sowed a deep mistrust in the mind of contemporary man for any authority beyond the field of empirical observation. Once accepted, it relegated to the dust bin as irrational prejudice, flabby emotion and enslaving propaganda, the irreplaceable authority of moral value, making all standards of justice and decency merely "relative."

This is not to say that the disciples of scientism steal from the poorbox, smoke opium, or seduce the vicar's daughter. In their so-called private lives they are much like any other human, but they have become susceptible to the appeal of a skepticism which eventually accepts the most brutish *realpolitik*, leading them to the most tragic heresy of our time, the belief that. ends justify means. Watching the captive Hitler youth, it struck me that Germany's form of national bolshevism was accepted with unique heartiness by the people most thoroughly committed to scientific method.

> "When right feelings are not supported by right thinking," Mortimer Adler has pointed out, "good men can be insensibly corrupted ... When the mind refuses to *see* the good and the bad things, repudiating any moral quality in things and actions to see, the will is blind, and blindly attaches itself to this or that through natural instinct, waywardness, or caprice."

During the war, when I was entrusted with the job of explaining to the troops what the fighting was about, it became obvious to me that the present generation was tailor-made for the totalitarian blindfold, and—since the virus today is Soviet rather than Nazi—for Communism. For though they were as good in *feeling* as any other generation of Americans, their *thinking* was conditioned by considerations which held the ethical as something irrelevant. The primary bases for their thinking were tissue needs, immediate workability, and power relations.

With the young people in schools and colleges who are drifting into the periphery of the AYD, of the PCA, and of the Wallace mystocracy, this ethical apathy is deeper and more conscious. The moral nerve has already been desensitized and there is no longer any pain when the Communizing youth leaders begin to pry it out. This desensitizing process begins with the destruction, cynically plotted, of any vestigial loyalties to men and institutions, and the instrument used is the Marxist theory of the class struggle. With this, the power to make ethical judgments is destroyed.

If every man is motivated by his economic position and his financial aspirations, if man's primary loyalty is to his purse and not to his principles—and if these pulls are unconscious—how is one to trust the ordinary channels of information. The daily paper, the preacher in the pulpit, the statesman and the professor, no matter what they say or how they act, are suspect. They are all participants in a continuous effort to mislead, to pervert, to hinder the forces of "progress" which are bound to triumph, mechanically, in a pre-determined historical process, say the Marxists. The class struggle, in effect, serves as a set of blinders, much as the theory of race supremacy served the young Nazi.

A great deal of superficial "evidence" can be piled on the impressionable mind to prove this point of a subverted press, clergy, and political leadership, all of which have "sold out" to the money interests for hard cash or for prestige. And insecure youth, seeing the inequities of society and fearful for his future, has soon shut out all the influences which might tear away the tightening blindfold. The "inevitability" of the workers' revolution, easily translated into the dictatorship of the proletariat, helps clinch the argument. In the development of regimented youth, this is of prime importance for it combines semantic confusion with moral disaffection.

The idealogical planners of the Communizing youth movements, the thinkers who draw their creed from Lenin and Stalin,
the slick young men who front for the Party in the AYD and the
other youth fronts, all know that the ethical basis of action is
nullified once you have made all history an "inevitable" process.
Dialectical materialism denies that at every step of our lives we
are faced with alternatives, that unlike beasts we are able to
distinguish between good and evil. By Marxist logic, the dictatorship of the proletariat—not a dictatorship at all, says the
apologist, and anyhow what about the Negro? the NAM?—is right
because it is inevitable. How many times have eager fellow
travelers told me that you can't hold back the dawn, that the
smart thing is to climb on the bandwagon now, back the winner,
get in on the ground floor? In other words, the new world order
is sold with all the trimmings that a shady promoter puts on a
phony bond issue.

The appeal of a young and victorious movement cannot be
under-estimated. Its effectiveness is widespread among the youth
who are not, as the sociologist Karl Mannheim pointed out,
innately "progressive" but rather aware that they have as yet no
stake in their society, no franchise to participate. Drama,
ritualism, totemism are supplied by the left totalitarians, giving a
glamor which tends to obscure the flapping backdrop of the
tawdry scene. The first hard knot is now tied in the blindfold, the
first section of the ethical nerve removed, when human nature, in
the struggle of class against class, is seen as debased, sordid. The
moral imperatives of ethical reason no longer exist. Mass purges,
slave labor empires, systematic assassination no longer offend—it's
all for the good of the world—and the criteria become speed and
success. If, in order to build the perfect society, all democratic
rights and human decencies are jettisoned, the novocained percep-
tions are not disturbed.

It is at this point that the earnest young seeker becomes a
casuist of first order. To make sense out of the two worlds we live
in, he must employ a double standard of political morality,
suppress facts, shut out the truth by smearing it, shout so that

what remains of conscience will not be heard. The basic American freedoms—of speech, of press, of religion, of association, from fear—these are just pretty speeches, he will say. But economic democracy, whatever that means, exists in the Soviet Union. Truth, from the lips of the capitalist enemy, ceases to be truth. Lies, from the loudspeakers of the Moscow radio, become the truth because they hasten the great day.

It is a happy moment for Lenin in his mausoleum when another sucker has swallowed his dictum: "The Marxian doctrine is omnipotent . . . It is complete and harmonious . . ." The blindfold is neatly in place. And, if you will observe, the coldly reasoning scientism has been gradually replaced by blind acceptance of an irrational doctrine. The rebel against authority, the believer in empirical truth, has performed an act of faith. The iconoclast is caught kneeling at Stalin's statue, clutching the *Problems of Leninism* in one hand, lifting a clenched fist, reciting a *Daily Worker* litany. Joseph Alsop put it bluntly when he said that Marxism is "a magic touch-stone . . . It does your thinking for you . . ."

For many young people, the Marxist blindfold is temporary. After a while, they drop it. For many, too, there is a chance at reclamation. For others who remain in the AYD-PCA periphery too long, removing the blindfold does no good. An acid in its folds has eaten their eyes away. They are permanently lost. Whether they drift from one Communist front to another or actually join the Party is not really very important . . . they act the same.

All loyalty for country, for family, for friends becomes secondary in their worship of the Soviet Union. If betrayal of their country is demanded, if they are told to spy on their friends, if they are ordered to turn in their relatives, so all embracing is their devotion that it is sure to be done. It is sometimes hard for us to believe this, but an abundance of evidence, incontrovertibly damning, thrusts itself at us to demonstrate its truth. The Report of the Royal Commission in Canada which investigated the theft of atom secrets is one shocking and revealing document attesting to the hold of the Communist ideology on its adherents, showing to what lengths they will go in its service. *The Secret Battalion* (digested in the October, 1946, *Plain Talk*) is even more wryly effective, coming as it does from Professor Harold Laski whose sympathies are very much with the Stalinizers.

Can we reclaim the lost or mislaid segment of our postwar generation? Can we re-indoctrinate the young people with the ethical and moral principles they have rejected, restore their respect for honor, decency, and the functioning goodness of man? At first glance, the task is of heroic dimensions, but it can be accomplished by working on the borderline cases—on the young people who have not accepted the blindfold but merely shut their eyes. They have uneasily accepted much which revolts their moral sense, but only because the totalitarians offered them a direction, a goal, and the comradeship of joint effort.

Sudden and shocking events, like the Hitler-Stalin pact and the recent Soviet attempt to sabotage the Marshall plan, have made some of them break away. But it is foolhardy, if not criminal, to wait for the Communists themselves to give us the ammunition. We must find our own ways of reconstructing the basis of democratic obligation in the present generation, of revitalizing the instinct for survival, of reawakening loyalties dormant but not dead.

Once during the war I was confronted by an audience of over a thousand Italian prisoners, sent to us from a PW camp for political rehabilitation. For thirty uncomfortable minutes I tried to explain democracy and the democratic process to these men who had lived all their lives in an environment which held our way of life up to ridicule. From these men to whom "liberty" was a meaningless word, there was not a smile, not a snigger, not a boo. Neither rhetoric nor humor moved them. They thought I was crazy—or lying.

Yet in some thirteen weeks, we had implanted in them a feeling of responsibility and participation. We showed them that the scales of justice can be evenly pitched. We showed them that democracy worked—that a *democratic* American army was triumphant over a *totalitarian* German or Italian army. We showed them that there can be obedience without compulsion. We showed them that democracies can tell the truth, even when it hurts, without collapsing. When these men were shipped out to quartermaster depots, they had begun to acquire a working faith in themselves and in the potentialities of a democratic system.

What we did for imprisoned Italians, we can do for free American youth. But if the totalitarian money-changers are to be driven from the temple of man, it can be done only by ceaseless effort: by sending people into the schools and colleges to talk, observe, counsel; by eternal vigilance which will prevent Communist infiltration of youth groups; by continually and dispassionately exposing the Communist and fascist totalitarians and their propaganda. But vastly more important: it must be demonstrated to the present generation that it has a stake in our democratic civilization, a stake not to be jeopardized by flirtations with death. It must be made clear that the world is not made up of enemies, that the ethical imperatives of our time are made up of self-evident and eternally durable truths.

Man does not live by bread alone, nor are political problems solved by polemic generalities. The totalitarians offer the youth of this country hard bread and black circuses. Can they be led away from the grim red path, back to the straight and open road? The answer is not in them, but in us . . .

Catholic Information Service
1947

The Alger Hiss Story

*Let no one do himself the disservice of assuming that
this brief treatment of the Hiss story means he need
not read Toledano's* Seeds of Treason. *The article, as it
appears here, is fine. The book is great.*

In Lewisburg Penitentiary, a man waits for liberation. The steel
walls of his cell do not merely confine him; they hold out a world
not of his choice, an enemy world of men who live and pray and
bless their Maker. In this world which he holds alien are many
who honor him—rich, respectable, or scum of the earth. Yet this
man is a traitor and a Communist. His name is Alger Hiss.

In many ways, Alger Hiss is a man without a country, a man
who can say "This is my own, my native land" only with that
crocodile irony which is the special bounty of treason. Alger
Hiss's "own" land is marked by a red stain on the maps of Europe
and Asia, a land where freedom burns feebly and in few souls.
Tyranny and terror are its shibboleths, betrayal and bondage its
bywords.

Millions can answer the question, Who is Alger Hiss? What he
may be is someththing else again. His name, in its contradiction
of symbols, adds to the bafflement: *Alger*, the almost comic
personifier of the rags-to-riches stories; *Hiss*, the onomatopoeia of
the spitting serpent. Neither the name nor the man who bears it
add up, to most Americans. To them, he is a mystery wrapped up
in an enigma. He is the Traitor rampaging in a land which, by its
very goodness, cannot understand treason. He is the Communist.

Yet alien though he may be, in a nation which has absorbed
the alien and made it native, Alger Hiss is no mystery. If he has
deceived his smug and powerful friends, it is because they have

not really experienced him. For to experience him, in the tepid flesh and the cold blood of his nature, is to know him.

I experienced Alger Hiss. I experienced him in the pages of congressional hearings as he twisted and turned to evade the inexorable questions of Richard Nixon; in the compassionate words of Whittaker Chambers; in the two trials, as he sat and I sat on hard benches while history closed an old account; at the moment of sentencing, as he stood to throw back into the teeth of justice the words of Judge Goddard.

The insight into Hiss's nature came in flashes—and in some cases the intuition did not explain itself until much later. There was the curious episode during Hiss's first appearance before the Un-American Activities Committee. It took persistence and repeated questioning by Nixon to elicit from him the name of one of the government officials who had brought him to Washington—Felix Frankfurter. On the face of it, Hiss was protecting Frankfurter from the guilt of association. But was he? Or was he perhaps serving notice on Frankfurter and others that, if the ship sank, Alger Hiss would not stand alone on the bridge. The enigma is its own answer.

There was Hiss's "explanation" to his friends, to those who had rallied around him but stirred uneasily when his testimony became too ringed in obscurity and contradiction to be totally convincing. Hiss offered "answers," far-fetched and vile, which poured slime over Whittaker Chambers even when they were not believed. Was Hiss a man fighting for his life and not finicky about the weapons at hand? This would be plausible and to a degree justifiable. But the stories, mutually exclusive, poured the same slime over those whom he professed to love and cherish—his wife and his stepson.

And there was Hiss's behavior on the witness stand in the first trial. Self-possessed, almost amused at the hulking prosecutor who had never hobnobbed with presidents and dictators, he tried insolence once—correcting Tom Murphy's grammar. It was successful with the chittering ladies who made up his courtroom claque. But most of the jury and the uncommitted spectators blinked their eyes, for the commissar had suddenly broken through the tea-party manner. Hiss dropped the insolence immediately, retreating behind his teacup.

These were the intuitions, nestling in the niches of a sturdy structure of evidence which Prosecutor Murphy built. The facts are a matter of legal record, and they have been supplemented since by the belated confession, from a senatorial witness stand, of Nathaniel Weyl, who knew Hiss as a card-carrying, dues-paying member of the Communist cell in Washington which Harold Ware organized. But the trial of Alger Hiss left many questions unanswered—not the questions of his innocence or guilt, for no amount of sapping by the Hiss cult has been able to topple the solid monolith of his guilt; but questions of the man himself, of his motivation and his evil, of the factors which made him a Communist and the forces which led him to compound his treason where others like Klaus Fuchs were to make partial penance in redhanded confession.

Does the story begin in the boy Hiss, growing up in a Baltimore as yet unsoiled by the grime of this industrial century, carrying on his back the burden of the *lumpen bourgeoisie*? Does it begin in the ambition of a widowed mother who projected a terrible frustration into a nature both gentle and adamant?

Was it then?

Or was the seed transplanted from the heart of Priscilla Fansler, who became Priscilla Hiss, a woman small and implacable, feeble in the wind of controversy but determined in the gale of history? Perhaps it was a virus, endemic to the tainted ideological kitchens of New York, which made monsters of the Rosenbergs and a Bolshevik of Alger Hiss. Unwept and unhonored, dead to the country which offered him both honor and tears, Alger Hiss sits in Lewisburg Prison—and the questions hover about him.

Start, then, with the boy Alger, growing up in a Baltimore which was no longer a community and not yet a modern city. As a schoolboy, he drew spring water from Druid Hill Park to sell in town, raised and sold squab, and played with his public-school classmates. But there lurked in the dark corners of his mind the specter of a father self-destroyed, the razor clenched in a bloody fist. Did the specter walk, many years later, when his sister writhed to her death after drinking Lysol, or a brother took the longer road with more conventional liquids? The mark of Cain-within-Abel must have been a weight on his soul, till he traded it for the more encompassing destruction of the society which should have claimed his loyalty.

Certainly something itched and tortured when, as an undergraduate at Johns Hopkins, he tried to seize stability and place, all student kudos, the fleeting glory of the campus leader, Phi Beta Kappa in his Junior year; top rank in the ROTC; editor of the college daily; member of the elite clubs—even the drinking club, though he was not a drinker; president of the dramatic society; a "smoothie" at campus dances to which he escorted leading Baltimore debutantes. And what of the desperate failures: a Rhodes Scholarship not won; rejection by the track team; and worst of all, loss of the Alexander Barton Cup for the student who had done most for his classmates—awarded to another! Instead; he was elected the "best handshaker."

No matter how much he had, he wanted all, and failing that, what he had became nothing. "Today Johns Hopkins, tomorrow the world," he could have said. The solid acceptance would overcome the rocking instability, the tremulous step of the insecure. The charming smile, the easy manner of the stabilized rich, the dignity of carelessness—all these could be his, heartfelt and enclosed.

These tensions could have catapulted Alger Hiss with Horatio Alger precision into a great law career. The brilliant mind and the will to success were there, ready at hand. The mind was closed to the gentler arts—to Shakespeare and music, to the books and the cadences that fill the heart with more transcendent longing. The fugal conflict of words and ideas was not for him. He was geared for the pragmatic and the instrumental, for the demonstrable theorem and the practical result.

It was this conventional outlook, this worship of the materialistic, which he took with him from the consecrated Babbittry of Baltimore to Harvard Law School. And the practical man is most prone to the spirit-rappings of Conan Doyle and Karl Marx. At

Harvard, the corruscating genius of Felix Frankfurter lay in wait, crouched to leap at whatever ties of Christian tradition still bound Hiss to the American past of his fathers. The soul, however, is not shaped by one fatal interview. Harvard seethed with the Sacco-Vanzetti case which, whatever the injustices involved, was the opening phase of the Communist victory over the American intellectual. In the context of the case, Professor Frankfurter was a hero. So too was Professor Francis Sayre, later to be Hiss's superior in the State Department.

There were others roaming the sophistical acres of Harvard, men who moved from the academic grove to the Communist *cloaca* with astonishing directness. Among them was Lee Pressman, forming then to the pattern of the American commissar—half-steel, half-lead, an opportunist with an ideology. Pressman had the organizational approach; success to him was an accretion, work and detail compounded. He was the first conscious architect of Hiss's Communism, moving with his friend to New York and Washington, to the International Juridical Association and the Harold Ware cell. The other influence was to come later.

At Harvard, Hiss proved that his ability and his ambition, which had been tested in the provincial puddle, could also triumph in the metropolitan lake. He was graduated *cum laude* from the Law School after capturing its highest honor, the editorship of the *Law Review*. Frankfurter opened the door to legal prestige for him by sending the young man to Washington as Justice Holmes's law secretary.

Hiss was rather amused by the patriarchal Supreme Court justice, carrying stories to his friends of Holmes's behavior, his tastes, his troubles. The old jurist was tired and troubled; his invalid wife had just died; he needed companionship. The Law, which stands above men but must also be of them, had begun to frighten him. Who could remain Olympian before the growing American revolution? He turned to philosophy and poetry for comfort and vindication. "How about Culture?" Hiss would say, the irony in the quiet voice directed as much against Holmes as against the idea of seeking solace in philosophical speculation, and he would read to him. The irony went deeper—an old man in a dry month being read to by a boy, the old man who promulgated the doctrines of "guilt by association" and "clear and present danger" being read to by a boy who would strike at the pinnacled Law in a manner which the Nineteenth Century mind of Holmes could hardly conceive.

It was in this period that the second fatal, and binding, interview occurred. Alger Hiss married Priscilla Fansler. Each marriage is set in its own destiny. Some are made in Heaven; this one might well have been made in Moscow. For Priscilla Hiss bore her own frustrations, her aggressions and tortures. Serious beyond humor, dedicated beyond redemption to unformulated goals, she carried on her conscience the scars of a broken marriage, of a Puritanical childhood, of a purposeless will which, world without end, invites the Devil.

On the surface, Priscilla Hiss was prim and repressed, pickling her passion in acidulous wit. But in her heart, she was the Walter Mitty of the revolution. The women who knit while the tumbrils roll were not her idea; she wanted to hold the reins in her hand. She was not a Communist at the time of her marriage to Hiss, but there is little doubt that she dreamed of Charlotte Corday—and as a Corday *manquee,* she made her mark on Alger. Boston, when Hiss began his practice of law in that city, was too small, too confined for her. She pushed him into taking a position with the law firm of Cotton & Franklin in New York.

Lee Pressman was in New York. So too was the International Juridical Association, an offshoot of the International Labor Defense, which was the Communist Party's legal arm. Pressman drew Hiss into the I.J.A., but Priscilla found more direct political action in the Morningside branch of the Socialist Party—a branch which had already taken more than half of the thirteen steps into the Communist Party. There were no guillotines handy, but soup kitchens for the unemployed served a temporary purpose. This was the induction into Communism for the Hisses, in no way remarkable or dramatic. Thousands went through like experiences, drifting into the party perhaps, then drifting out. But the grappling hooks bit deep into the Hisses.

At precisely what point the Hisses took their disloyalty oath, no one knows. But it is clear that when Alger joined the March on Washington of the New Deal, brought into the AAA by Lee Pressman, he was already one of Stalin's elected. More of his colleagues than Americans like to believe had taken the vows of political continency along with Hiss; he was part of a Communist cell in the AAA which eventually spread its infection throughout the federal government.

The Communist movement is a totality, and as a totality it has certain built-in imperatives. It must reject God as an authority above man unless it can convert God to Marxism-Leninism. It must reject free will and enshrine historical determinism and dialectical materialism, or free-ranging minds will challenge its dicta. It must be conspiratorial and dictatorial, even within its confines of strength, or the open hearts of men may find themselves in opposition. It must cultivate dishonor, for honor itself has its own imperatives. It must nourish treason, for in a totality only the Traitor can be trusted.

The Communist Party which Alger Hiss joined had still to begin its systematic rape of U.S. libertarians. (In its "third," or bloody, period, it was calling Franklin Roosevelt a "fascist.") Hiss did not join out of a misguided love of Thomas Jefferson or Abraham Lincoln: He was motivated by a rigorous acceptance of Leninist dogma. Communism afforded certainty and power to counter his life's insecurity.

Once he had accepted it, everything followed logically—the clandestine activities of the Ware cell, the first secret meetings with his apparatus superiors, the encounter with Colonel Boris Bykov of the Red Army's Fourth Bureau, the step into outright and systematic espionage. His eye did not flicker when he was asked to turn over top secret State Department documents to the Soviet apparatus; his hand did not tremble when he delivered them. Night after night, the documents were brought home for busy fingers to tap out on the old Woodstock. This was the Hiss contribution to the planned destruction of the United States.

But if, in a general way, Alger Hiss had collaborated in the would-be death of his country, he contributed directly and consciously to the murder of an American woman in Moscow—a woman who had left a child behind in the United States, whose crime was that she was married to a Soviet agent caught in Stalin's great purge. She was "Mrs. Robinson" or "Mrs. Rubens," a frightened woman who walked into the American Embassy in Moscow to report that her husband was missing. What American officials knew of her and transmitted to the State Department, fell into the hands of Alger Hiss. He recognized its significance; he knew what it would mean to the Soviet secret police; he sent the information back to Moscow, via apparatus courier. This was the death warrant, written out in Hiss's hand. "Mrs. Rubens" died. The small slip of paper on which Hiss made his notes is her monument.

Two trials, two books, have covered the grim and shocking record of Hiss's activities in the gray years between 1934 and 1938. It does not need recounting. But more than the record, there was the face and the manner of the man as he sat in court, listening and watching intently as the prosecution neatly laid each piece of evidence in place—a cool, arrogant face showing emotion only when the jaw muscle twitched slightly; and always, the hands clasped carefully on his lap, one thumb slowly rubbing the other. Or Hiss, during the recesses, standing outside the court-room door, smiling and bowing to the friends who clustered about him, as if the trial were merely a vulgar circus put on for the benefit of the *hoi polloi*. But beyond the opacity of expression, the watchful eye never rested.

But if the record of those busy years has been nailed down in law beyond the peradventure of a doubt, what of the later years? What of the time when a nation at was was proving that neither depression nor the coddling of a paternalist President could damage its virility? Tall, urbane, well-tailored, and smiling, Hiss remained at his post—still loyal to his disloyalty. The Hitler-Stalin pact did not shake him. Pride of country did not lift the revolutionary night from over his tent. Untouched by the itemized account of his treason which nestled in security files, Hiss continued to rise in the State Department, holding an impregnable outpost in the camp of the enemy, his people.

With the years, his power grew: busy at Dumbarton Oaks; busy at Yalta, where the world's future was sold for a mess of Stalin's promises; an architect of the preposterous Berlin settlement which left that city an island in a sea of Red. And the betrayals: the Polish government-in-exile, with the third largest combat force in Europe—delivered; China, exhausted by seven years of war—delivered; Korea, split in two—and delivered.

But the driving ambition to have and to hold, the will to treason, never lagged. The Hiss of Yalta, the Hiss of the United Nations conference in San Francisco, was still the boy who had won the scholarships, who had taken over all the clubs, who had graduated *cum laude* from Harvard.

The heat was on now; congressmen were pressing for his dismissal. But Alger Hiss worked steadily toward one last accomplishment. In the last weeks of 1945, Hiss had a plan, subtle but vast, for revolution by reorganization. It is marked in the files as the "Hiss Plan for Reorganization of the State Department." With it, in the files, is the quiet analysis of a State Department security officer, concerned over Hiss's "Svengali-like influence on the mental process" of Edward Stettinius—a Secretary of State who died in the tragic sense of his own failure. In mingled "admiration and horror," the security officer warned that should the Hiss Plan be put into effect, "the Hiss group will have achieved infiltration in, or control of, four critically strategic points, i.e., (a) UNO itself, (b) the UNO delegation, (c) State Department, and (d) Bureau of the Budget . . ."

Hiss's "reorganization plan" was his last warbled note in the State Department. Before he could impose it on a President tossed and plagued by problems beyond his comprehension, Hiss saw the danger flag flying. The ice had grown too thin even for so light-footed a skater. But he was still the success boy. From the State Department, he went to the Carnegie Endowment for International Peace—basking in its respectability, enjoying the $25,000 a year he earned as its president. The stage was smaller, but opportunity still presented itself.

When the Marshall Plan was devised, he was on hand, a participant in a citizen's committee. His contribution was unique;

he suggested that the Marshall Plan billions be administered by the United Nations secretariat—a group well salted with men who had left the United States government two steps ahead of the loyalty program.

Play the black and the red comes up. The Carnegie Endowment was Hiss's last play. The rigged wheel suddenly went honest and Hiss was caught. Eventually he went to prison for the minor crime of perjury. All the king's horses and all the Park Avenue commissars could not save him. The smiles, the bows, and the lies failed in the face of the immutable evidence. Even the appearance of Supreme Court Justice Felix Frankfurter, coming full circle to testify as a character witness, was unavailing. American juries are not easily awed, and the stink of treason was strong.

But in his cell, Alger Hiss can take comfort. Though he has become a symbol throughout the country, the figure of a new Benedict Arnold, Columbia University professors weep for him; a British peer writes a sorrowing book about him, collecting his royalties in advance from American millionaires. To them, he is a symbol too, but of "a generation on trial."

The generalization is too broad, but to a degree they are right. Part of a generation sinned with Hiss, still sins with Hiss, and sits in prison with Hiss. It has not heard the quiet voice which speaks in the dark night. It has not opened the Book of Jonah or read the burning line, "I do well to be angry, even unto death." It has not learned that when a soul divests itself of God, Evil takes possession. And not having heard, not having read, and not having learned, it has earned a damnation which Reason cannot chill.

The American Mercury
June 1953

ALGER HISS: A REMINDER

*Millions saw the television show that occasioned this
article. Sadly, most of them must have missed the rich
significance of the event, as here chronicled. Why, in an
industry where every hiccup of every ingenue seemingly is news, this truly newsy story was so poorly
covered is beyond me.*

W hen Alger Hiss's lawyers moved for a new trial, seeking to
rehearse in court their tired contention of "forgery by typewriter" and the argument that the entire American legal system
was corrupt, they were asked one simple question by Federal
Judge Henry W. Goddard.

Was there, he said, "a shred of evidence" to sustain their plea?

"No, your Honor," they answered.

This should have ended the comedy of Hiss's pretensions. The
case he had built up in the press consisted of a lame and
meaningless affidavit from a "documents expert" whose major
claim to fame was her efforts in behalf of the convicted
communist spies, Ethel and Julius Rosenberg. So empty a defense
could impress only those who believe that anti-communism is a
crime—but that treason is simply a form of nonconformism.

Yet from the moment that Alger Hiss was confronted with
hard, irrefutable evidence of his espionage (and worse) before a
Congressional committee, a grand jury, and a Federal court, he
has had at his side a noisy group of influential adherents who
have proclaimed his innocence or minimized his crime. We now
find the confusion compounded by Howard K. Smith, a television
commentator, and James Hagerty, former press secretary to
President Eisenhower and now vice president of the American
Broadcasting Company.

Given the history of the Hiss Case, it would be too much to
expect that they are the last. The Smith-Hagerty caper, however,
is particularly shocking. Since television was the medium, Smith

and Hagerty, despite their protestations concerning motivation, were able to abuse their great powers to poison the well of public opinion and to attempt the rehabilitation of a man—not merely a convicted felon who betrayed his country's secrets to the Soviet Union, but one whose entire political life was one great communist lie.

The Smith-Hagerty action in giving Hiss a forum, on a program designed to kick former Vice President Richard Nixon at a moment when he was down and vulnerable, has justly aroused many Americans. They feel that an insurance company might have secured more desirable means to sell policies. But the American Broadcasting Company was simply following a course of action which came naturally to others of otherwise decent reputation.

That zealous stalwart of the American Civil Liberties Union, Morris Ernst, delivered himself of the opinion that Hiss was not guilty on the basis of Hiss's self-serving book and with the startling confession that he had never bothered to read the court record.

Earl Jowitt, an unemployed Labor peer whose distaste for things American did not include the Yankee dollar, put together a curious volume in defense of Alger Hiss so full of "errors" that Doubleday, the publisher, honorably called back and destroyed the first edition.

Helen Buttenwieser, a heavy contributor to the bail fund of Soviet spy Robert Soblen, used her Park Avenue home as a rallying point for the Hiss defenders during the trial. After the jury pronounced his guilt, she sat in the courtroom weeping. And in New York legal circles, she passionately argued his defense.

Who were these people impugning? In taking up the cudgels for Hiss they were subscribing to his assertions that everyone was lying but himself, that he had been framed by President Truman's Justice Department; by the Federal Bureau of Investigation; by Thomas Donegan, a former FBI official of impeccable reputation who as special assistant to the Attorney General had presented the case to the grand jury; by respected members of the House of Representatives, of whom Richard Nixon and Karl Mundt (now a

senator) were but two; by a trial jury; by Judge Goddard; by the
Court of Appeals for the Second District, which included Judge
Augustus Hand who gave a lifetime of distinguished service to the
Federal judiciary; by the Supreme Court, whose dicta we are told
are the law of the land; and by what Alistair Cooke chose to call
the "drunken" American press.

These confusers were lending their support to Hiss's contention that his conviction came about because the American public
was "obsessed" with "an unreasoning fear of communism"—and
that the real culprits who stole classified State Department
documents for the Soviet Union were "persons whose identity
(Whittaker) Chambers has never made public . . . officials . . . charwomen . . . messengers . . . someone else."

The solicitude for Hiss goes back to the time when the cold
and ugly evidence was beginning to mount. The *Christian Science
Monitor*, which reported in 1946 that "more than one congressman, when the subject of leftist activity in the State Department
is mentioned, pulled out a list of suspects that was invariably
headed by Mr. Hiss," began collecting an anthology of testi-
monials to prove that charges of Hiss's communist espionage were
false. Individuals acted spontaneously.

"If there is anything I can do," wrote Dean Carl B. Spaeth of
the Standord law school and a former State Department official,
"I know that you will call on me." Francis Sayre, U.S. representative on the U.N. Trusteeship Council, felt "distressed and
keenly regretful that you are being subjected to unfair and totally
unjust accusations." Clarence Pickett, executive secretary of the
American Friends Service Committee, suggested that Hiss's lack
of "total recall" demonstrated his innocence. Senator Herbert H.
Lehman expressed his "complete confidence in your loyalty" and
found Hiss's testimony "forthright."

Ralph Bunche called the hearings "an utterly shameless attempt to smear your good name." Scores of others added their
mite—and the letters were duly mimeographed and distributed by
Professor James T. Shotwell of Columbia University. In her
column and in personal correspondence, Mrs. Eleanor Roosevelt

attacked Hiss's accusers and argued that were he a communist, she would have known it.

What was the crime to which they so valiantly blinded themselves? Was it "nonconformism" or "liberalism"?

Because the Constitution narrowly defines treason as an "overt act" giving "aid and comfort" to an "enemy," Hiss could not be tried as a traitor, even though the United States has been at undeclared war with the Soviet Union for many years. Because the statute of limitations had run out, Hiss could not be tried under the punitive terms of the Espionage Act of 1917. He stood trial, therefore, under the perjury statute for denying that he had been a communist spy.

The formal charges against Hiss were (1) that he had not been associated with Whittaker Chambers after January 1, 1937, and (2) that he had not turned over classified State Department documents to any unauthorized person for transmission to the Soviet Union. The date of his association with Chambers, former courier for a Soviet apparatus, was of importance because the documents and the so-called "pumpkin papers" turned over by Chambers to the government bore dates in late 1937 and early 1938.

On both counts, the prosecution proved its case beyond a peradventure of doubt. It showed that the secret documents in question had been typed on a Woodstock machine which Hiss conceded had been in his possession at the time and to which Chambers had no access. It was demonstrated through independent testimony that Hiss and Chambers had been in close contact after 1937, and that Hiss lied repeatedly in an effort to deny that affiliation. Such matters of record as bank accounts and car registrations—of great significance but too complex to recount in a brief analysis—solidified the evidence against Hiss.

(Hiss's argument, tentatively offered before the grand jury and later whispered to reporters, that Chambers must have crawled through a window of the Hiss house one night to copy—without being discovered—a four-foot stack of documents, was never presented in court. The grand jury reaction had been laughter, and Hiss's lawyers were too wise to try it in the presence of the public. In fact, the trial record shows such an airtight case that it becomes obvious why the defense devoted most of its efforts to the smearing of Chambers rather than to any cogent rebuttal.

But this is only part of the story. During the trial, the government was hampered by fear of reprisal on the part of those who could have testified to Hiss's communist activities and by the refusal of the State Department to open up its records to the Justice Department. After Hiss's conviction, new evidence against him began pouring in, and Congress succeeded in breaking down the State Department's wall of secrecy. Today, Hiss could easily be convicted without the testimony of Whittaker Chambers.

As a result of what is now on the record, it can be argued that Hiss's lesser crime was espionage. In the late thirties and in the forties, Hiss did far more damage to this nation by twisting and corrupting United States policy in a manner obviously designed to do the Soviet Union the most good.

Here, in brief, is a small part of the new evidence:

1.   On February 19, 1952, Nathaniel Weyl, a former member of an underground communist cell in the Federal government, testified that he had attended secret communist meetings with Alger Hiss in 1934 and had seen him paying his party dues.

2.   At the same series of Senate Internal Security subcommittee hearings, former Ambassador William Bullitt told of a conversation with French Premier Daladier in 1939. Daladier warned him that French intelligence had discovered that two State Department officials, brothers named Hiss, were Soviet agents. Bullitt answered that he had never heard of the Hisses and added, "That isn't even a name. It's a noise made by a snake." Subsequently, he met Alger Hiss and informed State Department superiors of his conversation. He was ignored.

3.   In 1946, a political gossip columnist published the complete order of battle of British troops fighting communist guerrillas in Greece. An investigation by Deputy Assistant Secretary of State J. Anthony Panuch disclosed that this information, so damaging to the anti-communist military effort, had come from Alger Hiss.

4. As director of the Office of Special Political Affairs, Hiss used his influence—against the direct order of Secretary of State Byrnes—to find employment at the United Nations for a group of Soviet agents then in the Federal government who were feeling the heat of the first loyalty-security investigations. When called before the Senate subcommittee in 1952, 27 of these key men in the U.N. hid behind the Fifth Amendment. A Federal grand jury investigating the episode reported "startling evidence" of infiltration at the U.N. by "an overwhelmingly large group of disloyal United States citizens"—the men Hiss had recommended.

5. In 1946, the United States was in the midst of important negotiations with Panama for renewal of leases to air bases necessary for the protection of the Canal Zone. Though there was strong communist agitation in Panama against this, the negotiations were proceeding satisfactorily. The Canal Zone is Panamanian territory for which the United States pays rent. But Hiss insisted that the zone be reported as an American "possession" to the U.N. This caused a furor in Panama, and Hiss was told never to do this again. Then, without notifying the Assistant Secretary of State for Latin American Affairs, Hiss listed the Canal Zone as an "occupied territory" in a report to the U.N. Trusteeship Council.

On the day the story appeared in the newspapers, Hiss could nowhere be found. He was not at his office in the State Department nor did he keep any of his appointments. Finally, he turned up, late in the afternoon, at the office of Acting Secretary of State Dean Acheson to say that he was "oh, so sorry," it was just a mistake. As a result of this "mistake," the negotiations for the air bases fell through and there was a wave of anti-American feeling in Panama.

6. When the records of the Institute of Pacific Relations were examined by the Senate Internal Security subcommittee, it was discovered that Hiss worked hand-in-glove with this organization. According to the subcommittee, the IPR was "considered by the American Communist Party and by Soviet officials as an instrument of communist policy, propaganda, and military intelligence." It was Hiss's role to arrange for quiet meetings between high State Department officials and now-identified Soviet agents.

Repeatedly, he also appointed pro-communists to important State Department policy-planning groups. These agents, we now know, were in large part responsible for convincing the department that the Chinese reds were really "agrarian reformers" who should be supported by the United States—and that the anti-communist Nationalist Chinese should be deprived of American aid at a time when they were in a life-and-death struggle with red military forces.

The documents Hiss turned over to the Soviets made them privy to some of our most carefully guarded secrets (one document is still classified and could not be submitted in evidence during the trials.) By working with other Soviet agents, he was able to plant the seeds for the Yalta agreements, to prepare the way for the downfall of China, and to lay the groundwork for the Korean war. He was not the most important man in Washington, but one State Department memo describes his "Svengali-like influence" on Secretary of State Edward Stettinius.

For his espionage, he served a term in Lewisburg Prison—boasting to his fellow inmates that he was covering up for Franklin D. Roosevelt. For doing his best to subvert American foreign policy, he has remained relatively unscathed. The public airways are offered to him and a great television network is willing to jeopardize its standing and its advertising revenue to rehabilitate him. Some Park Avenue doors were closed to him when his wife left him—for non-ideological reasons. But there are always others who are ready to propagate the myth that, despite the clouds of witnesses and the mountains of evidence, he is the victim of "patriotic hysteria."

American Legion Magazine
February 1963

The Noel Field Story

This is just one of the very many true mystery stories of Communist intrigue which, were there more reporters interested, would stock our shelves with lively reading far more hair-raising and perhaps a bit more honest, than the ersatz dreams of the spy thriller kings of the day.

After five years in a Soviet concentration camp, Noel Field and his wife, Herta, have chosen to remain behind the Iron Curtain. Or so the Communist government of Hungary, which has given them "asylum," announced. But were the man and woman recently interviewed by the U.S. consul in Budapest really the notorious Communist agent and his wife? Or were they two imposters? Would the secret police let out of its hands, even temporarily, a man who can open so many doors in the labyrinthine corridors of the Communist espionage? Would it release one of Alger Hiss' comrades in perfidy? Men now at liberty in the U.S. shudder at the thought.

For Noel Field was a significant figure in prewar and wartime Communist operations both here and abroad. His name crops up in tantalizing fashion in the annals of the Communist apparatus. That he occasionally ran on the same track in the Communist underground railroad as Alger Hiss is known; but what cargo they were carrying remains a mystery.

Noel Haviland Field—tall, aristocratic, neurotic, and the son of a distinguished Quaker family—moved into the Communist orbit in the 1920's, long before the New Deal ferment had made the Party an avocation of millionaires and social climbers. In 1928,

Vernet. (Many Communists were sprung from Le Vernet, but anti-Communist refugees were not so fortunate.) In the course of his work, he met Erika Glaser and Laszlo Rajk. Erika, an attractive brunette then in her teens, had already won her chevrons in the Communist cause. She was "adopted" by the Fields, although there were rumors that she and Noel were romantically attached. In the postwar years, Rajk became Foreign Minister in the Hungarian satellite government.

The collapse of France, after the phony war, sent Field skittering off to Geneva where, somehow, he became the European respresentative of the Unitarian Service Committee. His offices were a meeting place and a way station for refugee Communist leaders and traveling *apparatchiks* who made good use of the funds which trusting American philanthropists donated.

When the United States entered the war and set up its super-secret Office of Strategic Services, Noel Field and Erika Glaser were at hand and ready to do their bit. Allen Dulles, who ran the Swiss end of OSS, considered Field a "Communist idealist." Field reportedly received sums of money from Dulles for underground work in Germany. He is said to have then happily passed this money over to the Communist Fries Deutschland committee, which stashed it away for later use against America and the free world.

The end of the war found Erika moving onward and upward with the American Army. One of the first to reach Berlin after the surrender, she moved about freely, running a minor-league Mata Hari operation, spending much time with OSS officers, and having access to the secret material strewn about their offices. Field returned to Paris and his old job with Unitarian Relief, then lost it for siphoning off its funds to Communists. He wandered about Europe, a shabby man supported by God knows whom.

The Communists he had befriended in the Geneva days had all risen to high places in the satellite governments, but they did nothing for Field. One of them, in fact, was the cause of his downfall.

when he joined the State Department's Western European division, his enthusiasm for Communism was already in full flower—a poisonous flower which destroyed a promising career and left him without a country.

It was not until the mid-1930's that the Soviet apparatus, then functioning busily in Washington, marked him out as a recruit. Hede Massing, then a Communist operative, was given the assignment of bringing him into the apparatus. "I had no need to propagandize Noel," she has recalled. "He was already too passionately sold on the Soviets and eager 'to do something to help.' "

So eager was Field to convince Mrs. Massing of his devotion to the Soviet Union that he drove her late one night to the Lincoln Memorial and, standing before the Emancipator's statue, sang her the "Internationale"—in Russian. "I wasn't very impressed," she says. "It was cold—and I didn't understand the language." Her work of recruitment done, she was preparing to turn him over to a "contact" who would pilot him in the apparatus when she struck a snag. Alger Hiss had also been working on Field and wanted him for *his* apparatus. Hiss and Mrs. Massing met and amicably settled the jurisdictional dispute. "After all," Hiss is reported to have said in graciously relinquishing his claim, "we both work for the same people."

Not long after, Field suddenly and inexplicably resigned from the State Department. He turned up in Geneva, working for the International Labor Organization of the League of Nations—and for General Walter G. Krivitsky, chief of Red Army Intelligence in Western Europe. Just what Field's function was remains one of the many secrets which died with Krivitsky when the Communists "suicided" him in a dingy Washington hotel room in the early 1940's. And what knowledge, indirect or otherwise, Field has of the murder of Ignace. Reiss, the celebrated Soviet agent who was murdered in Switzerland by the NKVD for denouncing Stalin, may never be known.

By the late 1930's, Noel Field had moved on to other activities. In the guise of a relief worker, he was busy among Spanish Loyalist refugees at the French concentration camp at Le

A wave of arrests was sweeping the Communist world, as Stalin made one of his periodic clean-ups of Red leaders, and the NKVD decided to use Field as a whipping boy in the trials that were being prepared. In May, 1949, he disappeared from his hotel in Bratislava. Two months later, his architect brother, Hermann Field, who had gone to Warsaw in search of Noel, disappeared. Shortly thereafter, Noel's wife, Herta, disappeared in Prague.

In September, 1949, Noel's good friend, Laszlo Rajk, went on trial for treason in Hungary. He "confessed" that he had worked with Noel Field for the FBI (sic) and the OSS as an "American imperialist agent" to undermine the Hungarian government. Field's name continued to pop up in "confessions" of East European Communists, always attached to the accusation that he was an American "spy."

Meanwhile, Erika Glaser had gotten married and was living quietly with her ex-GI husband, then studying at the University of Geneva, and her two small children. Now she felt that the NKVD was closing in on her. Unable to get an American passport because of her past activities, she packed up her family and moved secretly to a small French town. "I feel myself in danger of the same hands that have taken Noel, Hermann, and Herta," she confided. This did not stop her from making contact with her old underground friends, in an effort to learn Noel's whereabouts and fate.

In August, 1949, Erika telephoned an old admirer, Leo Bauer, who ran the Communist radio station in East Berlin. He was nervous and evasive—and he wanted no part of Erika. When she pleaded that he meet her in the Western zone of Berlin, he coldly refused. But he reported the incident to his superiors who ordered him to arrange a rendezvous with Erika at Templehof Airport.

The manifest of the American Overseas Airlines registers the fact that Erika arrived from Frankfurt and cleared the Templehof customs. Bauer was not there to meet her. She was never seen again. Bauer was arrested in the Soviet zone, charged with being an enemy of the state and a co-conspirator with the "American agent, Noel Field."

For over five years, no word was heard of the Fields—Noel, Hermann, and Herta—or of Erika. It was generally believed that they were dead, or at best rotting away in the Siberian tundra. Then, in the summer of 1954, Josef Sviatlow, an important Polish Communist official, escaped. His story, given wide publicity by American authorities, involved the Fields. Sviatlow had been responsible for their arrest, he said, and Noel was "probably" dead.

The Soviets denounced him, of course, and then embarked on a curious course of action. Communist authorities announced that the three Fields were being released, with apologies and restitution for their false arrest. Hermann was released in Poland, spent some time in a Polish rest home, and then proceeded to Switzerland. He has remained silent. Erika's husband, now in the U.S., received what purported to be a letter from her, reporting that she was alive and well at the Vorkuta slave labor camp. Noel and Herta were "released" in Hungary, had an interview with an American consular official, and then disappeared again. The Hungarian Communist government announced that they had sought asylum there. All efforts by U.S. authorities to renew contact with them were fruitless.

The Communists had created the proper effect. To the world, Noel Field had renounced his own country in favor of the "worker's paradise." But there was a less simple explanation. *No one who had seen "Noel" and "Herta" after their release was in a position to know whether they were the same people who disappeared five years ago.* Once they had made their grandstand play, they melted away. Their former underground associates could breathe more easily. Like the other enigmas in Noel Field's life, this one would remain to perplex the world until the bloody dossiers of the Soviet secret police are opened—when the Soviet empire collapses.

The American Mercury
April 1955

Lincoln, Israel, and Freedom

There is in this little script of a single broadcast, in which Toledano substituted for George Sokolsky, a rich lesson for all those instant historians, right and left, who treat historic events and persons as mere adjuncts to current crusades and zeals.

We have had one day of oratory about Abraham Lincoln, and we will have another. For Lincoln's Birthday has become an excuse rather than a day of consecration. A thousand speakers have dug into the infinite variety of Lincoln biographies—or they have dusted off Carl Sandburg's massive and pretentious catalogue of the Lincoln years. And each of them has pulled out his quota of plums—the quotations to prove this point or that about the Great Emancipator.

It will be pointed out, I assume, that Lincoln was firm and stalwart and dedicated to the preservation of the Union. He will emerge stern or tolerant, sad or satiric—but never, I'm afraid, the man he was, the man of heroic indecisions, the champion of conciliation. "The Union must, and shall be, preserved," Lincoln said. And again, "I believe that this government cannot exist half slave and half free." These two quotations will be repeated over and over again tonight and tomorrow.

But how many will remember what Lincoln meant by the word "Union." It is clear from his utterances, but not from the ninety years of speeches which have followed them, that Lincoln did not mean a national state when he used the word "Union."

He believed in a Federal system of sovereign states, for above all he was a Constitutionalist.

The War Between the States was not fought to end slavery in the South but to prevent the South from imposing slavery on the rest of the country. In the Lincoln-Douglas debates, Lincoln made his position abundantly clear. "Wrong as we may think slavery to be," he said, "we can yet afford to let it alone where it is ... But can we, while our votes will prevent it, allow it to spread into the national territories and to overrun us here in these free states?"

So said Lincoln. And even when he signed the Emancipation Proclamation after three years of Presidential indecision, he did so, in his own words, as "a fit and necessary war measure for suppressing the rebellion."

Those who seek to depict Lincoln as an enemy of states' rights do him no justice. Those who invoke the veneration which surrounds his name—and who invoke it to plead for the supremacy of the executive branch falsify history. Lincoln knew that the limited sovereignty of the Federal government, checked and balanced by the limited sovereignty of the states, was the greatest—perhaps the only—safeguard of American liberty. In this he was merely reflecting the wisdom of Madison and Jefferson and Hamilton, and the other men of genius who fashioned the Constitution.

However, when Lincoln said that this nation could not long endure half slave and half free, he was speaking in terms of shrewd appraisal. For there is a dynamism which governs the affairs of men. And the dynamism of the industrial anti-slave North could not be contained by the agrarian pro-slave South. And the South had a dynamism of its own which could not be contained by the North. In a situation of this kind, containment was an ill-hatched hope.

This same is true today on a global scale. The United States and the rest of the free world were going to contain the mass tyranny. We were to keep the Communist world hemmed in. But all we succeeded in doing was to contain ourselves. We crippled the dynamism of liberation by our policy of containment—and we allowed the Soviet dynamism to roll on.

The Kennan-Acheson policy of containment, which has never been fully discarded, resulted only in retreat. It delivered the teeming millions of mainland China to the Communists. It lost us half of Indo-China. It is undermining our position in Japan and Indonesia. It unleashed the forces of Communist subversion in Africa. And tonight we can see what the policy of containment has brought us in the Near East.

Once again, the world faces the possibility of war, and we are containing it by allowing the Soviet government to pour offensive weapons into Egypt. These weapons will be used for one purpose alone—to crush the tiny and American-oriented State of Israel. This is not conjecture on my part. Says Premier Nasser of Egypt: "Israel . . . must disappear." Says Egypt's Foreign Minister: "We demand that Israel should vanish from the Middle East map." You can see that this is not a question of border disputes here or fishing rights there. This, for Israel, is life or death, survival or extermination.

And while the free half of the world has temporized and talked hopefully of containing the conflict, what has the slave half been doing? The Soviet dynamism, unopposed, has moved steadily to heighten the crisis. The whole world knows that the "peace-loving" Communists have been sending modern and powerful arms to Egypt—offensive arms with which to start the kind of war from which only the Soviet Union can profit.

But the world does not know in any detail what those arms are. From sources which I consider conservative and reliable, this is what I have just learned and I pass it on to you. The Soviets have sent Egypt:

   20 to 40 medium jet bombers,
   300 modern jet fighters,
   800 tanks, including Stalin tanks—the heavyweights of the Red Army,
   8 to 10 submarines, manned by Soviet and former Nazi sailors.

A corps of military technicians sufficient in number to command the Egyptian army down to battalion level.

Add to this the tremendous preponderance of manpower in the Arab states, mobilized on millions of square miles of sanctuary—and all aimed at the tiny strip of Mediterranean coastline which is Israel.

Standing between this Arab might and Israel is a small, tough, and determined army lacking most of the modern sinews of war. The Israelis have a handful of obsolescent jets which cannot intercept the Soviet bombers. They have no adequate anti-aircraft artillery, no radar, no anti-tank guns capable of piercing the armor of the great Stalin tanks.

I am not sure that the Arab might will prevail. For the Israelis have taken to heart some words of Lincoln which we seem to have forgotten. "Let us have faith that *right* makes might; and in that faith let us to the end dare to do our duty as we understand it." A man who fought in Israel during its war for independence said to me the other day that he was certain war would break out by April. He felt that Egyptian bombers would level the cities of Israel. But he was sure that, even without the defensive weapons Israel has called for, the tiny state would win in the end.

These are the stakes in Israel. These are the stakes for all of us, as Americans. Put aside the moral issues. Put aside all thoughts of the blood and toil which Jews have brought to the small receptacle of their ancient hopes. Forget, if you will, that many of the men on guard in Israel once saw the smoke rising from the crematoria of Belsen and Buchenwald. The crisis in the Near East is a crisis for this country and for the free world. For every sparrow that falls, the men of the Kremlin rejoice.

Yet in this terrible moment of decision, our State Department fumbles and dawdles. Has the dynamism of America run down? Have we forgotten the legacy of our own wars and our own sorrows? Or was Mr. Truman right when he said in his memoirs that our Near East specialists in the State Department are so blindly pro-Arab that they cannot see the dangers to the free world in an anti-Israel policy. Mr. Truman ascribed this state of mind on the State of Israel to anti-Semitism in the Department. Perhaps this is true, but I do not like to believe it. I prefer to think that our Near East specialists are victims of the psychology of containment. I prefer to believe that they are men of small scope who believe that evil can be restrained by barbed wire and kind words.

But the power, the might, and the glory of this nation can not be left in the feeble receivership of small men grubbing in the back alleys of our diplomacy. Despite the smiles and the bows of Geneva, we are engaged in a war for survival with the Communist world. And if we are to survive, we must first deserve to survive—by the breadth of our vision, by our dedication to justice, and by our sense of obligation both to ourselves and to others.

Half-measures will no longer work in the trouble spots of the world. The timidity of containment, in a world crying out for liberation, is an offering of counterfeit currency. It will not buy us any freedom. It will not buy us time. Conferences between France, Britain, and the United States will not prevail against the determination of the Soviet Union to precipitate a war in the Near East. Only a simple, categorical declaration by our government that it will not tolerate a breach of the peace—and the added warning that we will intervene if this declaration is ignored—only these can save the situation.

Lincoln, the conciliator—the man who carried his indecisions in the furrows of his face—learned in the great travail of his office that the time comes in the lives of men when they must openly resist. In the second year of the War Between the States, he wrote to Horace Greeley in the terms of his decision. "What I do about slavery and the colored race," he said, "I do because I believe it helps to save the union."

What we do to save Israel from destruction, what we do to defend any threatened nation, what we do to preserve the peace, we must do to save the Union and the freedom of the world.

Humanity cannot endure half slave and half free.

These are words to frighten some men. They would not have frightened Lincoln.

American Broadcasting Company
February 1956

Let Only a Few Speak
for Him

*This is about a man whom Toledano respected perhaps
above all others. It is about that man but it speaks as
eloquently of Toledano himself.*

Some men are touched by God, and in turn they reach out to
others the grace of their intuition. Such a man was Whittaker
Chambers. Only the foolish and the mediocre denigrated him. For
evil in its own way recognizes and respects the good, however it
may hate. Now he is dead, out of the mind's reach, a solitary
figure in the history he knew so well and helped to make. Those
of us who knew him, who shared his trust or had a sometime view
of the life he saw through those laughing, prescient eyes, can
reread his letters and weep and know the cold edge of our loss.
Why write of him when he has so much better written of himself?
Why beat hopelessly at a door that is locked and adamant in its
exclusion?

There is a reason. Whittaker Chambers was my friend, my
father, my brother—and sometimes my son. But this is my private
concern. A public duty resides in those who remain, transitory
between eternities, to speak of the dead. We do not honor them,
but ourselves. And if we utter our longing and sorrow, it is a
prayer to the God who made us and who will judge us at the End
Day. We also make our witness before a hostile world. He knew
what that hostility would be. Writing to me on Easter Sunday
1956, his fifty-fifth birthday, Whittaker Chambers said: "I hope
you have my obit ready. What fun the yappy little dogs will have.
I don't even begrudge it them, rest seems so welcome."

Through all the years that I knew him—the terrible time of the trial, the time of pain after the first heart attack, the time when he was forced by ill-health to absent himself from the felicity of the soil he loved so dearly—it was rest he wanted. This was something that his own nature could not give him. The desire for rest was always in conflict with an abounding sense of life. In the beautiful "back farm" to which he withdrew, he could look down a long vista in the summer quiet. He could wake early to hear the clamor of the birds, or step outside his door to feed the wild animals that did not fear his presence. But he surveyed far more than the pond and the trees and the far-away mountains. Sitting with friends on the small porch, his speech was rich in literary and historical allusion, all interwoven and all relating to the final conflict in which Christian civilization finds itself. The French Revolution, the marching sailors of Kronstadt, the death of the monarchic principle in England at the hands of Cromwellian mobs—these were all as vividly alive to him as the fighters in Budapest or his life in the Communist underground.

In a very precise way, he always saw himself in the past and in perspective. Writing to me and of me, yet really of himself, he could say: *"A man's special truth is in the end all there is in him. And with that he must be content though life give him no more, though man give him nothing. Must be content, that is, unless it comes upon him that wisdom itself is the ultimate folly, the ultimate presumption. I am myself so much in the sunset that all things cast their shadows eastward from me."*

He knew that he had made his witness, that he had stood before God stripped of pretension, humble yet unashamed. He had seen the Behemoth and never flinched, except for one despairing moment when death had seemed the single answer to a world gone so neurotic that it had forgotten the only pride not offensive to God: the pride of the man who is ready to fight and die for what he knows to be right and true. He was a symbol of that pride, and he had the intellectual courage to set his own worth high. Yet he knew that his witness might have been in vain, much like that of the Christian in the arena who felt the gladiator's sword pierce his flesh and felt the warm, red blood covering his loins.

After Alger Hiss had been convicted, when the yawping press expected exultation, he could write: *"The days that will diminish the echoes of the trial already reveal that I have an all but incurable wound. My good, intuitive friend, Marjorie Kinnan Rawlings, wrote during the first trials 'When this is over, I believe that you are planning to kill yourself.' In the literal sense, this was not true, but it was so close to my feeling from the beginning that I have never trusted myself to answer her. At the end of that day of turmoil in which I decided to put the Baltimore [espionage] papers in evidence, I thought 'Because of Esther and the children, I cannot pray to God to let me die, but I cannot keep from hoping that He will.' Now this feeling dogs me through these beautiful, unseasonable days and in the hours of the night when I wake. There keep running through my head two epitaphs that Byron saw in an Italian graveyard: 'implora eterna pace,' 'implora eterna quietà.' 'All they ask for is peace,' Byron noted. 'And that they implore.'*

"Add to this the feeling that it was all for nothing, that nothing has been gained except the misery of others, that it was a tale of the end and not of the beginning of something . . . , You cannot save what cannot save itself. These things happened because our sector of the world could not understand what was happening to it. It does not understand yet, nor does it understand this Case."

This was the theme that ran through everything he said or wrote. This was the cause of his impatience at many anti-Communists who saw the final conflict solely in terms of counterespionage, of disclosure, of military maneuvering. The battle was one of faith—and as the Crusades demonstrated, such wars were fought in grime and terror unknown to the tea-party pundits whose vocation was splitting hairs and making self-defeating distinctions. When a lady writer for one of the more rarified "little" magazines went through her exercises on the Case, Whittaker Chambers was at once amused and indignant. He was too charitable to assail her in print, to note her tardy record of recognition, but in the privacy of his correspondence, he cut close to the heart of the matter. *"The Chambers attitude, as he has said, is based on*

*respect of a common power to hold faith, at an intensity and
with a force, that the xxxxxx's do not know or admit. Is it nice?
Is dirt nice? Is death nice? Above all, is dying nice? And, in the
end, we must ask: Is God nice? I doubt it.*

> Der Gott der Eisen wachsen liess,
> Er wollte keine Knechte.

"And since you refuse to know German, I translate:

> *The God who made iron grow—*
> *He wanted no slaves.*

*"The world in which you and I exist and bow our heads before
the God who made it, is the world also of the atom bomb and
virus. The mystery lies beyond the lady's cerebration—or in yours
or mine. But if the neat, efficient, competent brain denies or
by-passes the mystery? That is the point whose bended edge
divides men into breeds between which mind may be an exten-
uator or a compromiser, but cannot change or assimilate the
breeds. And the breed of Hiss will always be nearer to the breed
of Chambers than it can ever be to the breed of xxxxxx. Because
the first two contain the power to hold faith; the second admits
only to the ability to entertain reason and a reasoned viewpoint."*

Whittaker Chambers was always a man of faith, and it was this
which kindled the love of millions who know that transcendental
hunger. As a very young man he saw what war and starvation had
done to a defeated Germany. He saw what depression could do in
a confident United States. And having been educated and trained
in that citadel of materialism, Columbia College, he thought he
discovered the antidote to these poisons in Communism. The
tentative and the wishful were not for him, and he gave everything to the solution which fitted his comprehension. He might
have been as great and productive a writer as this country had
ever known, but he tossed aside his personal ambitions in a cause
he believed was just. The polite Communism of the intellectuals
who hung their clothes on the hickory limb but never went near
the water was not for him. He plunged into the real business of

Communism—and only the grace of God prevented you and me from doing the same. But it was in his nature to realize that faith is but part of a trinity—that it is also incumbent of hope and love, the hope which is part of the human condition and the *caritas* which Christ at Golgotha gave us. And so, in fear and determination, he broke with Communism.

I began to know Whittaker Chambers in the early days of the Case—when the press with almost homosexual love was fawning over Alger Hiss, but lying in wait to pound Chambers with scatological questions. When I face my God, I will be confronted with many sins, but I will be able to say: In the hours of his sorrow, I stood by him and could give him friendship and love. It was a small thing—and repaid a million-fold with the gift of understanding. Of this there will be no more, for it would be obscene to clothe myself in his greatness. It is all there in his letters, in the poems he allowed me to see—but they are for my private comfort. God so loved the world that He gave His only begotten Son—and in my personal grief I can only say that without blaspheming, I know, I really know.

Whittaker Chambers is dead. For him there is rest. For us, there are only the simple words, *ora pro nobis*. In another age and another time, he would have stood by the seats of the mighty and guided their hands. In these times, he guided me through the thicket to the open plain where the light of God shines through—understanding of my weaknesses, but forgiving. And what can I offer in requiem? Let him speak in poems he wrote, imperfect but dear, and never shown to cruel eyes.

The bird sings,
releasing as it flies
the umbel of a flower that swings,
unimplicated, over stones
where the blood already dries
in fluffs of fur;
while expeditious emmets stir,
triggered mystically to feed,
before flies breed
maggots to compete.

And again:

> All things work together for good,
> as every field
> of springing grain
> is dunged with filth and death,
> and rots the falling rain
> which double duty dies,
> multiplying yield,
> and simulating peace;
> which is always for the ear
> that cannot hear;
> for the eye that is blind,
> or set behind;
> is always for the ending,
> never for the beginning, breath
>
> Is the web where hangs
> the suavely packaged fly
> that for only meaning has
> a little sizzling cry,
> whereby,
> confides to capable arachnid
> the monotony of the agony
> of its plea to die
> at once; and at the same time not
>   to die. . . .

Others can rehearse the facts and the events that made up the life of Whittaker Chambers. Others can weep more eloquently than I for a man who knew the fate incumbent in the bone. For myself—for those who love freedom and who have been reached by his greatness—only this is valid: He died a martyr. Let us say our goodbyes.

National Review
July 1961

History and the Class of '38

(Or, Cherchons le temps perdu)

*I do not happen to know any others of the ancient
gang Toledano writes about in this memorial. Knowing
Ralph has been pleasure, ordeal, wonder, trial, education and, perhaps above all, warmth enough.*

In the *nunc pro tunc* of our nostalgia, the recall is golden. Look
at the faces in the '38 *Columbian*. They stare out of the pages
confidently, as if the world of men to which they aspired were as
neatly ordered as the acres of Morningside. For them, the
hierarchical order which made sophomores of freshmen and
seniors of juniors was natural law. It seemed inevitable that
similarly and by small steps we would arrive each in his own way
to greatness. But we learned rapidly enough that beyond the
inscrutable gaze of Alma Mater time has a cold and iron whim.

That we thought as we did is a common enough failing of
college men, whether they stride toward the sunset in Ivy League
boots or roll out the barrel for Siwash U. Nothing that we read or
observed—not even the sometimes pitying, sometimes sardonic,
smile of our elders—marred the illusion. For like every generation,
we were seized of the *hubris* that the Class of '38 was unique—as
if history, having labored to produce it, could never again be so
felicitously fertile. Yet here, perhaps, we were not so lamentably
arrogant. If only in the context of our time's plague, we were
marked as few other generations had been since Adam's rib made
a fool of him.

319

In that civilized, third-person despair which characterized his *Education*, Henry Adams noted that a "law of acceleration" governs the pace of history. The accretion of technology, in its broadest sense, was not an algebraic or geometric progression. Beginning with the Industrial Revolution, man had careened ahead till he arrived at the historical application of $e = mc^2$ and the fission of human energy. The chronicles of the Class of '38 were the *quod est demonstrandum* of the law Henry Adams discovered and of the chain reaction it described.

Examine the context.

We were born, most of us, in the year that a whole civilization shattered itself against the bloody bastion of Verdun. Not merely men but a *Weltanschauung* tore its guts on that grisly battlefield. When the first war ended, the quaint lights that had gone out in 1914 could never be rekindled. They were replaced by a tawdry incandescence. In the years that followed, a cloud no bigger than the hammer & sickle moved across the horizon. A man named Mussolini took the night sleeper to Rome, dreaming of tinfoil grandeur. On the month, almost the day, that we took our scrubbed and shining faces to preparatory school, Leon Trotsky learned that his days at Alma Ata were numbered, that in his impending exile the Revolution he had made with Lenin would fall into Stalin's irrevocable receivership. A vast land mass and all its people were surrendered to Nechaevist terror.

By June of 1934, Hitler's legions were playing an *obbligato* to our prim Valedictory sentiments as we put away childish things and turned to Columbia. The Rhineland fell before we had paid our tuition at University Hall and chosen for our course of study those relics of a once-viable civilization. Still with us were the signs and trauma of the Great Depression, the dislocation of those societal arrangements which had glossed our world in security. The long, grey breadlines, the sorry anguish of men selling apples on streetcorners, the joint misery of the dispossessed and the dispossessors, the mass charity of WPA—these were everywhere about us.

And the year 1938, which gave us our collegiate identity, saw what had begun at Versailles come to a climax at Munich in the pathetic joke of "peace in our time."

In 1938, we left the hermetic world of the campus. At the moment of parting the years and the places changed suddenly—already cast in nostalgia. Bad days and adolescent sorrows were forgotten. All that remained were the sunset hours of Van Am quad, the beer and nonsense of the Lion's Den, the interminable debates in which we discovered new verities old to Athenian schoolboys. We remembered the sacramental bread-and-wine offered by teachers who fleetingly perhaps made it possible for us to glimpse the truth and grace of art and mathematics. In one of my books,* I paid tribute to some of those teachers:

> We saw our professors as through a glass brightly. Irwin Edman, a friendly, blond sparrow of a man, ran through Hegel's Idea-State, Spinoza's cosmic rearrangements, and the Aristotelian metaphysic, striking the notes with Mozartean grace ... Raymond Weaver, who had put so much of his life into the unveiling of Melville, offered us a taste of the bitterness which the world had served him. Like a beetle-browed Ahab, he pursued the white phantoms of the *chansons de geste*, of Dante, Boccaccio, Isidore of Seville, Pico della Mirandola, and Cervantes—navigating by the beauty, order, and harmony which had escaped his life. George Nobbe's Falstaffian guffaws whipped off the hobble skirts with which the academic mind had invested Donne and Sterne. Jacques Barzun and Lionel Trilling, both great teachers and opposite sides of a brilliant intellectual coin, involved us in their debates over history and letters.

Others, of course, drew their sustenance ·from teachers in different disciplines or of different temperament. Columbia was then, and must be now, full of teachers who made the enjoyment of learning both intellectual and visceral. What I wrote is personal to me. It is of a piece with that equally personal recall of John Jay's Fourth Floor where extracurricular activities resided: the mock rivalries of *Jester, Review*, and *Spectator*—and Eugene Williams sad-faced among the paste-pots; Ben Hubbard, who

---

*Lament for a Generation, 1960.

understood us far more than we liked to believe, seeing that our editorial exuberance did not get us into trouble with Dean Hawkes; the ear-shattering tympani concerts in the tiny offices— with Bob Lax on filing cabinet, Tom Merton on overturned wastepaper basket, Bob (Ain't Goin' Nowhere) Smith on desktop, and the rest of us, whether juniors or seniors, pounding whatever else made a noise; the amateur throat-cutting over editorial posts, ending in a solemn hearing before Student Board at which Herb Rosenthal won a Jester associate editorship; the jazz, poetry, and cheap-wine sessions of Philolexian; and all the attempts to be at once Stalky & Co. and Scott Fitzgerald.

This we enshrined, along with our infantile leftism, our Popular Front demonstrations, and the girls we kissed but did not marry. But we had little enough time to look back. Before we knew it, history was shifting into high. Careers barely started, the glow still bright on love and marriage, and our maturity not yet dry behind the ears, we were faced by the conjunction of communism and fascism in the Hitler-Stalin Pact, the outbreak of mankind's last "conventional" war, and the certainty that like our parents we would know the call of military duty.

The accelerated tempo of history caught us up—and to the credit of our marked generation it can be said that the Class of '38 put on its country's uniform without bravado or that rowdy boastfulness with which its elders had stormed out to pull the Kaiser's beard. We had already seen the betrayed idealism of friends who cut short their lives to fight in Spain. And we realized that however evil or inconclusive wars may be, there are times when men must fight if any vestige of what they hold precious is to survive. Victory for fascism—for any system which enslaves the human spirit, destroys the dignity of men, and denies a God-given free will—would have been an abomination. Patting household gods and making small goodbyes to wives and families, but putting out no flags, we accepted the responsibility.

E quindi uscimmo a riveder le stelle. And then we emerged, once more to see the stars—but to see them briefly. For history was now on the toboggan. Even before the last shot was fired, the Great Mushroom had risen over Hiroshima and Nagasaki—and the shadow cast by its monster cloud never left us. We were now both masters and prisoners of the Nuclear Age. Each proliferating scientific discovery extended man's vista—and humbled him. Before the war, we had prided ourselves on fast trains and speeding automobiles. But the world had scarcely become accustomed to the four-engine plane before the jets took over.

(I remember the first flight of the Intercontinental 707, the feeling that this mammoth of a plane could never lift itself from the runway, and less than nine hours later Moscow airport beneath our feet.)

But the jet was even then obsolescent—as outdated as our cliché awareness that God's little acre was precisely that. Before we had tamed our new knowledge, space reached out. Men were spinning in the sky and metallic objects bearing incredibly complex mechanisms were reporting on the planets and creating a new vocabulary for our children. In less than a lifetime we had traded in the Model T for the Agena B. It had taken man centuries to advance from a troglodytic existence, other centuries to invent the wheel. It took him five decades to convert a four-cylinder engine into a rocket with a million pounds of thrust. Only the soul remained to be automated.

But what progress could the Class of '38 really claim? It had answered none of the riddles that confronted Job or Pythagoras, Paul or Maimonides. In an era of limitless frontiers and exploding science, we were as earthbound as the inventor of the paddle. The world had changed, but the terror and resignation of the human condition were the same. Like a bad scriptwriter, the Class of '38 could say that it had merely produced "Son of Class of '38." Those of us with pretensions to philosophy might quote the Missal's *Sicut erat*, but this was hardly an answer.

Twenty-five years after we walked away from Morningside with misguided eagerness, do we have more to show than thinning hair or increased girth? By some standards, many of us may be considered successful lawyers, businessmen, writers, doctors, scientists, teachers. For better or worse, we have made the required contribution and offered our hostages to fortune. But the sad or comforting thought is that history outran us. We are Miniver Cheevys, still rattling the iron clothing of another age.

And perhaps, for all the speed of our toboggan ride (for all the history that has been crammed into our brief contemporaneity), we are not so special as a generation. Like all men who have searched in books for the meaning of the past and the promise of the future, we have learned that the gold of nostalgia is not an illusion. Like all other classes, we look back at the real adventure of classrooms and lectures, of ideas and ideals—even if we did not re-make the world we saw from that peak in Darien which was Columbia.

Those years are our own particular endowment—and we know now, simply, that it was once very good. There are new buildings and new faces on the campus, but it will always be the same for us and for those who follow us, world without end. Not history but humanity was our teacher. *Post jucundam juventutem,* but not quite yet *post molestam senectutem,* we can continue to sing *gaudeamus igitur* to Columbia—forgetting for a while the echoing end of that old student song.

Columbia Alumni Directory
Spring 1963